ROME

How to use this book

The main text provides a survey of the city's cultural history from the beginnings of Roman civilization to the present time. It is illustrated with paintings, sculpture, architecture and general views.

The map (pp. 238-39) shows the principal monuments, museums and historic buildings, using symbols and colours for quick reference.

To find a museum or gallery turn to Appendix I, which lists them alphabetically, with their address, opening times and a note on their scope and contents. The larger collections are sub-divided into departments. Page numbers indicate where these are mentioned or illustrated in the text.

To find a historic building or church turn to Appendix II, which gives a similar alphabetical list of important buildings, landmarks, monuments, fountains, squares, etc. Grid-references enable the most important places to be easily located on the map (e.g. S. Cecilia in Trastevere, CL., means horizontal reference C, vertical reference L).

For information on artists—painters, sculptors, architects, goldsmiths, engravers, etc.—turn to Appendix III. Here are listed those who contributed to the cultural greatness of Rome and whose works are now to be seen there. Each entry consists of a biographical note, details of where the artist's works are located, and references to the main text where they are mentioned or illustrated.

World Cultural Guides

in the nearby Corso. The reliefs then found passed to the Medici, in Florence; other excavations were carried out in the nineteenth century, and the last in 1938. Some reliefs were then added to the whole from the museums in which they had been preserved, except for a relief in the Louvre and some fragments still left in the Villa Medici (seat of the French Academy), which have been replaced by facsimiles together with some other missing parts from the lower frieze. The re-assembled Ara Pacis was set up again during the Fascist period inside a bleak cage-like enclosure typical of the sterile architecture of those times. Whether it should be left on that site and in its unsuitable cage is still a subject of controversy.

Some more detailed mention must also be made of the Basilica Julia in the Roman Forum. It stands in what was a site removed from the traffic, trade and customary affairs of the Forum. It was the Palace of Justice of the day, and therefore the symbol of Roman law (*Jus*). It was on three storeys, with a sumptuous perimeter and with a space separating the interior from the busy street; this space was formed by two

sacrifice, of his wife Livia, his son-in-law Agrippa, his stepson Drusus, and of the consuls and personages of the imperial court and the state, which are carved on the friezes covering it, constitute a realistic documentation of Roman life in the Augustan age. But the Ara Pacis is also the oldest sculptured monument left to us by Roman civilization. It is enclosed by a square screen surrounding the sacrificial altar. The figured reliefs appear on the upper part of the screen's outer walls, above friezes adorned with delicate decorative motifs. Other friezes decorated with garlands sculptured in relief adorn the inside wall of the screen. The Ara embodies the classical idea of a 'triumph', of dominion achieved. The personages follow one after the other in the imperial procession, motionless and solemn in their majesty. The same majesty is found in other official Augustan sculptures, like the marble effigy of Augustus discovered at Prima Porta (now in the Vatican Museum).

The Ara Pacis Augustae was lost to sight until the fifteenth century, when the first fragments of it were discovered under the Palazzo Fiano,

The Island in the Tiber lies between two ancient bridges: the Cestio on the left; the Fabricio, the oldest in Rome, on the right.

of the Empire and of his name, his Mausoleum and the Ara Pacis Augustae (the Altar of Augustan Peace), both not far from the river-bank, are still standing despite the damage and changes wrought by the centuries. Lastly, under the Tarpeian Rock, downstream along the Tiber between the Capitol and the Tiber island, Augustus completed the Theatre of Marcellus, which had been begun by Julius Caesar and which he chose to dedicate to his beloved young nephew, Marcus Claudius Marcellus. On one side of the Theatre he dedicated to his sister the Portico of Octavia, which still bears her name.

The Pantheon has come down to us today as rebuilt by the Emperor Hadrian, after a terrible fire had seriously damaged Agrippa's original construction. It is the orthodox monument with a central plan, the prototype of a classic perfection in architecture, like the Parthenon, a source of inspiration to other geniuses, among them Michelangelo. The Mausoleum of Augustus (in the modern and architecturally unattractive Piazza Augusto Imperatore) is also circular in form. In it the Emperor combined the Oriental idea of a magnificent tomb with the Etruscan idea of a tumulus. In its massiveness it corresponds in Roman art to the funeral majesty of the Egyptian pyramids. It was not the only monument of this kind; the tomb of Cecilia Metella, on the *Regina viarum*, the Via Appia Antica, and the tomb of Hadrian, which later became a medieval fortress, today the Castel S. Angelo, reproduced the same principle of the large-scale cylindrical construction; and that principle also appears in the elliptical mass of the Colosseum, the most lasting symbol of Roman architecture and of Rome.

Neither the Mausoleum of Augustus nor Hadrian's tomb have been spared the damage wrought by men and time. Hadrian's tomb, as a result of work done under the Popes and by architects from the Middle Ages to the seventeenth century, has emerged as an architectural structure of a modern kind (even Michelangelo had a hand in it, in a little chapel on a terrace); while the Mausoleum of Augustus owes to recent restoration its present appearance of a ruin which is never-theless structurally close to the original construction. Augustus had planned it as a great conical tumulus, 143 feet high, rising on a cir-cular base nearly 300 feet in diameter and covered with cypresses. All the chief members of the Julian clan were buried there with Augustus. His cinerary urn was in the middle mortuary chamber, together with that of his wife Livia — who, incidentally, had had built for herself at Prima Porta, near the city centre, a sumptuous villa adorned with splendid mural paintings. The mortuary chamber in the Mausoleum of Augustus was reached by circular corridors, following a concept more Oriental than Mediterranean.

Mediterranean, on the other hand, both in conception and in the nobil-ity of its sculptured figures, is the Ara Pacis Augustae, the Altar of Augustan Peace, which has experienced all kinds of vicissitudes from the time when it was erected (between 13 and 9 BC) down to the present day. The Altar, built to celebrate the peace established under Augustus throughout the Roman world after victories in Spain and Gaul, was intended by the Emperor to be a sculptural representa-tion of the epigraphic *Res gestae Divi Augusti* (the deeds of the divine Augustus). The portraits of himself, in the act of offering a

▷

The surviving columns of the Temple of Castor and Pollux, in the Roman Forum, dedicated to the Dioscuri (the Twins) in 484 B.C., after the victory of the Romans over the Tarquinians.

selves by scribbling symbols or other patterns — the *tabulae lusoriae* —
on the marble floor of the porticos), the house and Temple of the Vestal
Virgins, the Rostra (or platform for orators, so called because it was
originally decorated with the *rostra*, or beaks, of captured ships), the
Temple dedicated to his deified spiritual father, the Temple of Divus
Julius, and lastly, in the grandiose Forum which he opened in his own
honour, the Temple of Mars Ultor, commemorating the battle of Philippi in which the traitors Brutus and Cassius, slayers of Julius Caesar,
finally perished.

Augustan architecture was, in Argan's words, *programmatically* classical. In fact, in order to achieve regal style and language it went back
to the Oriental, Hellenistic, and even Etruscan traditions, all comprised
in the classical ideal of the antique.

Augustus did not limit his architectural undertakings to the centre of
the city, the Forum, but extended them also to the Campus Martius,
the quarter along the Tiber which was the natural outlet to the north-
west. In that direction his intelligent son-in-law, M. Agrippa Vipsa-
nius, had already been fruitfully employed in founding the Pantheon.
Agrippa also built arcades, baths, basilicas and bridges in that area,
which were eventually submerged in the city's modern building development. But Augustus's own constructions there, built to the glory

Forum of today, he embarked on the most extensive building projects ever undertaken, which were subsequently carried on by Augustus, the first Emperor of the Romans.

The Latin author Suetonius, speaking with a courtier's rhetoric, says of Augustus that he found a city of bricks and left it a city of marble. In point of fact, Augustus did not pursue Caesar's ambitious plans for the city, and his aim was rather to bring some administrative order into building development. The fundamental idea governing his town-planning was that of dividing the city into fourteen districts (*regiones*), in which the quarters with the nobles' palaces and the ordinary citizens' houses were to be equally distributed. There was not enough room for all the districts within the walls, and six were situated outside (*extra-moenia*), the last of them being on the right bank of the Tiber. This arrangement persisted throughout Rome's development during the whole period of the Empire. It is interesting to learn that Augustus introduced nocturnal illumination in the streets and passages of the city's centre. Buildings of his period include the Forum of his name (on the left-hand side of the Via dei Fori Imperiali going towards the Colosseum) and the great Forum with the main monuments in it, the Curia, the Basilica Julia (one of whose sides fronted on the most fashionable street of the day, where idlers used to amuse them-

Fragments of an ancient aqueduct in the outskirts of Rome can be seen today in their original rural setting.

The exterior of the Curia, in the Roman Forum, where the Roman Senate convened. Built, according to tradition, in the time of the kings, it was reconstructed several times up to Diocletian's reign and then transformed into a Christian church. Was restored to its original form in 1937.

were introduced, and, most important for the development of Roman art and architecture, the vaulted arch came into use; at first to replace the flat roof-coverings of buildings and then as an architectural feature in its own right (as in the imperial triumphal arches), and for bridges, gateways, and aqueducts. This building spurt reached its climax in the early decades of the first century BC, when Rome already stood on the threshold of the Empire. The Tabularium (78 BC), built by Sulla, is visible from the Forum as a sub-structure of the present Capitol, which was built by Quintus Lutatius Catulus as a storage-place for the State archives. Rome began to be adorned with marbles and sculptures (many of them Greek originals, especially in patrician houses), with wall paintings and luxurious furnishings. The antagonism between Julius Caesar and Pompey, around the middle of the first century BC, has visual expression in monumental edifices, intended to exalt the greatness of their respective patrons. One can still see — in the curve of the seventeenth-century houses — Palazzo Pio in Piazza del Biscione — the outer structure of the arena of Pompey's theatre, the first in Rome to be built of bricks (55 BC). Near the theatre stood the Curia Pompeia, in the place now called Monte della Farina, a few steps from Largo Argentina. It was before the Curia, on the Ides of March 44 BC, that Julius Caesar was struck down. Julius Caesar the *dictator perpetuus* (effigy in marble of Trajan's period, now in the Council Chamber of the Senatorial palace on the Capitol), has left his architectural mark in the ruins of the Forum named after him (on the right of the Via dei Fori Imperiali, coming from Piazza Venezia), which was the first structure, planned on a monument scale, of the most celebrated group of buildings in ancient Rome. Beside the Forum he also built the Temple of Venus Genetrix, from whom the Julian clan boasted descent, as an offering of gratitude for the outcome of the battle of Pharsalus (48 BC). In the Republican Forum, the Roman

Rome under the kings (Numa Pompilius, Tullus Hostilius, Ancus Martius, Servius Tullius, Tarquinius Priscus, Tarquinius Superbus) underwent considerable and rapid development, the city's expansion depending on each king's political needs, the character of his rule, and the circumstances in which he found himself involved. The original city was extended to take in other hills, the Janiculum and the Aventine. Important public works were built, such as the *Cloaca maxima* opened by Tarquinius Priscus; the outlet of this great drain, which discharged the water flowing down from the hills into the Tiber, is still clearly visible downstream from the Ponte Rotto (the Roman *Pons Aemilius*), though the fine terminal vault of tufa blocks that we admire today dates from only the second century BC. Temples and walls, wooden bridges over the Tiber, a city already large and fortified at its vulnerable points, constituted the urban inheritance which the royal era, ending with the despotic rule of Tarquinius Superbus, scornful alike of Senate and people, bequeathed to the Republic.

The republican era naturally produced architectural works of a more democratic nature, such as the Curia, or Senate, but it did not neglect the temples and the surrounding walls. The considerable portions of the so-called Servian Walls still visible today, in the heart of the city, are more likely the remains of an enclosure of the republican period, built after the burning of the city by the Gauls in 390 BC. And the fine group of four temples at different levels, three of them rectangular and one circular, brought to light between 1926 and 1930 in the present-day Largo Argentina, is also a notable example of the architecture of the republican period. Temple A had six frontal columns and surrounding columns of fluted tufa, most of which have been preserved. Temple B is circular, with seven columns still standing of the sixteen that surrounded it, and an impressive flight of steps at the entrance. Temple C is the oldest and the lowest in level. Temple D, the latest-built, has a high podium and is made of a more noble material, travertine.

The peaceful works undertaken by the republican rulers were brusquely interrupted by a series of wars against the Latins, the Etruscans, and the Volsci. But the real scourge that destroyed the major part of the existing structures was the invasion of the Gauls in 390 BC and the subsequent fire and pillage, which devastated the city to such an extent that the shattered inhabitants considered rebuilding it on a different site farther north. The good sense of the dictator M. Furius Camillus prevailed, and he managed to persuade his fellow-citizens to rebuild on the original site. For this reason he became the first to be known as *pater patriae*. The vast, enclosing Servian Walls of solid tufa in fact date from this period. Beginning at the Capitoline Hill, this amazingly daring structure marked a perimeter of seven miles, across valleys and over hills. Similar daring characterizes the impressive series of aqueducts, begun in 312 BC by the Censor Appius Claudius and continued and completed under the Empire; they rise majestically from the green of the Roman Campagna, dear to painters from Poussin onwards, to the romantic travellers of the Grand Tour, to writers and poets, and still an unmistakable landmark for visitors approaching Rome from the south. The aqueducts extend as far as the eye can reach, their interminable narrow arches aglow in the rays of the setting sun.

The city first acquired a monumental aspect in the second century BC. Columns embellished buildings, two-storeyed edifices were constructed, loggias were opened, decorations in stone, marble, or clay moulding

look down on the ancient city from a height or from an aeroplane above the winding Tiber, we get no visual picture of the seven hills (the Palatine, Quirinal, Viminal, Esquiline, Celian, Aventine, and Capitoline) covered by the later expansion of ancient Rome.

Nevertheless the Romulean city had something of the outward appearance of a town. Its social origins were not such as to imply the immediate rise of monumental architecture, but an ambitious design for expansion undoubtedly developed gradually in the first centuries of Rome's existence. During the reign of the seven kings the city's growth was determined by various influences, religious, civil, political, commercial, or bellicose.

The complex of tufa, bricks, travertine, storeyed marbles and columns that today makes up an evocative and romantic picture, alternating with green spaces and modern buildings and merging with the life of the city itself, lies displayed before the pilgrims from every continent like a single incomparable fabric. But it developed over the centuries in accordance with the needs of human beings, and with their history.

completed their rescue by suckling them. They were demi-gods, and the survivor of the fratricidal slaughter, Romulus, ascended into the heavens like a thunderbolt in a storm, to become the Roman god Quirinus.

When Romulus founded the city, the Etruscans had just reached the bank of the river. But by the time he had surrounded it with walls, fortified it, and created the *Pomoerium*, the intangible *Urbs* was already in existence. The *Pomoerium* was the sacred perimeter of the Romulean city which went, according to Tacitus, from the Forum Boarium, or cattle-market, where the Arch of Janus, the temple of Vesta, and the Temple of Fortuna Virilis stand today, to the Palatine, excluding the Forum Romanum, which was opened later. Today's visitor will find few vestiges of *Roma Quadrata* — some fragments on the Palatine, traces of a *pagus*, or hut-village, on the spur called Germalus (on the side facing the Capitol), an archaic vault inside the Forum, a consecrated area traced out in the Forum Boarium — mute reminders of those who once dwelt there. Even when we

Ponte Fabricio, which joins the left bank of the Tiber to the Island where Rome was born.

The City of the River

Legend, history and mythology may give a confused picture of the origins of Rome, but one fact is certain: the future capital of the most extensive empire of the ancient world, the *caput mundi*, had the most humble, even proletarian, beginnings. One day a small group of shepherds and traders settled on the square-topped Palatine Hill, then trackless and covered with vegetation, and later spread out onto the surrounding hills. The birth of this city was not unlike that of other cities of whatever future destiny, which rose on a hilltop and beside a river. At the foot of the Palatine flows the Tiber, the *flavus Tiber*, highway for the traffic and trade of ancient Latium, protagonist of Roman history and god and patron of the early inhabitants. The history of Rome began at the point where the crossing of the river was easiest: at the point, so the archaeologist Bianchi Bandinelli has recently affirmed, where the island in the Tiber lies today.

'Roma', according to remote Latin etymology, meant, in fact, *City of the River* — unless the word is taken even further back, to the *Ruma*, an Etruscan people. The bronze wolf of the Capitol, indeed, had always been regarded as an Etruscan work of art, possibly based on an Ionian Greek model. Now, however, serious arguments have been advanced for a different attribution. The sculpture, it is claimed, was a direct product of Greek art, and arrived via the Greek colonies in Southern Italy. So the Greeks too could lay claim to join the Etruscans, the Sabines, and the Latins in the formative process of Roman civilization. If the Capitoline Wolf, traditionally dated in the fifth century BC, is really a work of Magna Grecia, there is another point of fusion between Greek and Roman civilization.

A precise date for the foundation of Rome, *ab Urbe condita*, was handed down by tradition from the *Annals*: 21 April 753 BC. On that day — so history and legend unite in saying — Romulus traced the furrow outlining *Roma Quadrata* (the plan of the first wall was in fact trapezoidal). The twin sons of the God Mars and the Vestal Virgin Rhea Silvia, Romulus and Remus (who paralleled the fratricidal tragedy of Cain and Abel), had been thrown at birth into the Tiber. But the river retreated and left the twins high and dry, and the she-wolf

◁
The Capitoline Wolf (detail). Palazzo dei Conservatori. The famous bronze, age-old symbol of the mythical origin of Rome,
hitherto regarded as an Etruscan work of the late 6th-early 5th century B.C.,
has recently been maintained to be a work of Magna Graecia.

1503-13	Julius II (della Rovere). Michelangelo paints the Sistine Ceiling, Raphael the *Stanze* Rebuilding of St Peter's begun
1513-21	Leo X (Medici). Reformation begins in Germany
1523-34	Clement VII (Medici)
1527	Sack of Rome by the army of Charles V
1534-49	Paul III (Farnese) Michelangelo paints the Last Judgment
1585-90	Sixtus V (Peretti). Replanning of Rome begun
1623-44	Urban VIII (Barberini). Flowering of Baroque
1644-55	Innocent X (Pamphili)
1655-67	Alexander VII (Chigi)
1657	Bernini's Piazza S. Pietro begun
1700-21	Clement XI (Albani)
1798	Rome attacked and occupied by French revolutionary troops
1798	Proclamation of Roman Republic
1809	Rome made part of Napoleon's Empire
1814	Pius VII (Chiaramonti) restored to power
1847-78	Pius IX (Mastai-Ferretti)
1848-49	Revolution under Mazzini and Garibaldi. Short-lived "Roman Republic"
1861	Italy with the exception of Rome united under Victor Emmanuel
1870	Rome incorporated into the Kingdom of Italy and becomes capital. End of the temporal sovereignty of the popes, who retire into the Vatican
1922-39	Pius XI (Ratti)
1922	Mussolini's "March on Rome". Beginning of Fascist rule
1929	Lateran Pact between Vatican and Italy
1939-58	Pius XII (Pacelli)
1943	Fall of Fascism
1946	Italy a Republic
1958-63	John XXIII (Roncalli)
1962	Convocation of Second Vatican Council
1963	Election of Paul VI (Montini)

Significant dates
in the history of Rome

753 BC	Traditional date of the foundation of Rome
509 BC	Traditional date of the foundation of the Republic
390 BC	Sack of Rome by the Gauls
264-241 BC	First Punic War
219-211 BC	Second Punic War. Invasion by Hannibal
48-44 BC	Dictatorship of Julius Caesar
28 BC - AD 14	Reign of Augustus
54-68	Nero. First persecution of Christians
78-81	Titus
98-117	Trajan
117-138	Hadrian
161-180	Marcus Aurelius
193 211	Septimius Severus
211-217	Caracalla
284-305	Diocletian. Last persecution of Christians
312	Victory of Constantine over Maxentius
324-337	Constantine. Christianity becomes the official religion of the Roman Empire. (Arch of Constantine. First basilical churches)
410	Sack of Rome by the Goths
475	Deposition of the last Roman emperor
568-572	Invasion by the Lombards
590-604	Gregory the Great. Beginning of papal power
800	Coronation of Charlemagne in St Peter's
1084	Sack of Rome by Normans and Saracens
1143	Beginning of the Roman Commune
1309-67	Exile of the popes at Avignon
1347-54	"Republic" of Cola di Rienzo
1378-1417	The Great Schism
1417-31	Martin V (Colonna)
1447-55	Nicholas V (Parentucelli)
1458-64	Pius II (Aeneas Sylvius Piccolomini)
1471-84	Sixtus IV (della Rovere). Sistine Chapel built and walls decorated
1492-1503	Alexander VI (Borgia)

Contents

Aerial photographs pp. 44, 124, by Sostegni, Rome

End-paper illustration, plan of Rome, circa 1743

Here I am now in Rome, and have found,
it seems to me, a peace of mind
to last me a lifetime. To be able to see
it as a whole with one's own eyes,
even though I already knew the details
both of outer appearances and in
my own mind, is almost, I would say,
like beginning a new life.

J. W. Goethe, Italienische Reise

Translated from the Italian
by Muriel Grindrod and Geoffrey Webb

The World Cultural Guides
have been devised and produced by
Park and Roche Establishment, Schaan

SBN: 03-085984-0
Printed and bound in Italy by Amilcare Pizzi S.p.A.

ROME

Giovanni Carandente

154 illustrations
in colour and black and white

special photography
by Mario Carrieri

Holt, Rinehart and Winston, Inc.
New York • Chicago • San Francisco

contiguous arcaded corridors on each side, with triple rows of columns, the outer ones supported on pilasters. It was therefore, despite the spaciousness of the interior, a place essentially adapted to the comings and goings of its visitors, who moved about from one section of the porticos to another; these provided a psychological rather than real sense of separation from each other and from the rest of the Forum. It was, in fact, the ideal meeting-place for a community teeming with needs, and at the same time the official centre for legal consultations and the administration of justice, in short the headquarters of Roman law in all its authority. To this end the tribunal of the *centumviri*, the hundred councillors, met here. The basic conception of the building went

P. 20/21
A view of the Forum — the heart
of the ancient life of the Romans
— from the rostra (on the first
level at the left) to the Column
of Phocas and the other honorary
columns that line the Via
Sacra, to the stately colonnade
of the Temple of Antoninus and
Faustina. In the distance, on the
right, rises the 12th-century
Romanesque campanile
(bell tower) of the church of
S. Francesca Romana.

▷
The Tomb of Cecilia Metella,
on the via Appia Antica (the Old
Appian Way), built during the last
years of the Republic by Quintus
Metellus for his daughter. It is
among the most intact and splendid
funerary monuments along this road.

P. 24
The Temple of Vesta in the
Forum Boarium (detail), of the
time of Augustus, owes its name
(undoubtedly wrongly) to its
circular plan, which is similar to
that of the Temple of the Vestals
in the Forum.

back, as has been said, to Caesar. But its completion and rich marble covering, and the sculptures that certainly adorned the frieze of the first storey*, belong to the Augustan era and were typical of the solemn and noble conception of that historic moment which also prevailed in artistic development.

'We go up to the imperial palace [on the Palatine], the gigantic pillars, arches and ruins of which press skywards from amid the clusters of bushes moving in the breeze. At their feet, bathed in magical moonlight, is the symbol of a colossal imperial history, the Colosseum, like a gigantic stone bowl in which this Rome collected the blood of the world. Beside the Colosseum lies the Triumphal Arch of Constantine,

* US equivalent: second floor.

the boundary mark between paganism and Christianity, and everywhere, as far as the eye can reach, fragments of history emerge. An enchanted, magical silence reigns over them all. Among the ruins of the imperial palace an owl screeches. What went on here in those ancient times? Who passed through these imperial chambers? Augustus, Tiberius, Caligula, Nero, Domitian, the Antonines, Heliogabalus — the terrestrial gods and their daemons. Here were played out all the dramas of passion, of virtue and vice, magnanimity, madness, wisdom, and diabolical wickedness; every human sentiment found its expression here. Here the world was governed, squandered, wasted, dissipated in a night. Every age and sex has ruled here; here old men and women, young men and children, slaves and eunuchs have dictated laws. Now all is silence and death; the only sound is the plaintive cry of the owl as it flits among the deserted stone arches. From the other side the eye looks down on the eternal city, scintillating with a thousand lights, but it too is silent...'

These words were written by Ferdinand Gregorovius as he looked on the Palatine and the Forum one evening in the year 1853. After more than a century not much has changed, either in the aspect of that part of Rome or even in the romantic, funereal atmosphere described by the German historian. The Palatine and the Roman Forum, though now surrounded like any museum by an enclosure to which access is gained by a ticket bought at the entrance, have even today not become mere embalmed ruins. Almost the whole area can be surveyed from the terraces on the side of the Capitol.

Looking from the Capitol on to the Forum and the Palatine rising on its right, it is also possible to get a clear idea of the imperial city plan in a prospect reaching from the nearby Arch of Septimius Severus to the Arch of Titus — the two terminal points of the Via Sacra — and extending to the monuments on either side of the Via Sacra. These are: on the left, the Curia, where the Senate met (the present bronze doors are copies of the originals which Borromini transferred in 1660 to the entrance of the main façade of St John Lateran), the Basilica Emilia, originally of the republican era and reconstructed by Augustus, the Temples of Antoninus and Faustina and of Romulus, and the Basilica of Constantine; and on the right, below the slopes of the Palatine, the Basilica Julia, the Temples of Castor and Pollux, of Augustus, and of the Vestals (flanked by the Vestals' House and the garden adorned with statues, which successfully recreate the mysterious, removed atmosphere of the ancient area sacred to the vestal virgins). In the centre stand the *Lapis niger*, or black marble pavement, the honorary columns, and the Rostra, while in a picturesque corner lies the first Christian monument of the Forum, the church of S. Maria Antiqua, the first imperial building to be converted into a place of worship for the new religion which came into being with Christ during Augustus's reign.

Almost in the centre of the Forum, opposite the Curia and at a lower level than the other monuments, is a group of ancient remains that takes us much further back in time than the Augustan era. It bears a fictitious name, the Tomb of Romulus, and its discovery is of fairly recent date — 1899. All that may be seen at surface level is a square piece of black marble pavement, whence its name, the *Lapis niger*, or black stone. At a lower level, reached by a few steps, are the remains of an archaic altar and a *lex sacra*, or sacred law, thought to be a ban on profanation of the place, conveyed in an inscription in large archaic letters running from left to right and then from right to left, as in 'boustrophedon' inscriptions. This is the most ancient known inscription in Latin. It and the mysteriously symbolic character of the fragments of tufa give the place a special evocative atmosphere. Archaeologists will not swear that it was really the original site of Romulus' deification, but they think it likely that it was already a venerated place in the republican era. It too may have suffered from the devastations of the Gallic war in 390 BC. Perhaps the *Lapis niger* was set there only in Julius Caesar's time, during the extension of the Forum, to corroborate by the unusual distinction of black marble the veneration due to a place in which the founder of Rome was buried. Not far from the *Lapis niger* and the Rostra, towards the arch of Septimius Severus, is a circular base. It supported the *Umbilicus Urbis,* navel and symbolic centre of Rome and the ancient world. The Palatine as we see it today is just a square-topped height emerging between the depressions of the Circus Maximus and the Forum, projecting slightly towards the Tiber on its western side, where the river approaches the curve containing the Tiber island.

The importance of the hill fluctuated: at the time of Rome's origin, as we have seen, it was cardinal, then declined in the republican period, to flourish once again in the Augustan era. Claudius and Nero both had great interest in the hill, though Nero only built a transitory dwelling there, which was burnt in his own conflagration of Rome in AD 64: and it was modest indeed in comparison with his subsequent project, the *Domus Aurea,* or Golden House, the most luxurious and ambitious dwelling in Rome.

Nero's fire of unhappy fame destroyed two-thirds of Rome. This was why Domitian, the third of the Flavian Emperors, dedicated himself with the aid of his architect Rabirius to the reconstruction of the Palatine and of several other parts of the city. Domitian's palace corresponded to a somewhat different concept from that of the monumental architecture of the past. It consisted of a series of luxurious and magnificent reception quarters, and another set of quarters — what might be called today the guest quarters for courtiers' dwellings and for collective needs as understood at the level of an imperial court, such as the Stadium or Hippodrome and the *Terme,* or baths (these, however, were left unfinished by the Flavian emperor, to be subsequently completed by Septimius Severus). Septimius Severus once again interested himself in the affairs of the Palatine, which had been left to itself for some time (except during Hadrian's rule) in favour of other more pressing needs of the city.

The visitor who stands at any point in the Circus Maximus today will see spread out before his eyes the imposing high-arched frontals of Domitian's palace and the baths of Septimius Severus and, mentally reversing the prospect, he can also imagine the spectacle which the Emperor of the Romans must have enjoyed when looking down from the highest terraces of his house on to the Circus Maximus, filled during the games with two hundred and fifty thousand spectators. The Palatine also continued to be the imperial dwelling-place after Septimius Severus' day. But the luxury and splendour gradually waned. The only known restorations were by Heliogabalus, proverbial for his dissolute character and his passion for luxury.

After these brief overall descriptions of the Fora and their monuments, the reader will be looking for a more detailed account of their development and expansion. The series of Fora visible today was begun by Julius Caesar, prior to the Empire, and continued, one Forum after another, up to the time of the Emperor Vespasian. It therefore

The interior of the Curia, which, once the structure of the church of St Hadrian that replaced it had been demolished, was restored to its original austere simplicity.

represents an architectural span of over a hundred years. The Fora included a variety of great edifices — temples and basilicas, libraries and honorary columns, triumphal arches and tribunes — all of imposing size, remarkable for their decoration, and with varying effects of light and shade through the innumerable sculptures in relief with which they were adorned: the whole presenting a profusion of sculptured and embellished white marble which, in the blazing light of the summer sun, must have produced a blinding effect.

The area of the Fora extends from what is today the Piazza Venezia to the Colosseum and, transversally, from the hill of Magnanapoli (at the bend of the present Via Nazionale and Via Quattro Novembre) to the Palatine. The Forum of Caesar, the most ancient, which included the Temple of Venus Genetrix, is the first on the right of the present Via dei Fori Imperiali and thus lies at the foot of the modern white marble Victor Emmanuel Monument. Next come the Forum of Nerva (cut in two by the modern artery), the present enclosure of the Forum Romanum, and the Forum of Peace or of Vespasian (also cut in two by the road), with the Basilica of Constantine or of Maxentius beyond it. The first Forum on the left, going from Piazza Venezia to the Colosseum, is the late Forum of Trajan, also known as the Forum Ulpium (near the Basilica Ulpia and Trajan's Column). It was the last to be built and the most imposing. Its design is attributed to the imperial architect Apollodorus of Damascus, and it reveals an Oriental sense of display in the spacing of the buildings and in their grandeur

27

and variety. The Basilica Ulpia, which forms a background to it, is at a slightly higher level, and was like a vast *pronaos* before the Temple of Trajan (the ruins of which are completely buried today), while on each side of the Column of Trajan was a library, one for Latin books, one for Greek (papyri and parchments and also precious volumes on linen or ivory, which were preserved on quadrangular wall shelves); the very interesting remains of one of these libraries can still be seen today under the trees on the left of the Via dei Fori. After the magnificent Forum of Trajan came the Forum of Augustus, now completely excavated (approached from Piazza del Grillo), dominated by the majestic ruins of the octastyle Temple of Mars Ultor, an imperial *ex voto* for the battle of Philippi, mentioned earlier.

The other Fora (of Nerva or Transitorium and of Peace or Vespasian) have been swallowed up by the asphalting of the modern road which turns sharp left, and by the rhetorical constructions of the Fascist period, which subordinated respect for the sacred rights of archaeology to the senseless scenographic effect of driving a straight line from the Palazzo Venezia to the Colosseum.

The Amphitheatrum Flavium has been known as the Colosseum ever since the early Middle Ages (eighth century), perhaps because of its colossal dimensions (156 feet in height, the long diameter 205 yards, the shorter one 170 yards, and the external circumference 576 yards) or perhaps because it stood near the Colossus of Nero, a huge gilded bronze statue that Nero erected to himself after the burning of Rome, in the vestibule of the Golden House, at the foot of the modern flight of steps going up to the Temple of Venus and Rome.

The Colosseum was completed by Titus, the second of the Flavian Emperors, a year after he came to the throne. It had been begun by his father Vespasian eight years earlier. It thus took only a relatively short time to build this superb ring of travertine and tufa. The gladiatorial shows that inaugurated it, on the other hand, are said to have lasted a hundred days. It has been regarded for nineteen centuries as the symbol of Rome: 'As long as the Colosseum lasts, so the world will last', says an eighth-century prophecy. The architecture of the monument is closely connected with its function: an enormous human reservoir capable of holding 50,000 spectators and allowing them to leave it quickly, organized both above and below ground-level for every kind of games and gladiatorial contests. Five thousand animals are said to have been killed during the opening games, and a corresponding number of gladiators died, their fights alternating with land and naval 'battles'. The third Flavian emperor, Domitian, completed the amphitheatre, adding the last tier of seats. Alexander Severus restored the damage after it was struck by lightning in 217, and thirty years later the first millenary of the foundation of Rome was celebrated there by magnificent games and spectacles — contests between 2,000 gladiators fighting in pairs — and by the bloodiest slaughter.

The exterior of the Colosseum, a third of which is still intact, rises in four tiers, three of arches and the fourth of windows. The regulation

▷

The interior of the Pantheon. The great eye (oculus), more than 30 feet across, bordered with bronze and open to the sky.

(below) One of the picturesque approaches to the Palatine, the hill that preserves remnants of the early city and other, more splendid ones of the imperial age.

orders of Greek architecture, Doric, Ionic, and Corinthian, succeed one above the other in a sublime demonstration of theory. Much more of this famous monument might have been preserved today had not Emperor Honorius (AD 404) abolished by edict the *ludi gladiatores*, so that the Colosseum fell into disuse and lay open to spoliation. From the Middle Ages on, its travertine blocks were used for other constructions. In the fifteenth and subsequent centuries it became a veritable quarry for Roman builders. Not a few stones of the Palazzo Venezia, the Palazzo della Cancelleria, the Palazzo Farnese, and St Peter's come from this source. Another edict, this time by a Pope, put an end to the plunder. In 1750 Benedict XIV declared the Colosseum sacred to the blood shed there by the Christian martyrs (according to the then accepted tradition, though serious doubts have been cast on it today).

The Colosseum still stands, the perennial symbol of Rome; but Nero's Golden House, so ambitious and luxurious, has virtually vanished. It was a project as extravagant as it was colossal, brought into being by two Roman architects, Severus and Celer, whom Tacitus (*Annales*, XV, 42) describes as *magistri et machinatores*, corresponding roughly to super-engineers or building-contractors of today. It was called Golden because its interior walls were covered with gold, and also with ivory, gems and mother-of-pearl.

The only relic of all this opulence that the visitor of today can actually touch with his hand is the 'palace' which has been preserved practically intact in a hollow of the Colle Oppio, the Oppian Hill, buried under the Baths of Trajan (entrance from the Park of the Oppian Hill). The painted decorations of these caverns appealed to the standards of taste in vogue in the early sixteenth century, when the great geniuses of that time discovered them and greatly admired them. Raphael's *Logge* in the Vatican are a Renaissance transcription of them. The Laocoön group (now in the Vatican Museum), the work of the sculptor Agesander of Rhodes and his sons Athenodorus and Polydorus, dating from the second century BC, was discovered in a half-buried room of the Golden House in 1506.

The most fascinating parts of the House are the *cryptoporticus*, with square windows and paintings on the ceiling, the room of the gilded vault, and the famous octagonal hall. They give a sufficient idea of that majestic architecture and also of Roman wall painting of the time of Nero (corresponding to the fourth Pompeian style), executed here, according to Pliny (XXXV, 120), by the artist Fabullus. He spent his whole life on it, and we can believe Pliny when he says that Fabullus became the prisoner of his art within the high walls of Nero's crazy edifice.

Nero's dream was tinged by the myth of the Orient; Hadrian's dream, more cultivated and sophisticated than Nero's, aspired to a revival of Greece, while yet others, like the Praetor Caius Cestius', inclined more towards Egypt. The Pyramid of Cestius, near the Porta Ostiense, later included in the Aurelian Walls, was built by Cestius for his tomb and recalls the pretensions of the Pharaohs. With Hadrian, Roman architecture assumed a humanistic aspect. The Emperor wanted to live outside the city and near health-giving sulphur springs. Hadrian's Villa, near Tivoli (some 18 miles from Rome), with its *Canopus*, its so-called maritime theatre, the ruins of its columned four-sided portico (usually called the *Poecile,* from an unjustified comparison with the *Poecile* in Athens), and its Piazza d'Oro, remains, despite its mutilations, one of the most striking manifestations of the way of life of

A corner of the Basilica Julia, built by Julius Caesar (55-44 B.C.) and completed by Augustus. On its steps and on the marble paving slabs of its portico on the Via Sacra, the idle youths of Rome used to pass their time.

a cultivated man interested in art and literature. The building known as the Maritime Theatre was really a villa within the villa, standing on a little island surrounded by water and by a double ring of columns, an ideal place in which to read in peace and solitude. Baths and vast halls, monumental nymphaea, swimming-pools and stretches of water, peristyles, three theatres, two libraries, gardens and statues all amply justify the twenty years that the Emperor lovingly spent on them. The magnicent Canopus, or reproduction of the Serapeion (the sanctuary in the little Egyptian city of Canopus, to which, according to Strabo, pilgrims would go down the Nile from Alexandria), was built in accordance with Hadrian's wish to reconstruct such a place within easy reach of Rome. Recent intelligent restoration of Hadrian's Villa has revived it to a semblance of what it was eighteen centuries ago. The fine caryatids that border the canals are only plaster casts, but the originals are intact, kept safe from weather, in the Antiquarium on one side of the Canopus.

Theatres, circuses, and arenas served for the distraction of the populace, triumphal arches, honorary columns, and mausolea for imperial glory. Another type of gigantic edifice was characteristic of late Roman architecture; the *thermae* or baths. These were intended for both health and sport and as social meeting-places. They also existed in the imperial villas, for the private use of the court, but the most imposing baths were those built for popular use; the first of these, completed by the wise Trajan on the site of the ruined Golden House, has already been mentioned.

The thermal establishment was the most perfect product of contemporary building technique. It involved the collection and distribution of a great flow of water, and the adjustment of temperature at three different levels for the frigidarium, the tepidarium, and the calidarium; all this implied the proper functioning of many complex operations. Within the enclosure of the baths there were swimming-pools and sports grounds, rest rooms, and libraries, in fact everything required for therapeutic, educational, recreational and sporting needs, including gardens, arcades, and even places of worship. The baths were not only a place for social meeting and recreation, but also for meditation and disintoxication, a place both for communal life and for privacy, for spiritual catharsis and physical purification.

The contemporary visitor to the ruins of the majestic Baths of Caracalla, in the Via delle Terme di Caracalla, will find it difficult to realize that the perimeter of the original establishment was more than 2800 feet long and nearly 1500 feet wide. Its foundations were laid by Septimius Severus in AD 206, and it was opened ten years later by M. Aurelius Antoninus, known as Caracalla. His two successors continued work on it for another twenty years. The same combination of a bathing establishment and a place of recreation was reproduced in the Baths of Diocletian (begun in AD 289). These were on the Viminal, facing Rome's present-day railway station, and they are thus the first monumental buildings of the ancient city to welcome the visitor (although as soon as he emerges from the station he will also see on his right a considerable residue of Roman ruins, a portion of the so-called Servian walls actually belonging to the republican period after 390 BC). The Baths of Diocletian were slightly smaller than those of Caracalla, but the works they involved were so extensive that demolition and excavations virtually destroyed any difference of level between the two hills, the Viminal and the Quirinal. Ruins of the Baths can be seen here and there all over the area they once covered. The Museo Nazionale Romano, with its important collection of sculptures, mosaics and paintings, occupies a large part of the central block, or the Baths themselves. The tepidarium, however, is now occupied by the central nave of the church of S. Maria degli Angeli, built by Michelangelo in 1561 for Pius IV; he converted the large vaulted hall of the original building, treating the early structure with great respect. An elegant cloister with a hundred pillars, built in 1565, lies beside the church.

Trajan's Column (AD 113), which today stands isolated, was originally confined between the libraries of Trajan; it too can be likened to a volume of history, celebrating the Emperor's victory over the Dacians. The column, rising from a pedestal adorned by trophies, is of Parian marble, with a plinth at the summit on which stands a statue of St Peter by Tommaso della Porta (1587), replacing the original statue of Trajan. Around the column runs a continuous spiral band, 660 feet long, on which Trajan's achievements are faithfully depicted. The only interruption in the narrative is the figure of a Winged Victory

Only a few ruins remain of the majestic, once completely marble-covered, Basilica Julia, rising against the background of the Temple of Saturn.

in the act of writing (like a personification of history) the name of the conqueror on a shield, between the events of the first and second campaigns against the Dacians. Originally the parts in relief were painted and thus more easily visible from the atrium, the libraries, the Basilica Ulpia and the portico of the Temple of the Divine Trajan which surrounded it.

The unknown sculptor of this tremendous frieze, the 'Maestro of Trajan' (as he has been called by the modern archaeologist Ranuccio Bianchi Bandinelli, who has identified him stylistically), expounds, on the basis of a provincial and popular style, a new language. He takes something from the Hellenistic tradition but uses it in a modern way; and from the methods of Italic-provincial art he derives his vigorous narrative power and his passionate feeling of participation in the events portrayed, adding to it an urgent impulse of his own. The 'Maestro of Trajan' transformed an occasion for commemorative official sculpture into an astonishingly modern sculptural event. He was, in fact, the first authentically Roman sculptor.

In the same line of derivation is the author of the analogous frieze on the Column of Marcus Aurelius (AD 193). But whereas the first frieze is popular and realistic in style, the second is concise and expressionistic. In the sculptural scroll celebrating the victory of Marcus Aurelius over the Sarmathians and the Marcomanni, there is a greater contrast of light and shade, perhaps because this second column, which was dedicated to the Emperor and his wife Faustina, was, unlike Trajan's, planned for an open space where it would stand in full light. The sculpture of the period of Marcus Aurelius, moreover,

The façade of the Basilica Emilia in the Forum. Begun in 179 B.C. by the censors of the Emilian family. It was destroyed during the invasion of the Goths in the 5th century.

emphasized the anti-classicism which was typical of the late Roman era. Another example of this is the superb equestrian statue of Marcus Aurelius, in gilded bronze, incorporated by Michelangelo in the centre of the Piazza del Campidoglio in 1538. It was brought there from the Lateran. It owes its escape from destruction in medieval times to the fact that it was believed to be an effigy of Constantine and not, therefore, strictly speaking a pagan image. Traces of gilding are still visible on the bronze and are brought out when the sun shines on it; an ancient legend prophesied that the world would come to an end when all the gold disappeared.

The earliest development of Roman triumphal art went back to the third century BC. Indeed the custom of extolling the victor as a hero came into being at the time of the first Punic war. The first Roman monument with sculptured decoration dates, however, from 54 BC. It was dedicated to Paulus Emilius and to the gods, and was the forerunner of triumphal arches of the Augustan and Flavian eras.

All trace of many of Rome's triumphal arches has been lost; others exist in various provinces of the ancient Empire. The Via Sacra, in the Forum, is terminated at each end by the two survivors in that area, the Arch of Titus (after AD 81) on the highest point of the Velia, and the Arch of Septimius Severus and his sons Caracalla and Geta (AD 203). The Arch of Titus was erected by Domitian in honour of his brother

Titus, to commemorate the capture of Jerusalem in AD 70. The imperial triumph is immortalized in the two reliefs inside the arch showing the victor's *quadriga* and the captured spoils (among which is the seven-branched candlestick of the Jews). Resembling Hellenistic sculptures in their formal conception, these two reliefs, originally polychrome and gilded, reveal a new dramatic quality as compared with the Augustan art that preceded them. The figures stand out like living beings from the background, and perspective skilfully establishes their relationship to the surrounding space.

In the Arch of Septimius Severus, at the other end of the Via Sacra and thus back to back with the Capitoline hill, there are three archways on which the decorative structure of the reliefs is more composite. But the sculptures are unfortunately badly damaged. The arch was erected in memory of the triumph of the Emperor and his sons over Arabs and Parthians in Mesopotamia.

Triumphal in its grandeur is the Arch of Constantine, and it is also the architectural and sculptural symbol of the historic point in time when paganism gave way to triumphant Christianity. It is, moreover, a palimpsest of imperial Roman sculpture, for the many reliefs decorating it are of various different periods and styles and come from other dismembered monuments. Standing beside the Colosseum, at the end of the modern Via dei Trionfi, it marks the entry — or exit — of the ancient area of Rome that is most densely packed with archaeological memories. The small sections of the arch that actually date to Constantine's time — two medallions on the sides, the frieze on the smaller arches, and the base — reveal, as Berenson has said, a different conception of art, that of the decadent Roman Empire.

Another surviving arch, of the time of Constantine, stands in evocative archaeological surroundings in the Forum Boarium (which includes a rare example of a Greek-Italic temple of the first century BC, known by the (unauthenticated) name of the Temple of Fortuna Virilis, and another temple, consisting mainly of Corinthian colums, of the time of Augustus, erroneously called the Temple of Vesta, near two fine medieval churches, S. Giorgio in Velabro and S. Maria in Cosmedin). It is called the Arch of Janus, but archaeologists have ascertained that it had no connection with Janus, the god of peace and war, of housedoors, of beginnings — hence of morning, and of the first month of the year, *Januarius*. *Janus* refers simply, in Latin, to this particular type of arch with four façades. It too was a triumphal arch, and in its harmonious structure space and mass alternate, not only in its four crossed arches but also in the many niches intersecting its surface.

A similar alternation between the ponderous and the graceful, resulting from excavations in its massive walls or from the daring effect of its high barrelled vaults, may also be found in the Basilica Nova, known as the Basilica of Constantine or of Maxentius, begun by Maxentius around AD 308 and completed by Constantine after his victory over his rival in 312 in the famous battle *ad saxa rubra*, beyond the Milvian Bridge, on the Via Flaminia, *in signo crucis* ('in the sign of the Cross shalt thou conquer'). The spaciousness of this immense basilica still astounds us today, though only a third of the edifice remains intact. The play between the panels of the vaults seems to throw from space to space the despairing echo of a majesty on the verge of extinction. These are the last lamps to remain alight in the firmament of the Empire's glory. The upper foundations were on unstable ground, which caused its superb arches to collapse in the Middle Ages. There must have been a tremendous fall of masonry in which stones and colossal marbles, pillars and the imperial effigy itself were intermingled. Only the head of Constantine, with his great eyes wide open, was fortunately recovered; it now stands in the courtyard of the Palazzo dei Conservatori on the Capitol.

The Museo Nazionale Romano, in the Baths of Diocletian, the Capitoline Museum, the Palazzo dei Conservatori opposite, the Vatican Museums, the Borghese Gallery, the Barracco Museum, and also the private Torlonia Museum and Villa Albani are the richest repositories of Roman sculpture from the earliest days to the fall of the Empire, as well as of replicas of Greek originals that adorned imperial and patrician dwellings and public places. The collections were gathered by Popes and princes, beginning in the fifteenth century when, with the Renaissance, the feeling for classical antiquity revived. The oldest public collection in Rome and in the world was that in the Capitoline Museum. It was begun in 1471 by Sixtus IV, enriched by his successors, and opened to the public by Clement XII, the Florentine Lorenzo Corsini, Pope from 1730 to 1740.

Greek originals and replicas of the Roman era, Egyptian and Etruscan antiquities (the latter both in the Etruscan-Gregorian section of the Vatican Museum and in the splendid Museo Nazionale di Villa Giulia, in the Viale delle Belle Arti, itself a stimulating example of modern museum presentation technique), bronzes and marbles, sculptures in

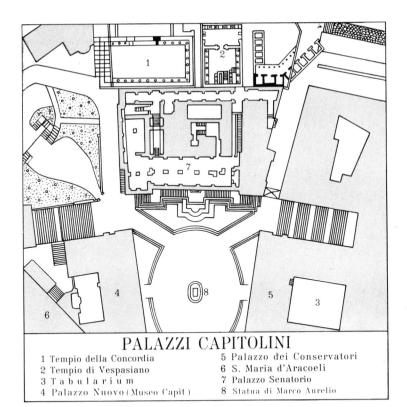

PALAZZI CAPITOLINI

1 Tempio della Concordia
2 Tempio di Vespasiano
3 Tabularium
4 Palazzo Nuovo (Museo Capit.)
5 Palazzo dei Conservatori
6 S. Maria d'Aracoeli
7 Palazzo Senatorio
8 Statua di Marco Aurelio

the round and in relief, sarcophagi and fragments of architectural decorations, effigies and busts (the finest series of busts of sixty-five Roman emperors, in chronological order, is in the Sala degli Imperatori in the Capitoline Museum), fantastic animals, goblets and precious marble vases — all these examples of ancient art can be seen in the rich collections of Rome's museums. The number of sculptures alone is overwhelming.

We know much less, on the other hand, about Roman painting. Written sources assure us that in Rome paintings were also done at the easel as well as on walls, but no examples remain except for the Egyptian Fayum portraits.

In the earliest times Roman painters continued the Etruscan tradition (familiar to us from the splendid tomb paintings of Tarquinia and Cerveteri), around the first century BC turning to Greek models, which they sometimes even copied faithfully, but it was not until a hundred years later, in the first century of the Empire, that they really began to give a better and more independent account of their art. From that period dates the large square panel portraying the wedding of Alexander and Roxana, known as the *Aldobrandini Wedding Scene* (Vatican Museums), which was discovered in the sixteenth century in a house on the Esquiline and at once held in high regard. Actually, this great wall-painting (roughly 3 by 7½ feet) has been found to be a copy. The figures do not stand out from the background and the perspective is uncertain: points of style and quality which in the Greek painting must have been fundamental seem to have escaped the Roman copyist of the Augustan period. The most notable and best preserved examples of painting of the classical era are perhaps to be found in the two Campanian towns of Pompeii and Herculaneum,

The Arch of Septimius Severus, one of the principal remaining Roman triumphal arches (A.D. 203), rises at the end of the Forum, at the foot of the Capitoline Hill and overlooks an intact section of a Late Empire pavement.

▷

The campanile of the church of S. Francesca Romana seen from the Basilica of Maxentius — a mixture of classical ruins and the remains of medieval and later periods.

which were destroyed by the eruption of Vesuvius in AD 79. In Rome there are the already mentioned decorations in perspective by Fabullus in the Golden House, and the older and more stylistically orthodox wall paintings which formerly adorned the walls of the Villa Livia at Prima Porta (Museo Nazionale Romano), showing charming scenes of fruit-trees and many-coloured birds against a background of open skies. The styles of tomb-painting, which from the third century decorated the underground Christian burial-places, the catacombs, also reflect the evolution in the methods of painting pagan subjects up to the fifth century when, with the erection of the first basilicas, Christian worship emerged into the light of day.

Another famous aspect of Roman pictorial art developed with the technique of mosaics. The floors of houses in Rome, Ostia, and the provinces were splendidly decorated with mosaics, black-and-white or coloured, made up of tiny or larger pieces, giving an extraordinarily mobile effect in the varying lights. The Villa Armerina, discovered a few years ago at Piazza Armerina in Sicily, is a highly instructive example of this art and of the exquisite technique of Roman mosaic craftsmen. There is no lack of splendid mosaics in Rome. They are to be seen in practically all the museums of antiquities mentioned above. In particular, those showing a still-life framed in rich borders and executed in many and varied colours (especially fine examples are in the Vatican Museums) display a type of pictorial art which in gradations of tone, vibrations of light, and chiaroscuro effects differs very little from, and sometimes surpasses, painting executed with a brush.

The Romans liked to spend the summer in pleasant places, whether close to or far from the capital. There was much sea and river traffic, their ports were highly efficient, and they built houses near them which sometimes actually formed towns or large villages. Ostia Antica, which takes its name from its position (*ostium*, or river-mouth, in this case the mouth of the Tiber), is 10 miles from Rome. The Tiber used at one time to lap the town just before emptying itself into the Tyrrhenian Sea. A flood in 1575 altered the course of the river, causing it to make a bend northwards. A little way beyond Porta Marina, the

sea also lapped the riverside town. It is easy to understand how important the town was commercially and as a port; it was Rome's gateway to all the regions of the empire. First Sulla and then the Emperors Claudius and Trajan fortified it with walls and strong port defences, opened harbours, established warehouses, and built out wharves. Ostia had as many as 100,000 inhabitants in an area of less than half a square mile.

A visit to Ostia, now in ruins but carefully excavated by modern archaeologists, gives one an idea of its past importance, which came to an end in the time of Constantine — thereafter it was to remain for centuries sunk in the marshy soil and in the grip of malaria. Divided into *regiones* (districts) and *insulae* (islands), Ostia presents a clearly defined and sensible town plan. It was studded with the massive shapes of public buildings: the various thermae (of Neptune, the Forum, and the Seven Sages), the Temples of Ceres, Rome and Augustus, the Mithreum (one of the eighteen sanctuaries of the original cult of Mithras that existed in Rome), the Basilica, the watchmen's barracks, the Capitolium (a prostyle temple of the time of Hadrian) dominating the Forum. Agrippa also built a theatre there on a semicircular plan, with a proscenium decorated with polychrome marbles. Septimius Severus and Caracalla restored it and it is thus certain that it was in use for theatrical performances throughout the imperial period (classical plays are now given there during the summer months). But private houses as well as public buildings were important in Ostia. Here as at Pompeii, we can get close to the daily life, customs and domestic habits of people in ancient times. One of these houses in Ostia, known as the 'house of the frescoes', is of interest for two reasons: because some of the rooms (the *tablinium*) are decorated with frescoes and have fine mosaic floors, and also because it constitutes as a whole a new type of dwelling, designed for several families like a modern apartment house, thus showing the change already taking place in Roman social customs during the Empire.

Early Christian and Medieval Rome

The Old Appian Way, the most familiar of the great consular roads, is bordered, in its first stretch out of Rome towards the south, with ancient tombs; it thus not only presents an evocative landscape of verdure and grey stones but is also a place dedicated to death. Like other sites of past civilizations — Byblos, the valley of the Pyramids, the Streets of the Tombs at Cerveteri and Pompeii — it recalls, with the funeral memories evoked by the tombs that line its borders, the respect of man in ancient Roman times for his ultimate destiny. In the same way, the labyrinth of catacombs that winds beneath the soil of Rome for some 60 miles was conceived by the early Christians as a memorial to the sublime moment of death.

Christian eschatology viewed death as a transition to the new era of the spirit opened up by the revelation of divine truth. The catacombs were thus the first place in which this mystery and the faith expressive of it found shelter and adequate outer form. The Christian funeral cult differed from the pagan, which manifested itself chiefly in the stele, the sarcophagi and other monuments erected skywards, forming

▷

The Domus Aurea (Golden House) of Nero, the most sumptuous residence of ancient Rome, which did not, however, survive its builder.

real architectural structures — or, for the poorer classes, in niches for cinerary urns which presupposed cremation, something abhorred by the Christians. From the architectural point of view, the catacombs had little significance. They were excavated out of the tufa deep in the bowels of the city, whereas architecture in general is produced by raising walls and enclosing spaces. Some Christian burial-places do nevertheless reveal the glimmerings of an architectural idea, if not precisely an aesthetic intent, for example in crypts, halls on a basilical plan, or three-tiered cells (*cellae trichorae*). They were, in fact, communal underground tombs, nor were they the first in ancient times.

We need only recall the perfect example at Hal-Safliemi, in Malta, which is of the neolithic period. The Basilica di Porta Maggiore, underground, of the first century AD, perfectly preserved and adorned with delicate stuccos, has exactly the appearance of a Christian chapel, but it was the place of worship of a mystic sect of another Oriental religion. Painting of the catacomb walls went on for more than three centuries, from the third to the fifth, and there were also sculptured reliefs and sarcophagi.

The Christian religion, both at its primitive clandestine stage and later, when it was officially recognized by the state (by an edict of

P. 42/43
The Cipolin marble column of the pronaos *of the Temple of Antoninus and Faustina, erected, by Senatorial decree, in the 2nd century A.D. in honour of Faustina, deified wife of the emperor Antoninus Pius, and dedicated to both after the emperor's death.*

◁
An aerial view of the Colosseum, which more than any other monument symbolizes the eternity of Rome. At the left can be seen the Colle Oppio gardens, which give onto the ruins of the Domus Aurea of Nero. At bottom right, the Arch of Constantine.

P. 46/47
More than half of the external travertine curtain wall of the Colosseum remains intact, with the superimposed Doric, Ionic and Corinthian orders which give the majestic structure the most solemn and austere nobility.

Plunder and destruction have not succeeded in damaging the splendour of the Colosseum. Eighty vaults give access to the arena, which held 50,000 spectators.

Theodosius in 380), was not concerned with artistic matters. Since it had to employ some form of figurative expression, it merely made use of methods taken over from pagan art. A large number of tomb-paintings have come down to us today, preserved the more effectively because they were hidden underground. Their subjects, whether explicitly expressed or by means of allegory, have an eschatological significance: the mystic communion in the hereafter of the soul with God. 'The earliest Christian images appeared somewhere about the year 200. This means that during roughly a century and a half the Christians did without any figurative representations of a religious character. It almost seems a pity', writes André Grabar, in his Mellon lectures on *Christian Iconography and its Origins* (Washington 1961), 'since this rejection of images never proclaimed *expressis verbis* by the theologians leaves us without archaeological testimony as to the spiritual state and reigning disputes of the Christian communities before the year 200.' The first figurative representations in Christian burial-places were in fact related to burial, showing little figures praying or the figure of the Good Shepherd (Christ the Shepherd of souls). Other figurative representations along conventional lines also appeared, sometimes symbolic, sometimes Biblical (frequent subjects were Daniel in the lions' den, the Resurrection of Lazarus, Noah's Ark, or Jonah and the whale). The most important feature is that the oldest tomb-paintings do not attempt to narrate an event but only to indicate it by means of a personage and a few attributes. The effect of this absence of narrative intent was that 'the paintings are schematic — that is, they are image signs, which appeal above all to the intellect and which imply more than they actually show' (Grabar). Another consequence is that many tomb-paintings, being over-laconic, have remained obscure or at least controversial as to their interpretation.

Christianity, undermining imperial unity, made proselytes in all classes, among the poor of the Suburra as in the court. Domitilla, after whom the largest Roman catacombs (in Via Ardeatina) are named, belonged to the family of the Flavian emperors. Sebastian was a valorous soldier in Diocletian's army, and the catacombs named after him are those which have been the most easily accessible throughout the centuries, and consequently the most readily plundered. Of their original four levels the second can be visited today (with guide) up to a crypt and a larger cavity beyond (*cumba*, or combe), from which perhaps the description *ad catacumbas* (the Greek *kata* meaning near) was derived. The relics of the apostles Peter and Paul were temporarily deposited in the Catacombs of St Sebastian. Among the most important catacombs are also those of Priscilla (of the *gens Acilia*, an illustrious patrician family) in Via Salaria (entrance at No. 430), containing the oldest representation in existence of the Virgin and Child (and the prophet Isaiah), of the second half of the third century, together with other frescoes interesting for the variety of their subjects. One chamber, square-sided and divided by an arch, has scenes from the Old Testament and a representation of the Eucharist, also of the third century. Not far from the Catacombs of Priscilla are those known as the Cimitero Maggiore (entrance at No. 6, Via Asmara), interesting for the mural paintings (a fresco of the Virgin adoring the Child is of the fourth century). Also of interest for their mural paintings (among them a representation of the *traditio clavium* — the handing over of the keys — of the seventh century and an interesting votive fresco, possibly of the same period or earlier, showing the Virgin, saints and the donor, the widow Turtura) are the Catacombs of Commodilla, an unknown Roman matron (in Via delle Sette Chiese, near the Basilica of St Paul outside the Walls); and, above all, the Catacombs of St Calixtus (just over a mile along the Via Appia Antica). Named after Pope Calixtus (218-22), originally a slave, who was persecuted by Commodus, rescued at the last moment, and elected head of the Christian community, these catacombs are on four levels, their windings following a most intricate course; they are especially notable as being the official place of burial of the bishops of Rome and the first Popes. Also buried there was St Cecilia, the youthful martyr of third-century persecutions (her sleeping marble figure here is a copy of the original made by Stefano Maderno in 1600 in the Basilica of St Cecilia in Trastevere: the sculptor represented the young girl as she was revealed on the discovery of the tomb, her body intact). The Crypt of the Popes, a gallery of the third century with cubicles and remarkable contemporary frescoes of the sacraments are the other major points of interest in these catacombs.

There were not only Christian but Jewish catacombs in Rome. Some of these are in Via Labicana, near the Christian catacombs of Marcellinus and St Peter; small and little-explored, they contain a number of frescoes of the third and fourth centuries. Other Jewish catacombs, not accessible to the public, exist beneath the park of the Villa Torlonia, extending for as much as five miles. More important for their

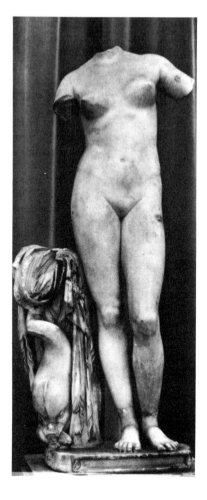

structure and decoration are the Jewish tombs in the vineyard of San Sebastiano, beside the Christian catacombs of that name (entrance at No. 119, Via Appia Antica).

The Jewish catacombs resemble the Christian in construction and decoration. In accordance with Jewish precepts, paintings did not portray actual figures but merely symbols, such as the Ark of the Covenant or the seven-branched candelabrum; inscriptions are mainly in Greek rather than Latin.

Paleo-Christian architecture, which came into being when Christianity secured recognition by the state, borrowed the models for its places of worship from classical architecture. The Christian religious edifice, however, was not based on the religious edifice of antiquity, the temple, but on a civic building, the basilica, and it kept that name. Another model used by the earliest Christian builders was the circular building with a central plan, derived in turn from the pagan tomb or mausoleum, and also from the porticos or nymphaea which had adorned thermal buildings. The basilica was intended by the Christians too as a meeting-place, the only difference being in the purpose of meeting.

The first buildings for Christian worship in Rome date from the fourth century, to the time of Constantine, Christianity's prototype-builder both in Rome and elsewhere. Obviously, these buildings were

being constructed simultaneously with late-Roman civil edifices, but there is a perceptible difference between them. The late-imperial edifice was in mixed styles and laden with decoration (it was the 'baroque' moment in classical art), whereas the Christian edifice was austere and in a single style.

The first basilicas in Rome were Constantine's Basilica of St Peter, on the Vatican hill, on the site where the leader of the apostles is said to have suffered martyrdom (*Tu es Petrus et super hanc petram aedificabo Ecclesiam meam* — Thou art Peter and on this stone will I build my Church — so Christ said) and above his sepulchre, as recent excavations have confirmed with the discovery of a Greek inscription of the time of Constantine, saying 'Peter is here', on the wall of the ancient loculus in the Vatican Grottoes; the Basilica, also dating from the time of Constantine, of St John Lateran, a few years earlier than St Peter's and established as the Cathedral of Rome; the suburban Basilica of St Paul, therefore known as *extra Moenia* — outside the Walls — on the Via Ostiense; and Santa Maria Maggiore on the Esquiline.

Only this last of the patriarchal basilicas retains its original fifth-century structure almost intact despite successive alterations (including the addition of the transept in 1290). St Paul's was completely destroyed in a fire in 1823, and what we see today is only a modern re-creation after the original style. St Peter's and St John Lateran have come down to us in the form given them by, respectively, the great architects of the sixteenth century (for St Peter's) and, basically, Borromini (for St John). In the church of S. Martino ai Monti, on the Esquiline (Paleo-Christian, but radically transformed in the seventeenth century by Pietro da Cortona), two ancient frescoes give an idea of the original form of the two interiors.

St Peter's was originally a vast construction with five aisles, preceded by an atrium with pillars, rich in mosaics, frescoes, and marble and bronze monuments, some of which are preserved today in the grottoes beneath the present basilica. The building of it went on for a number of years, roughly between 324 and 349. Pope Sylvester consecrated it to the fisherman of Galilee on 18 November 326. After more than a thousand years the edifice was reduced to a ruin, and Pope Nicholas V

decided to repair and reconstruct it. (A picture of the basilica at that time can be seen in a miniature by Jean Fouquet in the *Grandes Chroniques de France*, Paris, Bibliothèque Nationale). The Tuscan architect and sculptor Bernardo Rossellino embarked on the work of reconstruction in 1452 and continued with it for three years, up to the death of Nicholas V, when work was suspended, and for half a century nothing more was done except for a few repairs under Pope Paul II (Pietro Barbo). Julius II enthusiastically revived the ambitious plan, and Bramante, whom he asked to execute it, embarked on demolition of the Constantinian basilica with a view to raising in its place what he planned as a new Pantheon on the basis of a Greek cross. Work began on 18 April 1506; more will be said later about the subsequent developments.

The spaciousness of the ancient Constantinian Basilica of St Peter determined the stylistic character of all paleo-Christian architecture.

A foreshortened view of the Theatre of Marcellus, on the via del Mare, begun by Julius Caesar, expanded and brought to conclusion by Augustus and dedicated by him to his young nephew Marcus Claudius Marcellus, who died in A.D. 23. At the rear the columns of the Temple of Apollo Sosianus.

The altar of the *confessio,* above the martyr's last resting-place, was its focal point, visible from the entrance and the transept.

The needs of a dual function influenced the conception of this unusual plan. A recent theory to this effect has been advanced by Professor Krautheimer, and it merits careful consideration. As he points out, St Peter's Basilica, like the Catacombs, had its origin in the idea of a burial-place. It was in fact planned, on the one hand, to preserve the memory of the apostle (as is confirmed by the recent discoveries mentioned above), from that moment, or perhaps even earlier, an object of veneration, and on the other hand to render that *memory* accessible to the public, at the same time providing a suitable place for the consummation of rites.

The basilical conception had already developed with St John Lateran on a longitudinal axis, and it was visualized as a great empty space filled with light, symmetrical, harmonious, rational, and above all simple. The paleo-Christian basilicas and churches in Rome which have preserved their original structure confirm this view. Santa Sabina, of the fifth century (in Piazza Illiria, which takes its name from the church's founder, Peter of Illyria), with its fluted Corinthian columns, its solid arches between the nave and the aisles, its sober semicircular apse and its serene diffused light, is one such intact example. Clarity of form chiefly distinguished the architecture of early Christian times. From that clarity derived balance of masses, volumes, and spaces. Christian art, from its very beginnings, established its aesthetic canons free of theory, and almost unwittingly extended a bridge between past and present. With its severe spirituality, it implicitly repudiated the grandiose and challenging that were fundamental features of the imperial Roman structure, and the ostentatious affirmation of earthly possessions, dominion and power, all transitory things as compared with the eternity of the spirit!

Santa Maria Maggiore first rose, according to tradition, around 360, on a place indicated to Pope Liberius by a vision and by an exceptional fall of snow beneath the summer sun (hence its second name, Santa Maria della Neve). According to history (the *Liber Pontificalis*), the actual basilica was founded by Sixtus III, immediately after the Council of Ephesus (431) which had sanctioned the appellation of Mary Mother of God. Not all scholars are convinced, however, that the Liberian basilica was in the same place on which Pope Sixtus seventy years later raised his more magnificent construction. Contemporaneous with Santa Sabina, though it has come down to us less intact, Santa Maria Maggiore still preserves a considerable part of the paleo-Christian structure and almost all the mosaic decoration of Sixtus III's time.

The vast interior is divided into three aisles by forty monolithic columns with Ionic capitals on which the architrave directly rests. The mosaics of the triumphal arch date from the time of Sixtus III (the Pontiff's name appears in large letters in the centre), as do the thirty-six mosaic panels above the architrave. These represent the stories of Abraham, Isaac and Jacob (from Genesis) on the left-hand side and of Moses and Joshua (from Exodus and Joshua) on the right, with the idea of prefiguring the Advent of the Saviour, which appears together with scenes of Christ's childhood on the triumphal arch and views of the holy cities of Jerusalem and Bethlehem (in the spandrels) and the apocalyptic allusion (in the centre) of Christ's empty throne, symbolic of the expectation of His second coming to judge all men. The Sistine mosaics of Santa Maria Maggiore are a rare and precious document in the history of fifth-century art in Rome. They reveal a

Latin culture permeated by classical influences and, though they are the work of different hands, possess a unity of style which enables us to speak of a veritable Sistine Renaissance of classical modes. The figures in the Biblical series have a typically Roman strength and vigour, while the scenes on the arch have a more abstract, immaterial quality, by reason of the theophanic conception of the part of the structure that lies above the altar, the liturgical fulcrum of the basilical concept. Santa Maria Maggiore has continued throughout the centuries to have an artistic history of its own. Some nine hundred years after it was built, Nicholas IV (1288-92) restored the apse and added the transept. Jacopo Torriti, a Franciscan friar and artist, completed in the apse in 1295 the mosaic series of the glorification of the Virgin (as affirmed at the Council of Ephesus in 431) with the Coronation of the Virgin in the half-dome, which bears his signature and the date. Of the formal grandeur and chromatic splendour of this mosaic more will be said in the chapter discussing Roman pictorial art of the thirteenth century, which was a very important period in art. To the same period as Torriti belong the two series of mosaics (among them the scene of Liberius' foundation of Santa Maria ad nives), by Filippo Rusuti and his assistants, on the old façade, included in the modern portico of Ferdinando Fuga (1743-50). In Baroque times, before Fuga, work had been done on the apse and the sides by other illustrious architects, Flaminio Ponzio, Rainaldi, and Domenico Fontana, so that the whole magnificent structure stood as we see it today, with its massive parts scenographically disposed in such a way as to dominate the Cispian hill, one of the summits of the ancient Esquiline. On the right of Fuga's façade is the campanile, originally Romanesque but restored by John XI in 1377, the highest in Rome, with truncated spire, which was restored in 1615 by the Borghese Pope Paul V, who was also responsible for the sumptuous Pauline Chapel with frescoes by Guido Reni in the interior, to the left of the nave.

The Lateran Baptistery, though its structure dates from Sixtus III and its present appearance from Urban VIII (1637), was founded by Constantine and is the prototype of Rome's Christian edifices on a central plan. It was built on the site of the baths of a palace belonging to the Laterani family and hence traces its early descent, possibly directly, from a classical type of architecture. Its transformation under Sixtus to an octagonal form did not alter its structural principles but preserved the classical model. Together with Santa Costanza, also Constantinian (it was built as a mausoleum for the Emperor's daughters, Costanza and Elena) and Santo Stefano Rotondo, c. 470-83, relatively better preserved, it gives us a clear idea of Rome's first Christian churches on a central plan. The circular plan (surviving in S. Costanza and S. Stefano Rotondo) exemplified the rational idea which even primitive Christian architecture had grasped as being an essential of classical art: it is the most natural of structures, a circular wall with a roof to enclose a space within which light enters from several sources instead of from only one (as was the case in the Pantheon). In Santa Costanza a hitherto unknown idea was carried out. Mosaics (now partly restored) against a white background adorn the barrel-vaulting of the ambulatory, in other words the vault of the part most deeply in shadow, as if to lighten it with their vivid play of colouring. They represent vintage scenes among graceful vine-tendrils, perhaps in an allusion to the super-terrestrial world. Needless to say, a funeral concept also influenced the ideas behind Santa Costanza.

Lightness and space are the chief impression of the mosaics in the apse of S. Pudenziana (in Via Urbana), originally baths transformed into a basilica at the end of the fourth century, and also of the mosaics in the later S. Prassede (in Via S. Martino ai Monti), related to the former basilica perhaps merely iconographically, since the two titular martyrs were thought to be sisters. The apsidal mosaic in S. Pudenziana, which is contemporary with the construction, is of classical derivation in the individual parts of its composition, with its panorama of buildings aligned so as to give a prospect of Jerusalem (including façades of the two Constantinian churches of Golgotha and of the Nativity in Bethlehem), Christ in majesty, the Apostles foreshortened almost in the manner of Veronese, and the variegated and ethereal clouds, against which a golden cross stands out. The figure of Christ is a revival of the figure of the pagan Jupiter, severe and authoritarian, perhaps foreshadowing the earthly authority of His vicar, the Pope. In S. Prassede, built four hundred years later, at the time of Pope Paschal I (817-24), the triumphal arch and the apse (and also the Chapel of San Zenone, halfway down the nave) contain mosaics in a different style (Byzantine influences had in the meantine made themselves felt in Rome).

Byzantine influence came to Rome with the entry of Belisarius' troops in 536 and the reduction of the city to the status of a province of the Byzantine Empire. It bore fruit, despite the constant counterweight of the persisting classical tradition. In architecture, elements of Byzantine derivation are to be found in the ancient basilica of S. Lorenzo fuori le Mura (St Lawrence outside the walls), reconstructed by Pope Pelagius II (570-90), partially destroyed in the bombardment of Rome on 19 July 1943, and subsequently restored to its original state. Pelagius' building was superimposed on the earlier Constantinian basilica and established a connection with the tomb of St Lawrence in the catacomb beneath. In the thirteenth century the orientation of the Pelagian basilica was altered and it was extended up to the portico,

*(left) The Arch of Janus in Via del Velabro, near the Forum Boarium.
Dating perhaps from the Constantine epoch, but constructed of older materials.*

*(right) Part of the building of the Baths of Diocletian (A.D. 298-306).
Now houses the Museo Nazionale Romano (National Museum of Rome).*

thus becoming the presbytery of the new structural complex. The matroneum or gallery above the colonnade shows clear Byzantine influence. There is a similar gallery in S. Agnese fuori le Mura (St Agnes outside the walls) in Via Nomentana, where the effect is more picturesque, with the contrast between masses and spaces. The primitive church was founded on the catacombs of the martyr by Costanza, daughter of Constantine, in 342. The mosaic in the apse of the reconstructed basilica, of the time of Pope Honorius I (625-38), is one of the examples of Byzantine art in Rome which can bear comparison with the contemporary works in Ravenna. The stylized figure of St Agnes stands out against a field of gold, with a Pope on each side, one of whom, Honorius, the re-builder of the basilica, carries a votive model of it, in accordance with the iconographical usage customary from its earliest days in Christian painting.

Between the sixth and the eighth centuries people from Byzantium, Syria and the whole of the Christian Orient, and also barbarians from the north, flowed into the free port of Rome, which though politically in a state of depression remained wide open culturally. The various cultural trends penetrated the fabric of the city itself, influencing both in form and in content its architecture, painting, and decoration. Buildings preserved the basic paleo-Christian pattern, but they underwent transformations which gradually led to a new type of structure and a new aesthetic conception. The group of churches belonging to this period — or which were transformed from the original design during the period — speak for themselves. In S. Maria in Cosmedin, in the Forum Boarium, the colonnade was replaced by stretches of wall, and a new kind of space-rhythm appeared, with a different gap between masses and spaces (originally repeated at a higher level in the galleries, which were destroyed during restorations after AD 1000 under Popes Gelasius II and Calixtus II). S. Maria in Domnica (in Piazza della Navicella), built under Paschal I (817-24), with the broad nave and apse altering the usual relationship between the parts of a basilica, and SS. Quattro Coronati (in the street of that name), both of which were enlarged at that time, are further revealing examples of the gradual decomposition of the primitive basilical pattern. Architects in Rome were more concerned with the free values of masses rather than with the architectural canons and were gradually working out, among the many different influences and trends, a more elaborate and specialized and therefore more distinctive form of architecture. In this sense Rome too, if only in a limited way, shared in an active elaboration of the new building styles and of a new style of decoration. The first half of the ninth century was a time of development 'rich in new departures and appendices to the past' (Matthiae). A quite exceptional event had occurred on Christmas Eve of the year 800. Charlemagne, King of the Franks, had received the imperial crown from the hands of Pope Leo III in St Peter's in Rome, and was acclaimed by the Roman populace 'Emperor and Augustus'. The Pope had turned to him for aid against his enemies and was now giving him his reward. Charlemagne's father, Pepin the Short, had some years earlier donated to the Pope of Rome in exchange for his coronation (on that occasion in Paris) certain lands taken from the Lombards and by them from the Byzantines, and had thus laid the foundations of Papal temporal power. There is a silver coin which documents the agreement of the Papacy with the Carolingian monarchy: on one side it bears the monogram of Charlemagne, on the other that of Leo III. It could represent the concrete expression of the mutual respect of these powers.

The papacy of Leo III's successor Paschal I (817-24) was not a long one but three famous monuments bear his name. Two of them have already been mentioned, S. Prassede (to which we shall return shortly) and S. Maria in Domnica. The third building is one of the most celebrated in Rome, the basilica of S. Cecilia in Trastevere. It stands in the heart of a district whose fascination lies in its very contradictions: essentially a popular quarter, where ancient traditional crafts and trades are still pursued, it is one of the few places that offer the visitor an at least partially authentic sight of the 'Romans of Rome', as its inhabitants have aptly been called. In recent decades it has been invaded by an ill-considered and arbitrary town-planning policy, often tastelessly executed, while today it is the victim of misguided and artificial attempts to maintain its 'folklore' character — attempts to which transitory foreign residents, whether unconsciously or otherwise, often lend themselves. Santa Cecilia lies a little apart, but all the same it does not escape being assailed by establishments of noisy gastronomic vulgarity. It stands mysteriously behind a quiet garden with an ancient marble vase in the centre; behind it are Fuga's monumental eighteenth-century façade and the interior, whose basilical plan is barely perceptible amid the restorations of the eighteenth and nineteenth centuries. But in the half-dome of the apse there is a mosaic of the time of Paschal I, who appears in a lively representation on the extreme left (with the square halo, in accordance with paleo-Christian custom), beside St Agatha and St Paul. In the centre is the Saviour, and on the right are St Peter, St Valerianus, and his wife, the martyr St Cecilia; below is the symbolical flock of sheep. Stylistically this mosaic reproduces the themes of the mosaic in the church of St Cosmas and St Damian, but the paleo-Christian methods of presentation are supplemented by other elements which local tradition derived from the many different cultural influences it had absorbed. The appearance of the church is eclectic, combining widely differing relics of many centuries: Arnolfo di Cambio's canopy above the high altar (1283), the original of Maderno's marble statue of St Cecilia beneath the altar (already mentioned in connection with the copy of it in the catacombs of St Calixtus), the chapel of the Relics, designed

The Porta Maggiore, or Porta Prenestina, in the piazza of the same name, was built in A.D. 52 by the Emperor Claudius at the junction of the two consular roads of Prenestina and Casilina. It was restored and enlarged by later emperors.

by Vanvitelli, frescoes of the fifteenth and eighteenth centuries (the fresco in the ceiling, of the Apotheosis of St Cecilia, is by Sebastiano Conca), and the Roman constructions beneath the crypt. Beyond the interior façade, concealed by the eighteenth-century ceiling, is the most valuable work of all: the fresco painting of the *Last Judgment* by Pietro Cavallini, of around 1293. Entry (by special permission, through the convent of an enclosed order of nuns) is by a side-door.

Paschal I was responsible not only for the construction of S. Prassede and the mosaic decoration of its triumphal arch and apse but also for the building of the chapel of San Zenone, halfway down the aisle, which has come down to us practically intact, and is the most important reflection of Byzantine art in Rome. It was designed by the Pope as a little funeral chapel for his mother Theodora.

The early history of Rome calls for mention of another Roman Pope, Leo IV (847-55), and for other reasons besides the important pictorial decorations that he initiated in the Basilica of S. Clemente, near the Lateran, where, in a notable series of frescoes showing scenes from the life of Christ (on the left of the central aisle, in the lower church), he shows that he was himself a considerable artist, fully informed about the main cultural trends of the day, including Carolingian illumination and the compositional innovations of Western painting. To protect St Peter's and the adjacent areas from the increasingly alarming invasions of the Saracens, Leo IV surrounded them with

The Boy with the Thorn. Bronze.
Late Hellenistic art of the 1st
century B.C. Palazzo dei
Conservatori, Room of the Triumphs
of Marius.

solid walls and twenty-four fortified towers. Thus there came into being the enclosing perimeter of the so-called 'Leonine City', and with it the Vatican. In the course of the centuries these walls experienced many assaults; in 1084 they were almost completely destroyed by Saracen and Norman hordes led by Robert Guiscard. At the end of the fifteenth century the Borgia Pope Alexander VI decided to rebuild and strengthen them, and connected them with Castel S. Angelo by means of fortified corridors which enabled, for example, Pope Clement VII (Giulio de' Medici) to escape during the sack of Rome in 1527. Towards the end of the sixteenth century another Medici Pope, Pius IV, opened up a number of gateways in the walls which are still in existence. The perimeter of the Leonine City was much the same as today, part of it (to the south and west) following the enclosure of the Vatican City (some towers come within the modern perimeter) and part penetrating into the Borghi, the quarters to the north and north-east of Piazza San Pietro, from the Borgo S. Angelo to the piazza whose name is a reminder of the Leonine City of eleven centuries ago.

The Papacy of Leo IV marks 'the end of the last felicitous period of paleo-Christian architecture... After that date a long gap occurs in building activity in Rome, extending throughout the eleventh century, to be followed by a period in which architecture became definitely medieval' (Krautheimer, *Corpus Basilicarum Christianarum*, I). The establishment of the Commune (1143-44) and its free institutions brought with it the rebirth of the Capitol, where life had for centuries been extinguished; now the Senate was re-established there and it became once more the centre of democratic life, as it had been more than a thousand years before under the Republic.

Towns in other regions of Italy became flourishing centres during the period of the Communes, but in Rome, unfortunately, this awakening had no favourable effects on town-planning, and art continued to be almost entirely governed by church patronage. Only the stern fortified dwellings of the Roman patricians arose to dominate the scene; these were often superimposed on classical buildings.

In the middle of the twelfth century the Fabii, one of the many families that were then becoming powerful, built their fortress on the Theatre of Marcellus. Its arches became the substructure for the defensive bastions, a slope filled up the auditorium, and the Augustan monument lost its recognizable features for ever; later the Savelli (for whom Baldassare Peruzzi built two higher storeys in the sixteenth century) and the Orsini, in 1712, made still further alterations.

Another example of the spoliation of classical buildings by medieval construction lies not far from the Theatre of Marcellus — the Casa dei Crescenzi, in Via del Mare, which was erected in the twelfth century as a guard tower over the nearby crossing of the Tiber. It was built by Nicolò, son of Crescenzio and Theodora, as we are told in an inscription carved on its front.

No trace remains of medieval Rome as a whole, and the traveller can only chance on occasional relics of its civil architecture in the old quarters; but such islands do exist within the fabric of the city, reconditioned though it has been by the great transformations that

▷

Tivoli. Hadrian's Villa. The Canopus (detail). Built by the Emperor Hadrian (A.D. 125-134), it was the most luxurious and sophisticated of imperial villas. Hadrian reproduced there the works and artistic effects that had struck him most forcibly in the course of his travels.

began with the Renaissance, were continued in the Baroque period, and became intensified in modern times. In Trastevere, the Borghi, and the districts of Parione, Regola and several others, medieval vestiges emerge here and there, small in scale in relation to the surroundings, small houses, blind alleys, external staircases, brick arches, fragments of classical columns used as supports. A few medieval towers, repeatedly restored, transformed, or mutilated, rise up here and there against the skyline of the city; the Torre dei Conti (at the corner of Via dei Fori Imperiali and Via Cavour), built by Riccardo dei Conti di Segni, brother of Pope Innocent III, and celebrated by Petrarch; the Torre delle Milizie (in Piazza Magnanapoli), once a fortress of the powerful Annibaldi and Caetani families; the Torre Millina, or dei Mellini (behind Piazza Navona); the towers and ruins of Palazzo Onoriano (Pope Honorius III, Cencio Savelli) on the Aventine; and the fine campanili of S. Francesca Romana (1161) in the Forum and San Giorgio in Velabro, in the Forum Boarium, which bring one into the purely Romanesque atmosphere. According to Rivoire, the most typical Romanesque building in the city was the little church of S. Maria in Cappella in Trastevere, which, however, was radically restored in 1875 (a stone in the interior records the date of its foundation, 1090), still sober and elegant with its renovated façade and its tiny two-light campanile, similar in form to that of S. Benedetto in Piscinula near by (in Piazza Piscinula, where it stands opposite the medieval Casa dei Mattei, still showing some traces of its original elements despite repeated restorations). Indeed, when Rome was rebuilt after the devastation of 1084, it took on an increasingly Romanesque character, as can be seen in, for example, the transformation of SS. Quattro Coronati, the church and six-storeyed campanile of SS. Giovanni e Paolo on the Celio (recently restored) with its remarkable apse with blind arcading of Lombard origin, San Lorenzo in Lucina (transformed in 1650), and lastly S. Maria in Cosmedin, where Romanesque additions (the portico, choir, and seven-storeyed campanile with mullioned windows) give the edifice a contrasting structural and picturesque character typical of Roman architecture of this period.

Faithful to a tradition that even after so long a lapse of time was not repudiated, Roman builders who entered upon Romanesque constructive renovation neverthless accepted its rules only in part. They cannot be said to have produced a hybrid version of it, but certainly their decorative innovations produced a highly individual style. The alternation of brick and travertine in the campaniles resulted in a strikingly lively colour-effect, as did the insertion of majolica and enamel plaques of Byzantine influence. Some façades of churches of this period are

(above) Tivoli. Hadrian's Villa. The Canopus. Although the identifications of the place are hypothetical, with its long and narrow avenue with the pool in the centre surrounded by arches, columns and caryatids, it could be a copy of the Egyptian city of Canopus, fifteen miles from Alexandria.

▷

(below) Tivoli. Hadrian's Villa. The Poecile, with its pool recently restored among the olives and cypresses, freely imitates the famous Athenian arcade, Stoa Poikile.

P. 66/67

Tivoli. Hadrian's Villa. The Villa of the Island, also called the Maritime Theatre. The Emperor's delightful retreat is the ultimate expression of the refined taste which inspired the entire construction.

divided into a lower portico and a façade set further back, often decorated with mosaics. We can get an idea of this scheme from the church of S. Maria in Trastevere (though there the 1702 portico is by Carlo Fontana), in the centre of a typical *rione* and in one of Rome's most animated and popular piazzas. The fountain in its middle, also by Carlo Fontana, with the steps going up to it, accentuates the atmosphere of cordial intimacy, and in summer the place is like a lively open-air drawing-room. On the ancient façade of the basilica, with the characteristic coved cornice, the mosaics, unfortunately spoilt by restoration, and of such varying quality as to suggest different dates of execution, probably date from the second half of the thirteenth century, while the campanile is at least a century older.

Marble-workers were numerous and prolific in Rome in the twelfth century and after, their work being distinguished by the richness and polychrome effects of their ornamental designs, the typical placing of the inlaid or carved decorations (on doorways, bookshelves, screens, pulpits, vestment chests, and pavements) and also by its eclectic

Another view of the Canopus. The recent reconstruction (the originals of the sculptures are in the adjacent Antiquarium) scrupulously recaptures the supremely evocative quality of the imperial villa.

influences (classical models, Arabic geometrical patterns, and Byzantine fantasy of colouring); they represented the continuity of a family tradition of craftsmanship. Some of these marble-workers distinguished themselves by leaving their name on their works, and given the rarity of medieval sculpture in Rome prior to Arnolfo di Cambio (1240-1311) it may not be too much to describe such craftsmen as sculptors. A Niccolò di Angelo and a Pietro Vassalletto signed a carved candelabrum for the paschal candle in the basilica of St Paul's outside the Walls. A Vassalletto (Pietro?) signed a stray lion in the basilica of SS. Apostoli (in Piazza SS. Apostoli). The portico of St Lawrence outside the Walls (1216-27), classical in form and with strong variations of colour in the decoration, is attributed to a builder of the same family.

These Roman marble-workers are generally known as Cosmati (because the name Cosma was the most frequent among the various families), and their decorations as Cosmatesque. The above-mentioned paschal candelabrum is a work of sculpture of intensely plastic effect, with its decorations showing animals, leaves and fruits, monsters, and inter-

*Tivoli, Hadrian's Villa, The Poecile.
A part of the great surrounding
wall which was originally lined
with porches to provide shade.*

lacings, and with the delicate light and shadow effects of the Passion scenes. Architects handed down and confirmed the attribution to Vassalletto of the work in the portico and cloisters (where it is signed) of St John Lateran and in the cloisters of St Paul's outside the Walls. Cosmatesque decorations appear in numerous other churches of this period in Rome and its surroundings. The Cosmati were chiefly concerned with surface decorations rather than with sculpture in the round, but their method of ornamentation almost took the place of sculpture for more than a century, right up to the Gothic period, and despite the fact that the decorative parts of their work derived from older models (the Cosmati only rarely used figurative representation), it undoubtedly had an originality of its own and provided a valuable artistic complement to Roman architecture of the twelfth and thirteenth centuries.

As far as mural painting in the first two centuries of the new millennium is concerned, there was no lack of highpoints in the general panorama, and the enthusiasm for representation released after the restraints of the preceding period showed no signs of dying down. The first two significant manifestations revealed a strong feeling for narrative and a gradual detachment from traditional influences. The two series of frescoes that initiated this new pictorial trend, which were almost contemporaneous and also to some extent stylistically related, were those of the Marian Oratory near the church of S. Pudenziana (entry from the church) and of the vestibule and nave in the lower church of S. Clemente. The former probably dates from the time of Gregory VII (1073-85), who ordered work to be undertaken in the little oratory, while the latter is slightly later and also reveals an evolution in narrative style, rich in the spirit of naïve realism, but not going beyond it into folkloristic crudity. The representations in both cases are of lives of saints, shown with freshness and candour, at times perhaps reminiscent of the treatment already adopted in illuminated manuscripts. In both cases the frescoes initiate a new pictorial culture, Western and Romanesque, and also, more definitely, a new phase in painting.

About a century later (the church was reconsecrated in 1191) came the series of frescoes in the little church of S. Giovanni a Porta Latina (in the street of that name), founded in the fifth century and frequently restored since. The little church is today a rare example of renovation, for it has recently been accurately restored to its medieval state. The series of frescoes, showing scenes from the Old and New Testaments with the Elders of the Apocalypse, decorates the whole of the nave, but it has come down to us with serious lacunae. It is not impossible that the painter of S. Giovanni a Porta Latina may have taken as a model the mosaics that Venetian craftsmen had executed in St Peter's, which were lost when the Constantinian basilica was destroyed. He was certainly a worthy precursor of the trends that were soon to become apparent in Roman painting.

◁
(above) Portrait of a man. Terracotta. Etruscan, 2nd century B.C. from Falerii Veteres. Villa Giulia.

(below) The so-called Arch of Drusus near the Porta S. Sebastiano. Only one of the three vaults that originally composed this triumphal arch of the second century A.D. remain. The connection with Drusus (1st century) is erroneous.

This new manifestation may be said to have begun with the arrival in Rome of the Tuscan sculptor, Arnolfo di Cambio, and to end with Giotto's last stay there, in the first decade of the fourteenth century or a little later.

Arnolfo di Cambio, whom a contemporary 'license' of the Commune of Florence proclaimed as 'the most famous and expert builder of churches', for over twenty years, from around 1277 to 1300, spent much of his time in Rome. Not all the works he completed there have come down to us, and many are fragmentary and anonymous. He signed some of them, adding to his name the description of 'architect and Florentine' (though in fact he was born at Colle Val d'Elsa, not far from Siena). The 'official' sculpture of Charles of Anjou, which he may have modelled with the help of a collaborator, imperious in its programmatic celebration of the Angevin King as a Roman senator, was made in 1277. The work is on the second landing of the staircase in the Palazzo dei Conservatori on the Capitol (where there is also a high relief of a trumpeter by Arnolfo). In the semi-demolished tomb of the Annibaldi, in the Lateran, of slightly later date, the sculptor shows that he has already left behind his discipleship of Nicola Pisano and turned with open interest to the classical patrimony of Roman art, which in any case was implicit in his development as a *new* sculptor. Gothic forms appear in the architecture of the canopies of the two ciboria of St Paul's outside the Walls (1284) and S. Cecilia in Trastevere (1293), and similar characteristics must have been discernible in the destroyed Loggia of the Benedictions, which he built for Boniface VIII in St John Lateran. But a classical feeling animates the sculptures of the ciborium of St Paul's, where 'the angels resemble ancient Victories, and Eve is like a classical Venus' (Toesca). The strong modelling of the sculptures stands out among the lively decorations in Cosmatesque style (attributed to Pietro Oderisi, who was an outstanding personality in the group of Roman marble-workers). The classicism is accentuated in the Ciborium of S. Cecilia and the modelling there is stronger (S. Cecilia and S. Tiburzio on horseback, daringly foreshortened).

Rome served Arnolfo just as much as he himself was of service to the artistic atmosphere of the city and the impetus towards a creative art. The effect of giving and taking is bounded on the one hand by his pronounced sense of the Gothic, visible, in sculpture, in the surviving fragments of the Presepio in S. Maria Maggiore (in the chapel of the Oratory, renovated by him but restored by Domenico Fontana at the end of the sixteenth century) and on the other by the 'rough plastic tension' (Toesca) of his last Roman work, also now dismembered and fragmentary, the tomb of Boniface IV, in Old St Peter's, sculptures and reliefs from which are now in the Vatican Grottoes. Other works in Rome bear Arnolfo's print, sometimes of his own hand, sometimes of his ideas or influence: the strong bust, signed by him, of Boniface VIII in the act of benediction, in the Vatican Palaces; the sarcophagi of Cardinal Anchero in S. Prassede and of Honorius IV in the church of Aracoeli; a marble sculpture of St Peter in the Vatican Grottoes; and, last but not least, another more famous St Peter, the one in bronze in the Vatican basilica (against the last pillar on the right in the nave), a 'solemn simulacrum', the right foot worn away by the kisses of millions of pilgrims, which for long has puzzled historians. Some have dated it from the fourth or fifth century, but this perfect fusion in bronze is a work which undoubtedly reveals the direct influence of Arnolfo, even if it is not convincingly

The plastic reliefs on the interior of the Arch of Titus sum up the political significance of the imperial victory and emphasize the idea of the Triumph that inspired the construction of the arch.

by his own hand. The most plausible among the various alternatives seems still to be, therefore, the one advanced by Toesca, which attributes it to a gifted artist of the end of the thirteenth century, a follower of Arnolfo's methods, to whom Toesca also attributes a St Paul in wood in the Basilica of St Paul's, worn away to a mere stump because the faithful took to detaching flakes from it as relics for veneration, ceasing the practice only just in time to leave at least an approximate memory of the original to posterity.

In 1291 Pietro Cavallini was signing the mosaic panels of scenes in the life of the Virgin in the apse of S. Maria in Trastevere. 'He has something of the ancient, that is to say the Greek, manner', said Lorenzo Ghiberti, who so much appreciated his greatness that he described him as 'the most learned of all the other masters' (*Commentari*, II, 9; c. 1447). In the Trastevere mosaics, the iconographic scheme is Byzantine, and also the deep feeling for colour which, however, moulds the figures in a new way, enlivens the perspectives, creates distances, and gives plastic relief to the composition. 'In no other Italian pictorial representation before the thirteenth century', writes

Toesca, 'was colour so important, so that it became for the visual sense not merely an excitement but a revelation.' The donor of these mosaics, Bertoldo Stefaneschi (represented kneeling in the panel with the Virgin and the Apostles Peter and Paul, in the back of the apse) belonged to an illustrious family of art patrons. Cardinal Jacopo Stefaneschi distinguished himself some years later by other donations, the Stefaneschi polyptych, by Giotto and collaborators, formerly on the altar of the Confessio in Old St Peter's (Pinacoteca Vaticana) and the lost Giottoesque mosaic of the *Navicella*, of which more will be said below. Cavallini shows both greater maturity and a freer fresco technique in his *Last Judgment* in S. Cecilia in Trastevere, the only remaining part of the whole decoration ('he painted the whole of Santa Cecilia in Trastevere with his own hand', Ghiberti affirmed). The frescoes are on the inner façade, at a higher level than the eighteenth-century ceiling, and to reach it one has to go through the convent of an enclosed order beside the church (permit from the Vicariato of Rome).

Giotto was frequently in Rome. Controversy about the date of these visits by the great Florentine has been a topic of heated debate among critics both past and present. In 1904 Toesca achieved a partial solution to the problem with a decisive attribution. In the upper part of the transept of S. Maria Maggiore, hidden by the later ceiling (accessible only by special request), are some large *tondi* showing prophets, possibly of the same period as Torriti's apsidal mosaic, i.e. *c.* 1295. They give 'a new impression of the figure, noble and statuesque, different from that in the works of Cimabue and Cavallini: and it seems to be the first appearance of the art of Giotto.' Till recently these constituted the only evidence in Rome of the painter's obscure youth, and are comparable to the frescoes showing the story of Isaac in the upper area of the upper church in Assisi. Now a painted cross, unfortunately in poor condition, found in 1966 by Ilaria Toesca in the little church of S. Tommaso dei Cenci (near Via Arenula) to which it came from the Aracoeli, has provided new, moving and convincing evidence of the obscure youthful activity of Giotto in Rome (it can be seen at present in the Museo di Palazzo Venezia).

For the Jubilee Year 1300 Giotto painted a commemorative fresco in the Loggia delle Benedizioni at the Lateran, showing Boniface VIII with acolytes and a throng of worshippers. The small surviving fragment, restored in 1951, is in the right-hand aisle of the basilica. The date of execution of the mosaic of the *Navicella*, Peter's barque, originally in the quadriportico of the Constantinian basilica, is more controversial, but can probably be fixed at around 1313. Disfigured and restored fragments of this allegorical composition (showing Peter's barque in danger and Christ walking on the waters and reproving the fisherman for his little faith, in obvious allusion to the Church) are now in the portico of the Vatican basilica, and provide only a pale iconographic reminder of it, while other fragments in the grottoes and in a

P. 76/77

The Arch of Titus, at the top of the Via Sacra, with a view of the Colosseum, (at the right) was built by Domitian or Trajan to commemorate the victory of Vespasian and his son Titus over the Hebrews, climaxed by the destruction of Jerusalem in A.D. 70.

▷

*The Column of Marcus Aurelius (also known as the Column of Antoninus) in the Piazza Colonna. It was erected to celebrate Marcus Aurelius's victory over the Marcomanni, the Quadi and the Sarmatians (*A.D. *176-193?).*

village of Latium, Boville Ernica, are controversial as a result of their state of preservation and their questionable authenticity.

These works bring to a close the strange story of medieval pictorial art in Rome. For more than a century the city slumbered in relation to all the arts. True, the Capitol experienced renewed activity at this time, and communal life experienced outbursts of popular pride with, in the middle of the century, the Tribunate of Cola di Rienzo, when, among other things, by the expressed will of the people, the daring staircase of the Aracoeli was built, and Gothic churches, such as S. Maria sopra Minerva (originally founded on a pagan temple), were enlarged; but all other artistic enterprise came to a halt. The exile of the Popes in Avignon and the western schism threw the city into gloom, in the midst of which the Middle Ages drew silently to a close.

The City of the Popes

Despite the long schismatic crisis, the impoverished conditions of Rome's inhabitants, and the general lethargy pervading the city, the age of the Renaissance opened early in Rome, in the second decade of the fifteenth century: and if Rome, unlike Florence, did not at once find a Brunelleschi to set the stamp on its early architecture, it did see the opening — with Masolino, Masaccio and then Angelico — of a flourishing new era in painting. It had to make do with imported artists. With the election as Pope of Oddone Colonna, who took the name of Martin V, in 1417, the See of Peter returned, after 115 years and some French popes, to the great Roman families (the Caetani, the Orsini, the Counts of Segni and Tuscolo, the Frangipane and the Savelli), who had repeatedly held it in past centuries. The first care of Martin V was to repair the extensive damage to monuments wrought by a century of neglect. In the medals of his pontificate he sought to be remembered by posterity as having restored 'dirutas ac labentes urbis... ecclesias' (the city's decaying and dilapidated churches). In calling in artists from other regions, he did not display a humanist's discernment or the enterprising vision of a man of the new era. The courtly, regal style of international Gothic was certainly more to his taste than the deep human message of Masaccio; but he must be credited with the reviving of old customs, of once again making Rome the catalyst of different cultural forces and enabling it to exercise anew that power of attraction that had for centuries stood it in good stead.

Nothing now remains of the court paintings of Gentile da Fabriano (admired by Rogier van der Weyden when he was in Rome around 1450) or of Pisanello, in St John Lateran; nor is the two-sided triptych which Masolino da Panicale painted (perhaps with the aid of Masaccio in the side panels) still in its original place on the altar of the Colonna chapel in S. Maria Maggiore, where Vasari saw it: the work is now distributed between the Capodimonte Museum in Naples, the National Gallery in London, and the Museum of Art in Philadelphia. But other works have survived to throw light on this renaissance of the arts in Rome, now once more the city of the Popes. In a Gothic-style chapel of the church of San Clemente, Masolino, in about 1425, painted the walls and ceilings with frescoes showing the lives of St Catherine of Alexandria and S. Ambrogio, a Crucifixion on the farther wall, and the Annunciation on the exterior of the entrance-arch. In them he revealed his 'dreamlike wandering' — soft in modelling and pure in colour — in the late-Gothic world. But in some parts

A detail of the marble relief from the column of Marcus Aurelius celebrating one of his victories.

a more solid presence can be perceived. In a wide area in the lower part of the Crucifixion, 'a precise and complicated spatial circulation' (Longhi) can be seen which cannot be attributed to Masolino, the creator of purely illusory perspectives. In other words, we get a glimpse there of the presence of the young Masaccio, the 'new man' of the Renaissance. Other instances also exist of collaboration between the two artists (it seems unlikely that Masaccio's relationship with the old Masolino was that of a pupil or even an apprentice): the culminating example is the Florentine frescoes in the Carmine. In Rome, this collaboration may have been suddenly interrupted, which would explain Masaccio's limited and specific share in the Crucifixion: the riders daringly foreshortened, the 'new difficulty of the human form' (Longhi) in that perspective, the foreshadowing discernible there of the riders of Paolo Uccello and Piero della Francesca. (Piero della Francesca was also in Rome later, after the middle of the century, and painted in S. Maria Maggiore: a fresco showing St Luke, on the cross-vault of the former chapel of St Michael and St Peter, on the left of the Baptistery, has been attributed to him by Longhi.) At S. Clemente, indeed, not all the experts are prepared to admit the *modernistic* intervention of Masaccio, which disrupts Masolino's gentle figurative treatment, but it is nevertheless undeniable.

Among the little information we possess about Masaccio is the fact that he died in Rome, possibly in 1428, when he was not yet twenty-eight years old.

Martin V had also undertaken works in St Peter's and the old nucleus of the Vatican palaces. They were continued by his successor, the Venetian Pope Eugenius IV, in the midst of his considerable dogmatic difficulties with the Council of Basle and Florence. Indeed he could be said to have undertaken them at the right time, for the first years of his pontificate coincided with the presence in Rome of a number of artists: not only Gentile and Pisanello but also Donatello and Ghiberti, Michelozzo and Filarete.

According to an old tradition, Donatello enjoyed wandering with Brunelleschi in the ruins of the Forum and dug up, perhaps also drew, classical sculptures and architectural remains. It was he who, between 1432 and 1433, created with Michelozzo's collaboration, the marble Ciborium for the Chapel of the Sacrament (Martinelli) in Old St Peter's, now in the Sagrestia dei Beneficiati, in which Masaccio's humanistic vision is renewed in plastic form. The gravestone (badly worn) of Giovanni Crivelli (1432), with classical motifs, in the church of S. Maria in Aracoeli, is also by Donatello. Ghiberti did some work on the precious golden and bejewelled mitre of the Pope. Antonio Averlino, known by the Greek name of Filarete (lover of valour), humanist, sculptor, and above all goldsmith (he had been an assistant to Ghiberti), took on what was to prove the most difficult and laborious task: the bronze panels for the central doors of St Peter's; the work was as laborious as — in our own times, for other reasons but in striking historical similarity — the fashioning of the lateral door of the basilica by Giacomo Manzù for Pope John XXIII was to be.

It took twelve years to complete the bronze doors, elaborate and erudite as they were, 'stretched like a tapestry before an aperture' (Calvesi), but at last, in 1445, they were set on their hinges in the central doorway of the Constantinian basilica, whence they were later transferred to the new basilica.

In that same year or perhaps a little later, other famous artists came to Rome — Fra Angelico, Benozzo Gozzoli, and Jean Fouquet. Fouquet came there from Tours and stayed at the papal court for some time, at least three years with Eugenius IV, whom he painted with two companions in a likeness so striking that it caused a furore at the time: it has vanished, but it was exhibited for public delectation at least until the end of the sixteenth century in the Gothic church of S. Maria sopra Minerva, which in those years acquired a severe façade, later redesigned.

The fame of the Dominican 'Brother John the painter' — the Blessed Fra Angelico — must already have gone beyond the monastery of San Marco in Florence when Nicholas V, who succeeded Eugenius IV in 1447, commissioned him to paint his private chapel.

Angelico's frescoes were a first step in that advance towards grandeur, a veritable ascent to Parnassus, of which the Vatican was soon to be a unique example. It is probable that the Florentine artist was also responsible for other painting in the Vatican as well as that of the Pope's private chapel (known as the Cappella Niccolina), for a second and larger chapel, more or less on the site of the present vestibule of the Sistine Chapel, demolished in the time of Paul III, and also for a little study, mentioned in sources but difficult to identify. It is in fact uncertain whether some documents concerning payments in 1449 refer to it or to the Pope's private chapel.

Though Brunelleschi left no architecture of his own in the Vatican

One of the attractive approaches to the Palatine. The steep slopes which rise to the ancestral hill were dear to romantic writers.

(though he was almost certainly among the many artists and humanists surrounding Eugenius IV), its spirit is there, in the backgrounds that Angelico gave to his scenes from the lives of St Lawrence and St Stephen on the walls of the chapel of Nicholas V: a radiant message of Florentine civilization brought to Rome. The scenes in the early martyrs' lives are set 'in splendid basilicas or in the imposing vastness of Rome and its countryside', the figures 'are invested with that human dignity which is awareness of a moral conscience'. Angelico here transferred on a grand scale from the tiny *predelle* of his Florentine polyptychs 'his methods as an honest narrator, conferring on the individual compositions the solemn value of history in a humanistic sense' (Salmi).

The pontificate of Nicholas V amid its varying vicissitudes restored to Rome a forgotten happiness, and 'Roma felix' was the motto engraved on the medals coined to record it. The Emperor Frederick III was crowned in St Peter's, and a jubilee announced by the Pope was the occasion for a declaration of devotion by the people. But there were disasters too, among them the rebellion of the republican humanist Stefano Porcari, who with 300 Romans attacked Castel S. Angelo (but failed to take it and was hanged) and, above all, the fall of Constantinople on 29 May 1453, with which the Empire of the East came to an end.

During the second half of the century two other Popes — one Tuscan, the other Venetian — influenced Roman culture, each from his own particular angle. Almost at the juncture between the two pontificates an event of importance for the wide modern world also occurred in Italy. In 1465, at Subiaco, a little village not far from Rome, the first Italian book was printed, Lattanzio's *De morte persecutorum*. The discovery of the art of printing happened at the right moment to bring humanistic culture the fundamental support of diffusion. Of the two Popes, the first was a profound and enlightened humanist, whereas the other, coming from a city in which the love of classical antiquity had been little cultivated, was in some ways the reverse side of the medal.

Enea Silvio Piccolomini was born at Pienza, near Siena. He was the 211th Roman Pope, Pius II, but he continued to sign his writings on literature, history, cosmography, and other learned subjects, as well

A view of the Appia Antica, with one of the many tombs along its edges. This most important consular direct road to Capua was opened by the Censor Appius Claudius in 312 B.C. Towards 190 B.C. it was extended to Brindisi and became the road to the east. It was called the Regina viarum because of its splendid sepulchral monuments.

as his *Epistles, Commentaries*, and poetic compositions, as Enea Silvio, which might almost be a name from a neo-Platonic Academy. He had a perfect knowledge of Latin, and demanded of the compilers of his apostolic *breve* a Latin as classical as Cicero's. He had a genuine enthusiasm for antiquity and a great respect for the classics, like such scholars as Marsilio Ficino or Poggio Bracciolini. He granted amnesty to the Arpinati in the war against the King of Naples simply because they were citizens of Cicero's birthplace. During his journeys, in addition to concerning himself with the care of souls and with political

affairs, he also took careful note of the classical remains he came upon. Flavio Biondo dedicated to him, as to the most fitting recipient, his *Roma Triumphans,* which was the first exhaustive exploration of the antiquities of Rome (Poggio Bracciolini had already published a *Topography of Ancient Rome* in 1447).

Pietro Barbo, Cardinal of Venice, who on becoming Pope took the name of Paul II, was Pius' successor and his absolute opposite as regards cultural policy. Burckhardt has defined him as a festive Pope: and in fact he liked both sumptuous liturgical ceremonies, as Platina says in his *Lives of the Popes,* and gay secular festivals. He held them, with banquets for the people, in the piazza in front of the palace that he had built for himself, at the foot of the Capitol, when he was a Cardinal — Palazzo Venezia. If one were to excavate beneath the piazza and the palace, one might still perhaps find the medals and gold coins which — Platina hinted — he used to bury in quantities in the foundation of his buildings, with magic and pagan rite. He was no lover of the antique and took no interest in the adornments of classical culture, but he did not disdain to accept the flattery of an attributed descent of his family from the Aenobarbi — in other words from Nero. And the permitted one of his cardinals, Niccolò Forteguerri of Pistoia (buried in S. Cecilia in Trastevere, in a tomb sculptured by Mino da Fiesole, in 1473), to take charge of the first critical edition of the licentious comedies of Plautus and perphaps even to stage some of them.

The city that Paul II caused to resound with gaiety had, from the architectural standpoint, no coherent town plan, and the distribution of the buildings was purely casual. Consequently Rome in the middle of the fifteenth century, with its mixture of town and country, classical ruins and basilicas, medieval quarters and new constructions, must have presented a chaotic appearance. When the Palazzo Venezia went up at the foot of the Capitol and the Aracoeli stairway, the surrounding area was a valley with fields and gardens. There were, however, some patrician residences near by, that of the Colonna, beside the basilica of SS. Apostoli, and that of the Hungarian Cardinal Szecky, beside the ancient church of S. Maria in Via Lata, where the Palazzo Doria Pamphilj later stood.

The Palazzo of San Marco, subsequently called the Palazzo Venezia, of uncertain and disputed architectural paternity, begun in 1455, was undoubtedly the building that exercised the greatest influence on Roman architecture up to Bramante. Among the many civil edifices built in the second half of the fifteenth century by Popes, cardinals and nobles, it is the one that conveys to us the strongest architectonic impression. Guglielmo de Angelis d'Ossat has incontrovertibly proved its exact application of the *golden section*, in other words the purely intellectual application of the rules of geometry which was a feature of the architectonic doctrine of Humanism. The complex included a medieval tower and it later acquired from Rodrigo Borgia (Pope Alexander VI) a new tower — on the left of the façade — a square building and a courtyard; the ancient basilica of S. Marco was restored, and a portico added; at a later stage the exquisite *viridarium,* or garden court, was added, originally terraced and surrounded by an arcade (the court of the so-called Palazzetto Venezia which in 1910 was

▷

A detail of the Trajan Column. Erected in Trajan's Forum in the 2nd century A.D., *it commemorates the Emperor's victory over the Dacians and is the most important sculptural work of its kind.*

removed to behind the basilica to extend the view from the piazza of the Victor Emmanuel Monument, or 'wedding-cake', as English visitors have irreverently but perceptively named it).

The Palazzo della Cancelleria dates from some years later, between 1489 and 1496. It was built for Raffaele Riario, cardinal of S. Giorgio, enlarging an already existing building annexed to the paleo-Christian basilica of S. Lorenzo in Damaso. The attribution of the basic idea to Bramante (who according to Vasari was among the group of 'excellent' architects who gave advice about the 'resolution' of the palace and the basilica, in other words about the renovation and expansion of both buildings, while the work was actually carried out by Antonio da Montecavallo) has for long been discussed and rejected by historians because it clashed with the date of Bramante's arrival in Rome in 1499. The cardinal of San Giorgio, nephew of Sixtus IV, was an adventurous young man, a lover of antiquity and the arts. Tradition has it that he built the palace with money won in a night's gambling. He collected ancient sculptures, and they were the first that Michelangelo saw when he arrived in Rome at the end of June 1496: he spoke of them in his first letter from Rome to Lorenzo di Pier Francesco de' Medici, which is also incidentally the first letter of his that has come down to us.

The Palazzo Riario arose not far from another palazzo which Rodrigo Borgia, vice-chancellor of the Church and later Pope Alexander VI, had built for himself between 1460 and 1465 (today Palazzo Sforza Cesarini, in the Corso Vittorio Emanuele). The façade and sides of the Palazzo Riario and its courtyard with the loggia and staircase clearly reveal the influence of northern architecture, Lombard or Paduan in general, and even Venetian in the windows (Salmi). But it is above all its character, ample, solemn and noble, that distinguishes it from other contemporary buildings in Rome.

Sixtus IV (1471-84), a profound humanist, among his other merits enlarged the Vatican Library (a fabulous treasure-house of ancient illuminated codices, manuscripts, incunabula, precious bindings, and archives) and put it in the care of the celebrated humanist Bartolomeo Sacchi, known as Il Platina; the event is recorded in a fresco of Melozzo da Forlì, 1477, passed on from the old library to the Pinacoteca Vaticana. But his name is above all linked with one of the most famous buildings in the world, the great hall-like Sistine Chapel.

The paintings on the walls and ceilings of its majestic interior can be said to open and close, with the stylistic variations of their execu-tants, that supreme era of civilization in Italy known as the Renais-sance. It is not even known precisely who was responsible for the building of the walls themselves. One suggestion is Giovannino de' Dolci, a Florentine craftsman or perhaps only a master-builder; another, more recent and better founded, is Baccio Pontelli (De Campos). Construction was begun in 1473 and as far as the walls were concerned did not take long. The architectonic plan is the simplest imaginable, a bare rectangle with no incidental details, of perfect proportions (length 133 feet, width 45 feet, height 65 feet), illuminated by six windows on the long sides and covered by a vaulted ceiling with a flat surface in the centre. Within its great space the

▷

Originally, Trajan's Column was flanked by Trajan's Libraries in the Forum, and the reliefs were seen to better advantage. Now they compete with modern monuments such as the 18th-century cupola of the Church of the S.S. Nome di Maria.

paintings form an uninterrupted pictorial sequence. In the first instance, it had a single evangelical theme, with a continuous border of landscapes and figures, intended to give the illusion of an outer field of space inserted directly into the interior. The unity of the series of frescoes of the fifteenth century, in strict stylistic relationship with the decorations (the draped curtain below, derived from an antique model known from classical and paleo-Christian painting, and the simulated architecture), was broken in 1534 when, to make room for the *Last Judgment,* three panels by Perugino on the altar wall were destroyed and the *Capella maior* (as the Sistine Chapel is described in ancient documents) underwent Michelangelo's second titanic involvement (the first having been that of the ceiling frescoes). On 27 October 1481 four frescoes were finished and ten more were commissioned from the respective artists, who undertook to finish them by the following March. The artists were all either Florentine or Umbrian, and Vasari was too drastic in accusing the Pope of making a bad choice. The stories of the frescoes (nearly all of which have been subjected to revelatory restoration in recent years) were taken from the two

The Temple of Vesta in the Forum Boarium, now the Piazza Bocca della Verità. In the foreground the 18th-century Triton fountain by Carlo Bizzaccheri and Francesco Moratti, modelled on Bernini's in the Piazza Barberini.

Testaments, those on the left (beginning from the altar) from the Old Testament, those on the right from the New, with the obvious intention of linking the two sacred texts in parallel representation. Sandro Botticelli painted the second and the fifth on the left side and the second on the right, showing respectively the *Youth of Moses,* the *Punishment of the Rebels,* and the *Temptation of Christ.* All these scenes have many subjects, so that every panel is like a narrative, unfolded not only in space but in time sequence, undoubtedly in order to augment and amplify the meaning of Biblical precepts. According to Vasari, Botticelli's share in the work was particularly important because the Pope ordered him to 'become the leader' of the team of artists. He was in fact also responsible for some of the figures of pontiffs in the niches. But what is incontrovertible is that in the Sistine Chapel he reveals himself at a moment when he was at the height of his stylistic and dramatic powers. A contemporary reference forms the background to his scene of the *Temptation,* in which appears the façade of the Roman hospital of S. Spirito in Sassia (on the Lungotevere of that name) which, destroyed by fire in 1471, was rebuilt by Sixtus IV at

the same time that the Sistine Chapel was under construction. In the other two frescoes Roman monuments appear, the Arch of Constantine and the Septizonium of Septimius Severus in the *Punishment of the Rebels* and the front of a temple seen obliquely in the other.

Luca Signorelli painted, with collaborators (among them Bartolomeo della Gatta), the last fresco on the left wall, showing *Moses handing the rod to Joshua* (*Replicatio Legis scriptae a Moise* was the original title, recently uncovered during restoration). As Calvesi has pointed out, since this Biblical scene is opposite Perugino's *Christ giving the Keys to Peter*, the parallelism between Moses and Christ is obvious, and the link which the iconographic scheme aimed to assert between the Old and New Testaments is so explicit as to recall the analogous

idea of the *Parallel Lives* ot the Latin author Plutarch. The pointed interpretation gives a more concrete meaning to the fusion of humanistic and theological concepts which was intended to govern the whole conception of the cycle. The idea that Platina, councillor of Sixtus IV, was the inspiration behind the whole of the fifteenth-century decoration seems to be not only suggested but given manifest proof by these correspondences.

Perugino, in *Christ giving the Keys* (which Raphael was to have in mind in his *Marriage of the Virgin,* now in the Brera in Milan), brings this humanistic comparison between classicism and Christianity into an ideal formal balance. In the background of the scene, classical and *modern* buildings confront each other in perfect harmony, even

The Arch of Constantine. At right, the Colosseum. Built in 315 A.D., to commemorate the imperial victory over Maxentius at Ponte Milvio, the arch is the last triumphal monument of the classical age.

in the emphasis of the chromatic variations produced by the light, and in the idea of space in which they serve as perspective controls. When we recall the three lost frescoes beneath the *Last Judgment,* and the possibility that Perugino may have provided ideas for the *Journey into Egypt* (the first scene on the left) and the *Baptism of Christ* (the first on the right), in both of which the principal executant seems to be Pinturicchio, the Umbrian artist would seem to have played the most important role after Michelangelo in the Sistine Chapel. Of the other Florentines, the two Ghirlandaios, Domenico and Davide, painted the third panel on the right, the *Calling of the Apostles*, while Cosimo Rosselli, Fra Diamante, Bartolomeo della Gatta, Piero di Cosimo and Biagio d'Antonio are indicated by the same sources and by modern critics as authors of the remaining scenes: this is not the place to go in detail into the various reasons for these attributions. The two frescoes on the entrance wall are later restorations.

Michelangelo entered the Sistine Chapel in March or April 1508. His first designs for the ceiling are dated 10 May. On 27 July he went up on to the scaffolding and began work. He had had to decide, after much resistance on his part, to submit to the wishes of the Pope, the unbending Julius II. 'Since the ceiling of that chapel seemed to him

▷
Some reliefs contemporary with the construction of the Arch of Constantine; Roman legionnaires and barbarian prisoners.

The surviving majestic vault of the Basilica of Maxentius begun in A.D. *306 and not finished until the time of Constantine.*
In the summer, symphonic concerts are given amid the magnificent ruins.

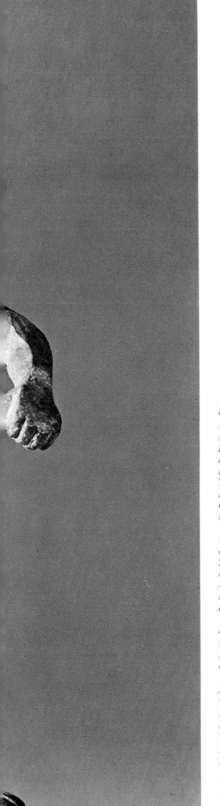

P. 96

*(above) A detail of the equestrian
statue of Marcus Aurelius in the
Piazza del Campidoglio. Bronze,
originally gilded (some traces of
the gilding are still visible).
The group was transferred from the
Lateran in 1538, and set up in the
Campidoglio by Michelangelo,
who designed the marble pedestal.*

*(below) The Cemetery of the Port
of Rome or the Sepulchre of the
Sacred Island. Contains hundreds
of modest tombs of the 2nd to
4th centuries A.D., of sailors,
artisans and small merchants
connected with the port.*

P. 97

*Votary Statuette. Small Etruscan
bronze, 2nd century B.C. Villa
Giulia. Antiquarium.*

P. 98/99

*The sarcophagus of the Married
Couple. Etruscan terracotta of the
6th century B.C. From Cerveteri.
Villa Giulia. More than any other
Etruscan work, it reveals a relation
to Ionic art.*

◁

*Minerva. Etruscan
bronze statuette, 4th century B.C.
Villa Giulia. Antiquarium.*

(above) The Apollo of Veii *(detail)*. *Polychromed clay. Etruscan, end of the 6th century* B.C. *Villa Giulia.*

◁

(left) Warrior. Decorative terracotta from the Temple of the Mater Matuta of Satricum. Etruscan. First half of the 5th century B.C. *Villa Giulia.*

a great and difficult labour, and mindful of his small experience in colours, he tried by every means to rid himself of this burden, putting forward Raphael instead,' says Vasari. On 31 October 1512 the frescoes of the ceiling were finished: it had taken little more than four years for that gigantic undertaking. In the nine Biblical scenes, whose order, following that of the fifteenth-century frescoes, runs from the altar to the entrance wall, Michelangelo traced the spiritual history of mankind. It seems that, to begin with, the plan of composition was extremely simple, with only the twelve Apostles in the spandrels and geometrical decorations in the central space (a design for it survives in the British Museum). Instead, in the end some three hundred figures populated the Sistine ceiling. They tell, in human terms, the story of the beginning of the world, from the division of light from darkness to the creation of the sun, moon and stars, from the separation of the earth from the waters to the creation of animals on land and sea; and then the origin of the human race, from the creation of Adam and Eve to their sin and their eviction from Eden; and then the origin

of evil, the flood, the sacrifice of Noah, his drunkenness, and the continuance of sin. The nine stories are supported by twelve majestic Seers who foretell the Redemption, seven prophets and five sibyls, and a great number of children. Meant to relate the stories of a remote past to the present, or perhaps to confirm its terrifyingly human dimension, enduring throughout the centuries, are the twenty nude figures (one of which, in the last panel towards the door, was completely destroyed by an explosion in 1798). An uninterrupted stream of literature has discussed these from every angle, advancing all kinds of interpretations.

The *Miraculous Salvations of Israel* in the corners and the *Ancestors of Christ* (from the Gospel of St Matthew) in the spandrels and lunettes of the window-openings conclude this 'dynamic and living organism of figures' (Woelfflin).

Emile Zola, contemplating the *Creation of Adam*, saw in the patch of sky that unites and separates the fingers of the Creator and of the first man a space both minute and immense, mysterious as the infinite. In fact, the mysterious vault of the sky does not dominate, but absorbs into itself the impenetrable bodies and the architecture enclosed within its perspective. The figures alone remain to witness the event of the Creation. Adam and Eve symbolically terminate it, in the act of leaving for ever the delights of Eden.

One must depart from the chronological order of this excursion through the centuries of Rome's artistic history to speak of the *Last Judgment,* for the Sistine Chapel is, in a way, the heart of our journey (as it is, in Rome, the heart of its various civilizations) and calls for a conclusion.

In order to paint the *Last Judgment,* commissioned by Paul III (Alessandro Farnese), seventh of the Popes in Michelangelo's life though not the last with whom he had to deal, Michelangelo had to sacrifice two of his lunettes with the *Ancestors of Christ* as well as the three frescoes of Perugino, in the lower area, and two windows. The preparation of the mural work alone took a year, from the spring of 1535 to the following spring, but in September the cartoon was ready. Michelangelo had the whole wall chiselled out and lined with a curtain of bricks. In addition, he sloped it so as to avoid the accumulation of dust. This device, however, made the fresco more vulnerable, especially in the lower part, to the smoke from candles and incense, hence its blackening.

The *Judgment,* begun in the autumn of 1536, was finished in October 1541. It was uncovered on 1 November, All Saints' Day, the same day on which, twenty-nine years before, the ceiling had been uncovered. Paul III, who had already seen many details of it, fell on his knees overwhelmed by the great apocalypse. With this human gesture the deeply-moved Pope inaugurated the legend of Michelangelo's *terribilità* (terribleness). The Romans were allowed to see it the following Christmas, but moralistic polemics were already in the air. Biagio da Cesena (who, according to tradition, is portrayed as Minos) and Aretino launched their darts against the plethora of nudes in the fresco. 'I am ashamed', wrote the latter to Michelangelo, 'at the licence, so unlawful for the spirit, that you have allowed yourself in expressing your ideas... that you should have done this in the greatest Temple of God... above the first of the altars of Christ... in the greatest chapel in the world, the very pivot of the Church. A luxurious bath, not a supreme choir, is the place for your work.'

The *Judgment* has often been compared in modern literature with Dante's supraterrestrial vision in the *Divina Commedia*, but the parallel was also anticipated by early commentators and by the first biographers, Vasari included, in the first edition of his *Life of Michelangelo* of 1550. And it was perhaps also because of these literary and secular (for that time pagan) comparisons that the Council of Trent, on 3 December 1563, a few months before Michelangelo's death, pronounced a vague condemnation of the *Judgment* and in general of unsuitable representations in churches. A pupil of Michelangelo's later had the thankless task of clothing the nudes; at least the author did not receive this affront personally.

Divided into three areas, the *Last Judgment*, which was painted entirely in fresco on damp plaster, shows the three kingdoms: at the top, the Heavens, with Christ as judge, the Virgin, and the Apostles, patriarchs, prophets, confessors and martyrs; in the centre the judged, with the chosen and the reprobate; and below the damned, with Charon and the demons of hell.

The Sistine Chapel before Michelangelo, when its ceiling was still as painted by the Umbrian artist Pier Matteo d'Amelia, in blue and gold, had constituted an organic example of architecture and pictorial and sculptural decoration of the early Renaissance. Within that framework came the elegant screen that divides the hall into two-thirds, and the *cantoria*, both in translucent marble, traditionally assigned to a team of three sculptors of different extraction and experience, the Tuscan Mino da Fiesole, Andrea Bregno from Como, and Giovanni Ducnovic (known in Rome as Giovanni Dalmata) from Trau. The two works may really have been produced by so many hands, but they nevertheless reveal a definitely Tuscan style.

Collaboration between these sculptors of different origins and the presence in Rome of others, both Roman and otherwise — Paolo Romano (possibly Paolo Salviati), the Florentine Simone di Giovanni Ghini, a problematical Mino del Reame, Isaia da Pisa, Jacopo di Andrea from Florence, the Roman Paolo Taccone, and all the other many collaborators — left in the city a rich collection of sculptured marbles (tombs, altars, ciboria) in a great many churches, the character of which can only be described as eclectic, contaminated in some cases by relics of Gothic, in others by ponderous interpretations of classical motifs. A typical Roman fifteenth-century monument is the tomb of Eugenius IV, 1447, now in the church of San Salvatore in Lauro (in the Piazza of that name), to which it was transferred from the old basilica of St Peter's; in it Isaia da Pisa, possibly with the help of others, tackled the problem of a sarcophagus with the reclining figure under a canopy with reliefs, within a framework no longer Gothic but fifteenth-century, although some details of the modelling of the figures bear traces of older influences. Workshops of sculptors from Tuscany, Lombardy and other regions of Italy toiled intensively to adorn the churches of Rome with marbles, especially tombs, forming a band of more modest craftsmen whose productions followed in the wake of the rare prestigious works which the great figures of the century had left there. Outstanding among these are two works in bronze of Antonio del Pollaiuolo, the tombs of Sixtus IV and of Innocent VIII, the former originally in the chapel of the choir of Old St Peter's, and now in the Vatican Grottoes. The latter, broken up and then reas-

A fragment of an 8th-century mosaic from the Vatican grotto. It represents Pope John VII (705-707).

sembled not entirely in accordance with the original (the sarcophagus with the reclining figure of the dead Pope was above, topped by the lunette; the Pope, blessing, was below), was transferred from the old to the new basilica, where it stands beside the second pillar between the nave and the left aisle.

The tomb of Sixtus IV is one of the masterpieces of Italian fifteenth-century sculpture: a strange, immense piece of polished workmanship, vibrant throughout its articulated bronze structure, a worthy humanistic memorial of the Pope who built the Sistine Chapel. The pontiff lies, according to noble custom, on the low tomb-slab, surrounded by the seven Virtues, supported by the Arts.

Though it has lost through dismemberment its original compositional unity, Pollaiuolo's other tomb, that of Innocent VIII, in gilded bronze with two representations in the round of the Pope and with reliefs on the background, reveals the nervous tension of the sculptor's energetic line. He may have been assisted in this work by his brother Piero. The twins who were added at this time to the fine original model of the Capitoline Wolf were also attributed to Antonio del Pollaiuolo, as has been mentioned earlier. This may have been done during the lifetime of Sixtus IV, who in 1471 donated the sculpture to the city of Rome and the Capitol. But another hypothesis suggests that the twins are by Piero rather than Antonio, in which case the work would have to be dated some twenty years later, when Sixtus IV was already dead.

Besides these two Vatican tombs, two others may be mentioned in this brief survey of the century's works of quality. One is the marble slab by the Florentine Andrea del Verrocchio showing the 'Madonna and Child', belonging to the Sistine Hospital of Santo Spirito (now in its official headquarters), which provides confirmation of Vasari's mention of Verrocchio's activity in Rome as sculptor as well as goldsmith, which last is more fully documented. The other, by the Sienese Lorenzo di Pietro, known as Il Vecchietta, is the tomb of Bishop Gerolamo Foscari in Santa Maria del Popolo, the authorship of which has recently been recognized by Pico Cellini.

The mortal remains of Innocent VIII, who died in 1492, were deposited in the tomb commissioned from Pollaiuolo by the Pope's nephew, Lorenzo Cibo, on 30 January 1498. Five days later the artist died — but for the past year and a half the Florentine Michelangelo Buonarroti had been living in Rome.

He had arrived there on horseback on 1 June 1496, full of hope and curiosity. The city that he saw was no different from Benozzo Gozzoli's depiction of it some years earlier in a fresco in a church at S. Gimignano, the village with the splendid towers near Siena, nor from that in the other painting, by an anonymous artist, of about 1498 in the Ducal Palace in Mantua: buildings of the past and present punctuated its profile; there was no town plan, and the monuments were casually scattered about like chess pawns within the urban area. The Cardinal of San Giorgio, Raffaele Riario, whom Michelangelo had gone to visit for the second time in his palazzo, asked him, as the artist records in his first letter from Rome, 'if I had a mind to do something fine. I answered that I would not do anything very special (like the ancient sculptures that I had seen in the Cardinal's collection), but that he would see what I would do.' And he added that, having bought a block of marble, 'I will start on Monday to work on a life-size figure.'

That first sculpture of his in Rome was the lascivious *Bacchus*, now in Florence. The cardinal refused it, and the banker Jacopo Galli bought it for his garden instead. It was followed at once by the *Pietà* in St Peter's. This was commissioned by a Frenchman, the Cardinal Abbot of St Denis, Jean Bilhères de Lagraulas, ambassador of Charles VIII to Alexander VI and the founder in Rome of the national church of his compatriots, S. Luigi dei Francesi, and also of the Trinità dei Monti, at the top of the steps from Piazza di Spagna. The contract for it was signed on 27 August 1498. Michelangelo, aged twenty-three, was described in it as 'Maestro' and 'Florentine sculptor of statues' and he undertook to hand over the work within a year. The sculpture was destined for the Vatican church of S. Petronilla, chapel of the Kings of France, which was later absorbed into the new basilica of St Peter's.

This famous group (restored to the first chapel in the right-hand aisle of St Peter's after its journeyings overseas in the late 1960s), the most finished of all Michelangelo's works, carved at the same time that Leonardo da Vinci was finishing his *Last Supper* in Milan and in a certain sense partaking of the novelty of Leonardo's approach, may have been the result of an intentional display of virtuosity, but this in no way diminishes its stature as an outstanding sculptural

(above) The apse of the church of S. Sabina on the Aventine.
The 5th-century building was completely restored between 1914 and 1938.

(below) The apsidal mosaic (detail) from the church
of SS. Cosma and Damiano. It is a work of the 6th century,
and was commissioned by Pope Felix IV.

invention, the first of its kind in the history of Western sculpture
since Phidias. The *Pietà* leaves behind it centuries of a vision of
three-dimensional form and opens the way to a new vision in which
reality and metaphysics, ethics and sentiment aim at the same spiritual
purification. The *Pietà* is always a representation of the mother's grief
for her dead son: but with Michelangelo the grief here attains the
sublime.

The Pope under whom it appeared, Alexander VI, was one of the most
powerful princes in Italy even before he came to the throne, father of
that Cesare Borgia, Duke Valentine (of Valencia, for the city of origin
of the Borgia family was Jativa, near Valencia), who was at the centre
of the struggle between Spain and France in Italy, and like him an
enemy of the most important aristocratic Roman families. The Pope
also saw, at the very beginning of his pontificate (1492), the ways of
the old world giving way to the new with Christopher Columbus's
voyage to the Americas.

His contribution to the artistic development of the Vatican was considerable, reflecting alike his policy and his aestheticism, both of which aimed to unite the prestige of the pontifical court with the pomp of the principalities, where luxury and fantasy were felicitously combined with purely aesthetic considerations. The apartment that he had made for himself in the Vatican palaces, and which still bears the name of the Borgia Apartment, yielded nothing in elegance of architecture and splendor of pictorial decoration to the famous palaces erected by Italian noblemen of the Renaissance in Mantua, Florence, Ferrara or Urbino. It faces on to the Borgia courtyard and the Cortile del Pappagallo, includes a tower, and was in part an adaptation of the building constructed by Nicholas V.

In the finest of its six rooms, the Sala dei Santi, on the Arch of Constantine, glowing in a golden light, which appears in the background of one of Pinturicchio's fresco scenes, is inscribed the attribute that Alexander VI chose to accord to himself despite his bellicose and violent character: 'Pacis cultori' (cultivator of peace). The scene is that of *St Catherine's disputation with the philosophers before the Emperor.* In the garb of the historical personages are contemporary figures, Duke Valentine and Lucrezia Borgia, Andrew Paleologus and Prince Djem, brother of the Ottoman Sultan Bajazet II, who came to Rome in 1489, and Pinturicchio himself.

Between the end of 1492 and December 1495, the Umbrian artist Bernardino di Betto, known as Il Pinturicchio, decorated these rooms, with the help of other artists on the ornamentation (among them Pier Matteo d'Amelia, author of the original star-spangled ceiling in the Sistine Chapel). The fantasy of the colours and the profusion of gold seem to emulate the ancient Golden House of Nero. In order, the Chamber of the Sibyls, of the Credo, of the Sciences and Liberal Arts, of the Saints, of the Mysteries of the Faith (followed by the Chamber of the Papacies — although that was rebuilt by Giovanni da Udine and Pietro Buonaccorsi, known as Perin del Vaga, in the time of Leo X) follow out the theme superficially dear to Alexander VI: the fusion of humanism and Christianity. The portrait of him, in the fresco of the *Resurrection* in the fifth room, kneeling in his rich cope embroidered with gold and jewels, ideally concludes the fifteenth century. The scenes, the stucco friezes, the wonderful ceilings, the rich furnishings combine to give an extraordinarily vivid impression: they are the appropriate seal to the art of the early Renaissance in the city of the Popes.

The new century, with its dramatic events and ideological contrasts, its doubts and its reforms, and with the new political and cultural outlook of the Popes, had as its protagonists in Rome the greatest artists of the time, who synthesized the theories and aspirations of humanism. This was the propulsive force of the cultural transformation that was occurring and it had arrived 'on the wings of a sense of conquest and success', justifying from the outset 'the illusion inherent in every triumphant ideology: that of the ability to rebuild everything from the foundations' (Chastel).

This was what Bramante aimed to do when he embarked on the rebuilding of St Peter's, even though, as Tafuri has recently said, one can regard as 'accidental the chronological coincidence' between the general direction of artistic thought at the opening of the sixteenth century and Bramante's arrival in Rome. It was above all the aim of the man who commissioned the new St Peter's, Pope Julius II (who first had to overcome the devotional difficulties involved in the destruction of

*Porta S. Sebastiano, at the urban end of the Appia Antica. It is the
ancient Porta Appia in the Aurelian Wall. It was
reconstructed in the 5th century by Honorius and restored in successive
centuries by Belisarius and Narsus.*

the venerated sanctuary of Peter, albeit visibly decaying), to affirm in
the new edifice the idea of cultural progress which the vaunted
magnificence of the Vatican, the radiating centre of Christianity,
demanded.

Once again Rome found itself at a turning-point in its history, whereby
it became the centre of power, thought, ideas and artistic trends.

Bramante's first buildings in Rome had already had their effect in
conditioning the atmosphere by their novelty of concept and execution.
These were the cloister of Santa Maria della Pace, the Tempietto of
San Pietro in Montorio, on the Janiculum, and the Cortile del Belvedere, in the Vatican, subsequently to be radically altered. All three
posed the problem of the relationship of architecture to its surroundings
and to classical sources, the first by the articulation of space and the
'mechanism of the orders', the second by its small proportions and its
evocation of the classical circular temple (and also of the Temple of
the Sibyl at Tivoli), and the third by its character of a refined image
of a classical model. Bramante's novelty coincided, perhaps not by
chance, with the synthesis and subtle analysis that Leonardo had
introduced into art and into the artist's consciousness. Leonardo had
been in Rome at least twice, but Bramante had seen him in Milan
at work on the *Last Supper* in S. Maria delle Grazie. The only work
of Leonardo in Rome today is the monochrome of *St Jerome* in the

111

Pinacoteca Vaticana, which, though impressive and highly introspective in its portrayal of asceticism, with its emaciated figure of the hermit in the bleak countryside, was still only a powerful sketch; and it was certainly not connected with any special commission (it turned up, incidentally, in a second-hand dealer's shop in 1820, and its origin remains obscure).

Another architectonic work by Bramante, the Belvedere Staircase, which mounts spirally in the narrow space of a quadrangular tower from the Cortile del Belvedere to the Gregorian-Etruscan Museum, reveals perfect proportions and a brilliant play of perspective. The small space seems to be set in motion by the vigorous windings, through five stages, of its spiral ramp, punctuated by the rhythm of the columns and the alternations of light concentrated on the masses and shadows deepening in the spaces.

In the reconstruction of St Peter's, Bramante aimed at a grandiose return to the paleo-Christian conception, but executed in new terms, even though the ingredients remained those of the ancient repertory: the Greek cross, the basilical conception of space, the dome as in the Pantheon model. The construction was a long-drawn-out affair and ended only a century-and-a-half later. What the visitor sees today is the result of the work of many artists, each succeeding the last with fresh changes of plan.

Bramante was appointed architect for the new basilica in 1505. The first stone of the building was laid, as we already know, by Julius II on 18 April of the following year. Bramante's first design of a Greek cross with four chapels in the corners, which reduced the plan to a square (according to Förster's reconstruction), had as its fundamental justification Julius II's wish to place his own monumental tomb, entrusted in that same year to Michelangelo, in the centre of the basilica. At Julius II's death in 1513 and Bramante's in 1514, the only portions erected were the four piers of the dome with the great arches of the four intersections. Next came Raphael, designated by Bramante himself, in collaboration with Fra Giocondo and Giuliano da Sangallo. The architect and artist from Urbino, who already had to his credit in Rome the buildings of S. Eligio degli Orefici and the Chigi chapel in S. Maria del Popolo (and, later on, Villa Madama), proposed the plan of a Latin cross, with lighter structures and more harmonious space. But Raphael's design made little progress, nor did the two that succeeded make any greater headway; and a return to the Greek cross was proposed first by Peruzzi and then by Antonio da Sangallo the Younger in 1537.

When, nine years later, Michelangelo was commissioned by Paul III Farnese to carry on the work, he at once reverted to Bramante's initial idea, although the reason for it — the erection of Julius II's monumental tomb in the centre of the basilica — was no longer valid. To Bramante's plan he added a more closely-knit structure, a solidly-woven perimeter, in strict relationship to the interior immensity, which he visualized as crowned by the majestic dome. Michelangelo saw only a part of his work completed. At his death in 1564 two sides of the transept and the great drum of the dome were finished, and the apse was quite far advanced. A fresco of the early pontificate of Sixtus V (1585-90), in the Vatican Library, shows the state of the work when the Egyptian obelisk had already been installed in the centre of Piazza San Pietro after its transference in 1586 by Domenico Fontana from the nearby circus of Nero (an undertaking memorable for the technical difficulties involved). And it was Fontana who, after

Porta Latina. It was opened by Belisarius (6th century) in the Aurelian Wall, and had one vault between two towers.

P. 114/115
A view of the Piazza S. Maria in Trastevere, in the heart of the ancient popular quarter. In the foreground a detail of Carlo Fontana's fountain (1692), restored in the 19th century.
In the background the Basilica of S. Maria in Trastevere.

Vignola, together with Giacomo della Porta brought the dome to completion in accordance with Michelangelo's design. In it the universality of the sixteenth-century conception found its fulfilment. The façade added to the basilica in 1614 by Carlo Maderno, projecting as it does beyond the dome, to some extent cuts off the view of it, diminishing its upward soar, which is better seen from the side of the Basilica, inside the Vatican City. The Loggia delle Benedizioni which stands above the central doorway is the place from which the Pope addresses the world *Urbi et Orbi*, and it is from here too that the world learns that another Pope has been elected by the conclave of the cardinals assembled in the Sistine Chapel. The clocks at the sides were added by Valadier; the gigantic statues crowning the whole are outlined against the sky, and from below seem quite small, on a positively human scale.

In the portico on the right is an equestrian statue of Constantine by Bernini, and on the left a statue of Charlemagne by an eighteenth-century sculptor; above the central entrance, much restored, is Giotto's mosaic of the *Navicella*, referred to earlier; and below are Filarete's central doors; the right-hand one, or Porta della Morte, being by Giacomo Manzù (1964), the most recent work of art of the many to

adorn the basilica throughout the centuries. The coat-of-arms of John XXIII in the pavement, executed in polychrome inlaid marbles, in commemoration of the opening of the Second Vatican Council in 1962, is also by Manzù.

Julius II began to take a lively interest in Rome itself in addition to the Vatican, more particularly after the city had emerged from the rigours of the plague, which began in November 1503 and lasted until the summer of 1506. In the twenty years between that date and the Sack of Rome in 1527, the city undertook a first partial attempt to bring some order into its town plan, with Bramante as adviser. To

The Cloister of S. Paolo Fuori le Mura (St Paul outside the walls). It was begun at the beginning of the 12th century and completed before 1214 by the Vassallettos.

Julius II's initiative belongs the layout of new streets, the Via Giulia, running from the Ponte Sisto (built by Sixtus IV to join the medieval district on the left bank of the Tiber with Trastevere) to the Vatican, and the widening of other already existing streets, the Via della Lungara, formerly Settimiana, the Via dei Banchi Vecchi, and the Via delle Botteghe Oscure. This was a first attempt to introduce social and hygienic improvements as well as to bring more dignity to the city. The width of these new streets was quite unusual for the times, when the *insulae*, or blocks of dwellings, still followed the medieval plan, with buildings crowded close to each other, leaving only enough

space for narrow alleys between (even today truncated indications of the *Insulae* and *Regiones* can be seen on many old street name-plates). The Via Giulia and the Via della Lungara, parallel to the river, proved an invaluable means of access to the Vatican, providing for a quick and convenient flow of traffic in both directions.

In this 'renewal of power' by the resolute pontiff (who took his name from a Roman predecessor (337-52), first Bishop of Rome and the first to assert the supremacy of the Roman Church, but also, not wholly obscurely, from Julius Caesar — indeed a medal of his pontificate bears the singular inscription 'Julius Caesar Pont II'), art never escaped beyond the bounds of political design.

The Stanze in the Vatican painted with frescoes by Raphael form no exception to this principle. Before him, the Stanze had first been decorated by Piero della Francesca, Luca Signorelli, and Andrea del Castagno, and the decorations were then being completed by a number of well-known artists: Perugino, Sodoma, Peruzzi, Bramantino, and Lotto. Julius II liquidated all the old paintings with a single gesture; of the new ones then in progress, Raphael, who secured the exclusive commission for the whole of the decoration, retained only the ceiling in the Stanza dell'Incendio out of respect for his master, Perugino, who had painted it. It was Bramante who had called Raphael, his fellow-citizen from Urbino, to Rome. But Julius II also grasped the greatness of the young painter, then only twenty-five years old. Born in 1483, Raphael, after a first apprenticeship with his father, went to Perugia as a pupil of Perugino. The *Coronation of the Virgin* in the Pinacoteca Vaticana, done when he was not yet twenty, belongs to this early Umbrian period, while the *Deposition* in the Borghese Gallery in Rome, painted in 1507 after the artist had spent some time in Florence and meditated on Leonardo and Michelangelo, reveals him as having already gone beyond the stylistic confines of the gentle green hills of his own region. Raphael arrived in Rome at the end of 1508. On 13 January 1509 he received payment for the Stanza 'di mezzo' (in between), or the Stanza della Segnatura.

The *Stanze,* as they are always simply known (and the name calls to mind the divisions of a poetic rather than an architectonic composition), are situated exactly above the Borgia Apartment in the wing of the Vatican originally built by Nicholas V. The rooms, which were not large and had cross-vaulted ceilings, became the new apartment of Julius II, who from the day of his coronation abhorred the idea of living in Alexander VI's apartment below and seeing '*omni hora... figuram praedecessoris sui, inimici sui, quem marranum et judaeum appellabat et circumcisum*' (every hour... the figure of his predecessor, his enemy, whom he called a pig, a Jew, and circumcised), as a papal master of ceremonies wrote in his diary! But Julius II never lived in the new rooms; they were not yet finished when he died. Like Nero, he had to content himself with living in a *Domus Transitoria,* a provisional dwelling.

The new apartment included, besides the three Raphael Stanze, i.e. the Stanza dell'Incendio, the Stanza della Segnatura, which was painted first, and the Stanza di Eliodoro, a fourth room, the Sala di Costantino (decorated under Clement VII, after Raphael's death, by Giulio Romano and assistants) and the adjacent Sala dei Chiaroscuri (now dei Palafrenieri), the room next to it, the Sala Vecchia degli Svizzeri (it was Julius II who instituted the corps of Swiss Guards, the first of whom had arrived in Rome in 1505), entered from Bramante's staircase, and the Cappella dell'Angelico, which communicated with the Pope's bed-chamber, now transformed into a chapel, while the annexed '*stufetta,* or bathroom, has become its sacristy' (De Campos).

The iconographical plan for the three rooms was dictated personally by Julius II. This is attested by Giovio, the contemporary biographer of Raphael. But there is good ground for thinking that the humanistic subtleties and doctrinal questions in the complete cycle go back to neo-Platonic philosophical ideas which Raphael himself had held ever since his Urbino days.

The first fresco to be painted in the Stanza della Segnatura (so called perhaps because the Pope used to sign state documents there, since this was his private study and library) was the *Triumph of the Church.* A mistaken tradition, going back to at least 1610, and originating in the group of personages on the left engaged in discussion, describes it as the 'Disputation of the Sacrament'. In the semi-circle, which recalls the apse of an unfinished basilica, is shown, instead, the adoration of the Divine Being, on earth in His eucharistic transubstantiation, in heaven in the persons themselves. A broad low horizon and an open sky create a mysterious hiatus between the two regions, earth and the empyraean. Many of the personages bear recognizable resemblances; Dante, Savonarola in a cowl, Fra Angelico, Bramante, and Julius II himself.

The *School of Athens*, on the opposite wall, framed in Bramante's monumental architecture (Vasari attributed to the architect the

The Romanesque cloister of the church of S. Cosimato in Trastevere (12th-13th centuries). A second 15th-century cloister with octagonal pillars is close by.

architectural part of the design: 'he disposed the buildings and then placed them in perspective in the Pope's room'), is the classical counterpart of the *Triumph of the Church*: the two 'stories' stand in reciprocal relation to each other, as did, according to humanistic principles, ancient thought and Christian thought. In the *School of Athens* too, there are recognizable figures in the assembly of scholars surrounding Plato and Aristotle: Diogenes, Epicurus, Ptolemy, and Pythagoras, and also Michelangelo, deep in thought, representing Heraclitus, Raphael, absorbed, beside Sodoma, and Bramante as Euclid, who seems to want to pacify 'the impatience of Julius II, making him contemplate, as if in a dream, the future Vatican Basilica' (De Campos). It has been thought that the figure of Michelangelo, in the centre of the foreground, may have been added by Raphael later; and in fact technical examination shows it to have been painted after the fresco was finished, on a superimposed coating of plaster. It also differs in style from the other figures, being sculptural like the Prophets in the Sistine Chapel.

The *Parnassus*, or the 'Triumph of Poetry', on the third wall is the allegory of the Beautiful, and thus continues, after the two aspects of Truth (natural in the *School of Athens,* supernatural in the *Triumph of the Church*), the exposition of the supreme Three Ideas of Platonic philosophy. The third idea, the ethical idea, or the 'Triumph of Good', is expressed in the next wall, dedicated to Justice, with the Virtues and the two episodes celebrating Law (on the right, ecclesiastical law, with 'Gregory IX presenting the Decretals to a jurist', and on the left secular law, with 'Justinian presenting the Codes of Law'). In both the representations, of Parnassus and of the allegories of Justice, there are still more recognizable likenesses: in the first, Homer, Virgil, Dante, Petrarch, Sappho, Ovid, Catullus, Sannazzaro, and — according to Tolnay — Michelangelo, appearing here as a poet, as the wreathed figure on the right near the laurels, turning towards us; in the second, Julius II as Gregory IX and beside him Giovanni de' Medici, the future Leo X, and Alessandro Farnese, the future Paul III. The quadrangular and circular spaces within the already existing geometrical compartment of the ceiling of the Stanza della Segnatura were also painted by Raphael.

When Raphael started on the frescoes for the next room, the Stanza di Eliodoro (1512), the ceiling of the Sistine Chapel was nearly finished. In the four frescoes — the *Expulsion of Heliodorus*, the *Miraculous Mass of Bolsena*, the *Delivery of St Peter,* and the *Meeting of St Leo and Attila* — there are dramatic vortices, now of movement, now of light. Unlike the stories of the Segnatura, which were connected only in idea with the present, through the iconographic personification by the artist's contemporaries of characters from the past, these frescoes actually *represent* the present, bringing it in, as on the stage today, as a 'play within a play'. In the Biblical story of Heliodorus whom the angels expelled from the temple in Jerusalem whither he had

▷

(above) The Torre delle Milizie, built by Gregory IX (1227-41) on a Servian base, towering over Trajan's Market and the Basilica Ulpia. It was reduced to its present height in the 14th century.

(below) The Romanesque campanile of the church of S. Cecilia in Trastevere (1113), among the most notable examples of the towers which punctuated the city sky in medieval times.

gone to steal (from the Second Book of Maccabees), the present is introduced by the papal court on the left, so that the fresco has been called 'a picture within a picture' (De Campos). Similarly, the *Mass of Bolsena* combines the historical event of the miracle accomplished in 1263 in the little town of Bolsena, in Latium, when drops of blood flowed from the host on to the chalice-cloth (still preserved in the cathedral of Orvieto) and the contemporary event of Julius II venerating the ancient relic. These portraits of living persons have a wonderful quality of synthesis and immediacy. Raphael captures them with a few essential characteristics.

Pietro Cavallini, The Nativity, *1291. A detail of one of the seven mosaic panels which the great Roman painter made for the apse of the church of S. Maria in Trastevere.*

It is not liveliness of colouring, but the luminosity of a dramatic night-piece that lights up the three sections of the *Delivery of St Peter:* a gentle moonlight in the awakening of the soldiers with the first flush of dawn on the horizon; a light reverberating with dazzling rays in the two angel apparitions. This is the first night-piece in the history of painting, except for Piero della Francesca's *Dream of Constantine* at Arezzo, to which — in the geometric solidity of the light — this fresco harks back, at the same time anticipating Caravaggio, Rembrandt, and even Vermeer.

The iconography reveals the inspiration of Julius II, who had been

titular cardinal of San Pietro in Vincoli, the church in which the chains of the apostle are preserved and in which, thirty years later, the Pope's tomb was to be placed, reduced, from the ambitious stature it originally had in Michelangelo's first plans, to the proportions of an ordinary sepulchre.

The fourth fresco, showing the *Meeting of Leo I and Attila* at the gates of Rome, had only just been begun when Julius II died. In the preparatory designs Leo I was given the features of Julius II, but when work was resumed, following the interruption of the Pope's death, he assumed the features of Julius' successor, the Medici Pope Leo X. And since the latter had already been portrayed as a cardinal in the Pope's suite, the papal court was seen to exhibit two identical profiles, one behind the other. Although the design for the fresco is Raphael's entirely, we begin to see the hands of assistants, and this is

An aerial view of Rome from above the Vatican Gardens.
In the foreground, the apse of St Peter's, with Michelangelo's cupola, Bernini's
colonnade, the Papal Palace. On a line with the Basilica,
Castel S. Angelo, which faces the Tiber, beyond which is the massive bulk
of the Palace of Justice. At the right, the dense Renaissance
quarter, the cupola of the Pantheon, the Victor Emmanuel monument.

increasingly evident in the frescoes of the next room, the Stanza dell'Incendio del Borgo, where typically *Roman* scenes are portrayed: the conflagration of the Borgo (the quarter adjacent to the Vatican) in 847, the battle of Ostia, two years later, between Romans and Saracens, the coronation of Charlemagne in St Peter's in 800, and the oath of Leo III in the same year: all foreshadowing or analogous to events in the Medicean papacy. Raphael's own hand is more probable in the *Conflagration* scene, in which there are still some noble pictorial passages, especially in the left part. Penni, the youthful Giulio Romano, and Raffaellino del Colle were the executants of the other frescoes, although the conception and preparatory designs must be regarded as Raphael's; he still had administrative responsibility for the whole, and was only partially relieved of it by the Pope when from 1514 on, as the architect for the building of St Peter's, he was

The 13th-century façade of S. Maria d'Aracoeli. The steep stair (122 marble steps) was constructed in 1348 as an offering by the populace, who had survived a plague. The tribune Cola di Rienzo was the first to ascend it.

◁
*A detail of the apsidal mosaic of
S. Cecilia in Trastevere, The figure
at the left is that of the living
Pope Pasquale I (817-824) who
commissioned the work and who
is therefore shown, according to
custom, with a square, rather than a
round halo.*

*The campanile of S. Maria
in Cosmedin, in Piazza Bocca della
Verità (12th century). Seven storeys
high, with two- and
three-mullioned windows, it is
among the most beautiful examples
of the Romanesque style in Rome.*

occupied, as we have said, with the plan for the reconstruction of the Vatican basilica.

But he had the time to complete the Logge (galleries) which Bramante had begun for Julius II and to design the whole ingenious plan of the decoration and even many of the sketches for the Biblical scenes in the vaults. The harmonious conception makes the Logge one of the most significant landmarks of the High Renaissance, in the gracefulness of its architectural lines, the subtle elegance of its decoration, and the noble and perfect harmony of its colouring. Raphael's achievement of balance is revealed here, a state of grace resulting from an intimate harmony between sensibility and vision. The thirteen arcades that compose it carry a rich network of ornamentation, partly in stucco relief, partly painted, which derives its origin from the decoration of the Golden House, which had recently been reopened and was constantly visited by artists. A number of pupils collaborated with Raphael in the Logge: but the unified conception remains, in the exquisite rhythmical movement with which the master imbued it.

The Vatican is also a treasure-house of other works of his: the series of ten tapestries for the Sistine Chapel, woven from his cartoons in Brussels in the atelier of Pieter van Aelst under the direction of Bernard van Orley, which were displayed for the first time below the fifteenth-century frescoes on Christmas Day 1519. Today they are all in the Pinacoteca Vaticana, together with Raphael's other easel paintings: the *Madonna of Foligno,* painted for the scholar Sigismondo Conti, of Foligno, in 1512-13, which shows a shadowy view of the Umbrian town in the background; the predella of the Borghese *Deposition* and the *Coronation of the Virgin,* youthful works to which reference has already been made; and lastly the great picture of the *Transfiguration* which the artist left uncompleted at his death, on 6 April 1520. On the following day the remains of the man from Urbino, who was only thirty-seven years old, were deposited in the Pantheon in an ancient sarcophagus.

Raphael often liked to sign his works 'Raphael of Urbino'. The *Fornarina* (now in the National Gallery in Palazzo Barberini) bears this inscription on the bracelet or ribbon which surrounds her left arm, with a suggestion of possession that seems to endorse the affection linking the painter with his model, a link about which some doubts have been raised by modern historians. The great luminous eyes of the peasant girl, the oval of the face, so realistic in its harmonious form, contrasts with the elegant nobility breathing from the image, which the leafy background, the light veil, the turban, and the gestures of the hands exalt to the height of a classical sixteenth-century female prototype. Raphael painted many other works during the twelve years

The austere basilical interior of S. Maria in Cosmedin, of the 8th century but with 12th-century alterations. The iconostasis (wall separating nave from sanctuary) and the other Cosmatesque marble decorations date from the 11th to the 13th centuries.

The so-called Bocca della Verità in the portico of S. Maria in Cosmedin. The ancient mask of a river god, according to popular tradition, would bite the hand of a liar if it were put into its mouth.

he spent in Rome while he was occupied on the Stanze and on architectural works. Not all of them have remained there but the visitor can complete his Raphael itinerary first in the Borghese Gallery itself, where, together with the *Deposition,* there are the early *Portrait of a Man* (*c.* 1502) and the *Girl with the Unicorn,* of 1505-06, recovered in 1932 from a disguise as St Catherine, which had been foisted onto it by an unwary restorer at the end of the seventeenth century.

In the villa which the banker Agostino Chigi built for himself between the Lungara and the Tiber, the most sumptuous dwelling in Rome in the sixteenth century, later known as the Farnesina, Raphael in his last period painted in fresco the ceiling of the ground-floor gallery, with the collaboration of Giulio Romano, Penni, and Giovanni da Udine, representing there the *Myth of Psyche,* from Apuleius' *Golden Ass;* while in the next room he himself had already painted, in 1511, in competition with Baldassare Peruzzi and Sebastiano del Piombo, authors of the adjacent works, the fresco of *Galatea on the Waves,*

Arnolfo di Cambio. Colle Val d'Elsa c. 1245. Florence 1302.
The Ciborium of the church of S. Cecilia in Trastevere, 1283 (detail).
The slender ogival cusp is among the most significant
of the Roman works by the Sienese architect and sculptor.

an essential work in his stylistic development, pervaded by classical humours and a subtle aesthetic idealism, extraordinarily balanced in its composition, rhythm, and colours.

Not much later than the *Galatea* is the *Prophet Isaiah* on the third pillar of the nave of the fifteenth-century church of S. Agostino (in Piazza S. Agostino, interior restored by Vanvitelli in 1760), revealing the emotion felt by the painter at the uncovering of the Sistine ceiling. The *Sibyls* frescoed in 1614 in S. Maria della Pace, commissioned by the aforementioned Agostino Chigi, translate this emotion in still more typically Raphaelesque ways. The Michelangelo-like plasticity of the figures is here supplemented by the fluid rhythm and the continuous, winding, entwining line, which modulates the forms in addition to moulding them sculpturally. The *Prophets* in the same church certainly go back to an idea of the master's and possibly to a design of his, but most scholars regard them as the work of assistants.

Agostino Chigi was a key personage in sixteenth-century Rome. His family had moved there from Siena at the time of Sixtus IV. His father had already accumulated a large fortune, to which he added considerably in the course of a few years. In 1509 he took over a Roman bank, but apart from that had unlimited funds at his disposal. A councillor of Julius II, he was also his financier at times of emergency.

This astute and cultivated merchant, around whom legends have gathered for centuries (he is said to have given banquets served on massive silver and gold plate which, at the end of the feast, he would throw into the Tiber beneath his balconies — but had fished up afterwards in a net), this far-sighted Maecenas, invited the architect Baldassare Peruzzi, a Sienese like himself, to build him a villa.

This villa, which later went to the Farnese family, became known as the Farnesina, to distinguish it from the monumental palace which that family had built on the other bank of the Tiber, and still bears that name today; taxi-drivers sometimes confuse it with the modern Farnesina, where the Ministry of Foreign Affairs is; while few people know that the little palazzo of Cardinal Le Roy, by Antonio da Sangallo the Younger, in Corso Vittorio Emanuele (which now houses the Barracco Museum, with a fine collection of ancient sculptures), is also called the Piccola Farnesina, though only as the result of mistaking the *fleurs-de-lys* of France on the façade for the Farnese lilies.

The Villa Farnesina was built by Peruzzi in its enclosing garden in accordance with an architectural plan that was quite new for its time: it is a composition of articulated structures, with two lateral wings projecting beyond a central loggia. Peruzzi revealed in this construction an unusual preoccupation, that of building for town surroundings. He was in fact to repeat the same plan soon after, in Palazzo Massimo (in Corso Vittorio Emanuele), with a convex façade echoing the curve of the street.

The decoration of the interior of the villa on the Lungara was entrusted by Chigi to some of the best artists then available, to the Sienese Giovanni Antonio Bazzi, known as Il Sodoma, to Raphael and his numerous assistants, and to the Venetian Sebastiano del Piombo who had recently arrived in Rome. A work by the last-named has only recently (1969) reappeared as a result of restoration, a limpid

▷

The interior of the church of S. Maria sopra Minerva (around 1280, but refurbished in the 19th century). It is among the rare examples of Gothic architecture in Rome, despite its marble facing and the polychrome decoration which was added between 1848 and 1855.

lagoon landscape in soft tones of blue and pink (which had been covered up, possibly during the nineteenth century) in the fresco of *Polyphemus*, next to Raphael's *Galatea*. In the same room Sebastiano del Piombo, the painter who more than any other brought in person to Rome the luminous colours of Venice, painted in fresco, in the high lunettes, scenes from Ovid's *Metamorphoses*, while in the ceiling Peruzzi painted the constellations. In one of the lunettes, the *Metamorphoses* series is inexplicably interrupted. In the last lunette on the left-hand wall as one enters is an enormous youthful face, with wide-open eyes and an intense plasticity of feature. It is painted in monochrome directly onto the *arriccio*, or base coat, in other words before the addition of the coating of plaster for the fresco. Tradition says that it was the work of Michelangelo. And indeed one is tempted to believe it and to imagine that it may have been a portrait taken from life: of one of the young apprentices who were working at the

The picturesque ruins of the medieval Caetani Castle on the Appia Antica, near the Tomb of Cecilia Metella.
The ancient halls of the noble dwelling, today uncovered, contain fragments of sepulchres in the vicinity.

Farnesina; that Michelangelo, standing on the scaffolding, may have skilfully drawn him unobserved, in order to show how, according to him, the perspective involved in looking up to that height from below should be understood.

Il Sodoma has left in the villa his masterpiece, the *Marriage of Alexander and Roxana* of 1511-12, in a room on the first floor next to the Hall of the Perspectives. The delicious frieze in a room next to the ground-floor loggia is by Peruzzi.

The Farnesina, which houses some offices of the National Lincei Academy, is also the seat of the National Print Cabinet, with one of the most important collections of old drawings and engravings in Italy. The charm of the garden surrounding the villa that lies peacefully within its enclosure opposite Palazzo Corsini remains unchanged, except for the reverberation of traffic along the nearby Lungotevere, which increasingly threatens both the security of the frescoes and the structure itself. In its green quiet the visitor can picture Michelangelo's *Bacchus,* as it stood in a similar garden of the same period, in the vineyard of another banker, Jacopo Galli, to whom it originally belonged.

After completing the *Bacchus* (which Shelley strongly disapproved of for its lascivious character) and the *Pietà,* Michelangelo had left Rome. He came back in 1505 for the first approaches to Julius II about the papal monument in St Peter's. It was intended to be, rather than a tomb, a sculptural representation of the Renaissance idea of a Triumph, that worldly idea that had excited the fancy of emperors, captains and poets, which was now to be combined with the triumph of the Church, the Faith, and the Pope himself. For this purpose, Michelangelo had several times visited the marble quarries of the Apuanian Alps. For this purpose, a mountain of marble had been

The Ponte Nomentano on the Aniene River, tributary of the Tiber, near Monte Sacro. Damaged during the invasion of the Goths, it was restored in the 15th century by Pope Nicholas V.
Dear to painters and poets since the 17th century.

brought to Rome and stood unused in the piazza in front of the basilica. The Pope, meanwhile, had changed his mind, and his tomb, which was to have been enlivened by more than forty sculptures, was never erected in St Peter's. The tomb that, more than forty years later, was placed in San Pietro in Vincoli embodied the last and most modest of the six designs projected. Only the *Moses* reflects the sculptor's defiant encounter with rugged nature as he stood alone before the gigantic spectacle of the marble Alps. 'I find I have lost my youth, bound to this tomb', he wrote...

Fairly quivering in his momentary inactivity, the majestic prophet sits in the same attitude as his fellow-prophets painted on the Sistine ceiling. His inner energy vibrates on the surface of the marble skin; veins, tendons, muscles bursting out in barely-restrained tension. Also by Michelangelo, but of later date, are the sculptures at the sides:

Rachel or the *Contemplative Life*, and *Leah* or the *Active Life*. The great marble tabernacle and the other sculptures certainly derive from Michelangelo's design but were executed by the master's assistants. The other sculptures which he did for the tomb, some of them unfinished, are in Florence (Galleria dell'Accademia) and in the Louvre. Rome possesses, in addition to the *Pietà* and the *Moses,* one other sculpture which is indubitably by Michelangelo, and another that is probably his. The first is the *Risen Christ* on the left-hand side of the high altar of S. Maria sopra Minerva. It was commissioned from the artist in 1514 by a canon of St Peter's and three other Romans. But the first version he made in Rome was left half-finished because a black vein appeared in the marble just on the face of Christ. The second version, from another block, was finished in Florence in 1520 and sent to Rome by sea from Pisa the following year. A pupil of Michelangelo, Pietro Urbano, went with it, and on arrival he touched up some parts that had been left unfinished (in the feet, in the hand bearing the cross, and in the nose and beard of Christ). Urbano's finishing touches did not please Metello Vari, the only surviving member of the four who had commissioned it (the others had meanwhile died), and Michelangelo declared himself ready to do the sculpture again (that would have been for the third time). But Vari also asked for, in compensation, and obtained, the version with the dark vein (which Michelangelo had left in his studio in Rome) and put it in the garden of his house, where it was still standing in 1556, after which it was lost. Though not one of the sculptor's masterpieces, the *Risen Christ*, with the remarkable contrast between the powerful nude and the small head with its delicate features, has a certain importance in the master's stylistic maturation because it reveals for the first time the new conception of form that Michelangelo a little later developed in the Medici tombs in Florence. The *Risen Christ,* like the nudes in the *Last Judgment,* suffered the ignominy of a later covering of chaste drapery of gilded bronze, and a covering was also added to protect the foot worn away by the kisses of the faithful. Francis I of France wanted the cast of it and of the *Pietà* to adorn one of his chapels with 'the things which I am assured are the best and most exquisite of your works', as he wrote to Michelangelo on 8 November 1546. And Michelangelo agreed.

A *St John as a Boy* in marble, situated in a niche at the door of the sacristy of the church of S. Giovanni dei Fiorentini (built by Leo X as the 'national' church of his fellow-citizens, on the Lungotevere opposite St Peter's), was identified in 1958 by Roberto Longhi as a probable work of Michelangelo's youth, of 1492-93. It is certainly of considerable quality and as far as style is concerned would correspond to those early years of the sculptor. But other scholars have believed the youthful *St John,* which is mentioned by Condivi and Vasari, to be a different sculpture from the one in Rome; while other old records refer to the work as having gone to France and there been reduced to fragments.

Michelangelo conceived his first independent architectonic work at the age of forty-one, and not in Rome. But in Rome he subsequently did do some architectural work, though he often modestly asserted that such work was not congenial to him. In Rome he was both architect and town-planner, if we take into account the supreme monument that the Piazza del Campidoglio in this sense represents — a complex equalled in grandeur of design, in the whole history of

Gentile da Fabriano (attrib.). Fabriano, c. 1370 - Rome 1427.
Annunciation. Panel. Vatican Pinacoteca (Picture Gallery). Gentile came
to Rome in 1425, in the service of Martin V and painted frescoes,
which are now lost, in S. Giovanni in Laterano (St John Lateran).

sixteenth-century architecture, only by the fortifications with which
Michelangelo had surrounded Florence.

After the Sack of 1527 Rome stood in great need of expert town-
planning. The Capitol, as we see it in old engravings, was still a
rugged hill, the summit all ridges and hollows; thus the first thing
to be done, when in 1537 Paul III Farnese and the civic Guardians
decided to tackle it, was to level the piazza and define its limits on
the Aracoeli church side. The old Senatorial Palace in the background,
the appearance of which was completely altered, the flight of steps
approaching it, placed centrally in relation to the palace, the transfer
from the Lateran and the erection of the equestrian statue of Marcus
Aurelius in the centre, the trapezoidal plan of the open space with the
two palaces diverging from it, were not coordinated operations arising
out of a single initial design, but they can be said to have rendered
in concrete form, albeit in guises that altered in the course of the
work, Michelangelo's own ideas. For the front of the Senatorial Palace,
he had envisaged two storeys of equal importance, accessible by a
stairway of two flights. Of this idea all that remains today is the
flight of steps with the statue of two river-gods, the Tiber and the
Nile. The flight of steps indeed derives from the two ancient sculptures its 'ascending, symmetrical and articulated form' (Bonelli). The
Senatorial façade was constructed after Michelangelo's death by Giacomo della Porta (1583-89), when Martino Longhi the Elder had only
just finished the central tower. It seems reasonable to suppose that in
the original stage of planning a remarkable display of ancient sculptures was intended for the hill, the ideal centre of Rome and the most
majestic place in which to commemorate its ancient civic grandeur.

Besides the river-gods, in fact, a great Jove was to have occupied the centre niche, but its place was later taken by a statue of Minerva, found at Cori, which was given the more fitting name of Dea Roma. As the centrepiece of the piazza, on a pedestal of his own design bearing the arms of the Pope and the city, Michelangelo set up the statue of Marcus Aurelius; it stood — and stands — at the point of convergence of all the lines of perspective, standing high in itself and additionally so, both in reality and by illusion, because of the slight convexity of the floor which acts as a focal nexus between the wings of the great hall, open only on one side, dominating the city and solemnly and nobly detached by its own magnificence from the urban conglomeration below.

Gentile da Fabriano, A miracle of St Nicholas. *The saint saves a boat from shipwreck. Detail of the polyptych painted by the artist for the Quaratesi family. Vatican Pinacoteca (Picture Gallery).*

The design for the pavement of the elliptical floor of the piazza, already used by Michelangelo in 1527 in the Biblioteca Laurenziana in Florence and taken from similar mosaic decorations, both classical and medieval (an analogous design, as Goldscheider has noted, is in the Baptistery in Florence), was carried out more or less faithfully in 1940. The design was known, as indeed were all Michelangelo's plans for the reconstitution of the Capitol, from the prints of the Frenchman Etienne Dupérac, engraved between 1567 and 1575.

The *Dioscuri* and the *Trophies of Marius* on the balustrade of the central approach also belong to the pageant of ancient memories of the original conception and so too, for a time, did *La Lupa* (the *She-Wolf*), which stood on the façade of the old Palazzo dei

Lucas Cranach the Elder. Cranach 1472 - Weimar 1553. Pietà (detail) panel. Vatican Pinacoteca, Room V. It is among the rare works of the German artist in Rome.

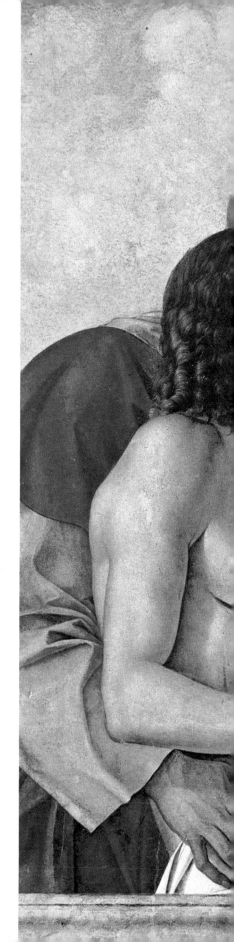

Giovanni Bellini. Venice, c. 1430-1516. Pietà. The cyma (crowning moulding) of the polyptych from the Pinacoteca of Pesaro, which the artist painted for the church of S. Francesco of that city. Vatican Pinacoteca.

Conservatori. Work on the new façade of that building was going on when Michelangelo died, on 18 February 1564.

The third phase of his direct intervention on the Capitol, following the setting for the Marcus Aurelius statue and the flight of steps for the Senatorial Palace, had begun the previous year, and the artist had again employed a collaborator. For the Palazzo dei Conservatori this was the architect Guidetto Guidetti, who became executor of the master's plans for a short time, from February to the autumn of 1564; then he too died and was succeeded by Giacomo della Porta, who continued to respect Michelangelo's original idea; as it was also respected, at a distance of several decades, by Rainaldi, who in 1655 built the Palazzo Nuovo, or Capitoline Museum, on the other side of the piazza. It is customary to generalize about the complex problem

Leonardo. Vinci 1452 - Cloux 1519. St Jerome. Vatican Pinacoteca, Room IX. The monochromatic painting, unfinished, was found in the 19th century, cut into two parts. The artist, protected by Cardinal Giuliano de' Medici, lived in Rome from 1512 to 1517.

of the sixteenth-century reconstitution of the Capitol and to attribute its authorship solely to Michelangelo. Modern criticism, however, has distinguished more objectively between the master's original conception and the work carried out by his friends and successors: between the two there is certainly a difference of feeling, if not of substance. The piazza, majestic and solemn, harmonious as are few others in the world, the first piazza in modern Rome to be created according to a regular plan, the actual draft of which has disappeared and certain details of which were perhaps given only verbally, remains for visitors from every continent Michelangelo's Capitol.

Michelangelo's work on the fabric of the city of Rome was not confined to the Capitol and St Peter's. During 1546 he was working almost exclusively on architecture, for in that year he began the reconstitution of the Capitoline piazza with the senatorial flight of steps, and at the same time he was at work on Palazzo Farnese and on the first model in wax of the dome of St Peter's. Palazzo Farnese had been left unfinished by Antonio da Sangallo the Younger, who died in that year. Michelangelo designed for it the central balcony and the coat-of-arms, the upper windows and the frieze of the cornice on the exterior, and the top floor of the inner courtyard. But he did not finish the building; it was completed in 1589 by Vignola and Giacomo della Porta. Now the seat of the French Embassy to the Republic of Italy, its sumptuous salons are entered from Sangallo's majestic hall and a vast staircase. The gallery on the first floor was frescoed between 1597 and 1604 by the Bolognese artist Annibale Carracci, who had as collaborators his brother Agostino, Domenichino, and Lanfranco. The frescoes of the Farnese Gallery are the most important event of painting in Rome at the time of the transition from Mannerism to Baroque. In the great figures the monumental methods of the Sistine Chapel are still in force, but a new animation and the intense variation of the colours bring them into tune with the new century just beginning.

Michelangelo showed himself, in his adaptation of the Tepidarium in the Baths of Diocletian as the Church of S. Maria degli Angeli, highly respectful of the ancient conception of space; in the Nicchione del Belvedere (subsequently altered), he adhered fairly closely to Bramante's original plan; and in the exterior of the Medici chapel in Castel S. Angelo (which goes back to the time of Leo X), he showed a temperate readiness to adjust to the surroundings. In the late Porta Pia, however, begun in 1561 and executed with the aid of numerous collaborators, he gave a more explicit idea of his architectonic and urbanistic vision of a city such as Rome. He designed and projected other architectural works (for the church of S. Giovanni dei Fiorentini, for the Sforza chapel in S. Maria Maggiore, for an altar in S. Silvestro in Capite, for the tomb of a friend in the Aracoeli church, for a bridge over the Tiber, for a flight of steps in three stages, part of a daring scheme to join Palazzo Venezia to the Quirinal, etc.). Some of these works were carried out, some left unfinished, some never begun. The 'unfinishedness' was a problem of Michelangelo's architecture, as it was of his sculpture. It was not always due to chance or circumstances, to the artist's dissatisfaction or his successors' disregard: 'even if the not-finished was a method and a system, its matrix was anguish, an anguish so authentic and involved (*engagé*) that he was unable to be rational about his own productions' (Zevi) — which, in consequence, the modern visitor to Rome will unhappily never be able to enjoy.

Palazzo Venezia in the piazza of the same name.
Begun by the Venetian Cardinal Pietro Barbo (later Pope Paul II)
in 1455, completed by his nephew twelve years later. It was the papal residence
for a century, then passed into the hands
of the Venetian Republic, whence its name.
Its architect is unknown.

The Modern City

The sixteenth century has been called the 'century of Rome'. Before
it ended, the foundations of the modern city had been laid, a new
society had been born, and from all its vicissitudes had emerged,
following the religious crisis, the Catholic revival (Erasmus, Calvin
and Luther had planted strong roots in the individual and collective
conscience). These events coincided with a profound transformation
of the city. 'The Baroque spirit', as a modern town-planner has written,
'is the spirit of Rome; it is a spontaneous generation, offspring of the
place itself, and indigenous' (Quaroni). The cupolas of the Counter-
Reformation punctuated the sky of the city, which assumed a new
profile against the clouds and the red sunsets — no longer the profile
of columns arising to cleave the air, of white marbles, curving arches,
and the sloping roofs of the ancient basilicas.

From the middle of the sixteenth century to the mid-seventeenth,
Rome was like a busy workshop. The old formless aspect underwent
a radical transformation: bit by bit it was replaced by a rational urban
network. The first 'town plan' was drawn up by Sixtus V in 1585 and
carried out for the most part by Domenico Fontana. Not only did the
best architects of the day cram the city with churches and solemn-
faced palaces built of stone and even more of travertine, but also wide
streets were cut through to join together the most famous basilicas

The 16th-century courtyard of the Palazzo della Cancelleria (Palace of the Chancellery) in the piazza of the same name. The sumptuous building was begun in 1483 by Cardinal Scarampa Mazzarota, continued by Cardinal Raffaele Riario, first Roman protector of Michelangelo, and finished in 1517, after various interruptions.
It has housed the Vatican Chancellery since 1870.

and for the first time provide for a flow of traffic. The basis of all this plan was essentially religious and political but also economic and social, because Rome was no longer confined within the perimeter of the Aurelian walls, because the population had by now grown tremendously, and because new practical needs were urgently arising in every quarter. Sixtus V broke through the circle of the anachronistic walls and with great foresight created long-distance cross-routes, but he also created new centres and axial routes, and annexed to the urban nucleus the large still-uninhabited areas of the gardens and vineyards on the Pincio, the Viminale and the Esquiline. Before everything else he endowed the city with a new and efficient aqueduct, purchasing the water from the Colonnas near Palestrina, so that soon the famous fountains of Rome were flowing. The first, named Aqua Felice, in Piazza San Bernardo alle Terme, was built by Domenico Fontana in 1587, with Giovan Battista della Porta, Flamino Vacca, Leonardo Sormani and possibly Prospero Orsi from Brescia collaborating on the sculpture. Great straight lines were traced by Fontana between the main points of the city. The architect did not bother about the ups and downs of the land but drew long-range perspectives of which the scenographic vertex, at the convergent points, was formed by obelisks (which had come into fashion after the obelisk was set up in Piazza San Pietro), or by groups of sculpture (like the *Dioscuri* in Piazza del Quirinale). S. Maria Maggiore, which was enlarged externally at that time, was their centre of radiation. The system of streets went out from that church in the form of a star, if not precisely according to the design of the ideal city of the Renaissance (as Giedion has rightly pointed out), at least partly because such a pattern was related to what had been done by preceding Popes and was, in any case, farsighted in its vision of the city's future development.

The visitor who sets out today from the high flight of steps outside the apse of S. Maria Maggiore, and walks down the straight road he sees before him, can go along the old Via Felice and Via Sistina (only the second still has its original name) and arrive at the Trinità dei Monti, following the line traced by Sixtus V (who before he became Pope was Felice Peretti, and gave his name to the first stretch of road). The Corso too, which from ancient times was the continuation of the consular Via Flaminia from the Ponte Milvio to the Capitol, thus thrusting a wedge from the extra-urban artery into the heart of the city itself, was first systematized by Sixtus V and Domenico Fontana. It was Fontana who designed the high pedestal of the Antonine column and erected on its summit (as Tommaso Della Porta had done on Trajan's Column) the gilded bronze statue of St Paul (and it is obvious how closely it corresponded to the spirit of the Counter-Reformation to top the lofty monuments of antiquity with the figures of saints). Piazza del Popolo also had its obelisk, visible from far off in the narrowing prospective. The Corso was then known as Via Lata, and though it was not yet the animated centre of city life that it was later to become, it nevertheless had its illustrious palazzi such as, for example, Palazzo Aldobrandini, later Palazzo Chigi (now the seat of the Presidency of the Cabinet), for which Giacomo della Porta did the designs. Many of the houses in the Corso had their façades painted in fresco or covered with mural designs, and this gave a particular character to the street, as indeed it did to the whole of Rome in the sixteenth century. It was a fashion which, born in Venice, had moved to Florence, and it caught on in Rome more than anywhere else. Masters like Raphael and Peruzzi adopted it, but its chief exponents were the Mannerists, Polidoro da Caravaggio, Taddeo and Federico Zuccari, and Maturino da Firenze; more than two hundred houses on both sides of the Tiber were festively painted in many colours in this way, as if their façades were adorned with permanent tapestries. But these unusual decorations were far from permanent, being doomed to transitoriness from their position, exposed to the rain and winds, and from the fragile nature of the plaster. The passer-by lingering in the old quarters will find some faded trace of them in the Ponti *rione*, in a house in Via della Maschera d'oro (No. 9) near Via dei Coronari (where there are many antique shops), in the Parione *rione*, in the old Palazzetto dei Massimi (in Via dei Massimi) and in two houses in Via del Pellegrino (Nos. 64 and 66), and in the Regola *rione*, rather better preserved, in Palazzo Ricci in Piazza de' Ricci (built at the end of the fifteenth century by a Florentine family, the Calcagni), which passed in 1576 to the possession of Cardinal Ricci of Montepulciano.

Sixtus V had a predilection for the Quirinal Palace, summer residence of the pontiffs, which had been begun by Gregory XIII in 1574 and was in use up to 1870 when, with the ending of papal temporal power, it went to the Italian state. Since 1946 this sumptuous edifice (in which at various times famous architects had a hand — Domenico Fontana, Maderno, Bernini, Fuga — and which contains a valuable collection of art treasures) has been the seat of the Presidency of the Italian Republic. The piazza in front of the Quirinal Palace was not the only one with which Sixtus V concerned himself: he also opened up other piazzas in every quarter, from S. Maria Maggiore to St John Lateran and from S. Lorenzo fuori le Mura to the Baths of Diocletian. The radical operation he carried out on the ancient body of the city provided a framework for the future building programme, a framework which in fact was taken into account at least until 1870.

The patrician families showed greater arrogance in the building of their palaces and in their decorative pretensions; the churches vied with each other in height within streets too narrow to enable one to see them without twisting one's neck. Ancient remains were wantonly encroached upon. On the ruins of the theatre of Cornelius Balbo, the Crescenti and later the Cenci built their palazzo like an island of stone upon a hill (Monti Cenci), almost as solid in appearance as the bastions that Antonio da Sangallo had built between Porta S. Sebastiano and Porta S. Paolo. Giulio Mazzoni had decorated a much more ornate edifice for Cardinal Bernardino Spada, the Palazzo Spada in Piazza Capodiferro, today the seat of the Spada Gallery and of the Consiglio di Stato. The Villa Medici on the Pincio (since 1803 the seat of the French Academy) also had fine decorations by Annibale Lippi, who built it for the same Cardinal Ricci who had bought the palazzo with the murals.

Jacopo Barozzi, known as Il Vignola, left a deeper mark on Roman architecture with his high, severe buildings, governed by rigorous laws of perspective, spacious and almost stark in their articulated vastness, but also varied by picturesque contrasts. The church of the Gesù (completed by Giacomo della Porta), is characteristic, as is the Palazzo Farnese at Caprarola (40 miles from Rome), begun by Peruzzi and Sangallo, in which Vignola dissolved the compactness planned by the two first architects into 'a light and airy chiaroscuro, really Correg-

One of the façades of the Villa Farnesina on the Lungara, constructed by Baldassare Peruzzi (1508-11) for the banker Agostino Chigi; its interior was decorated by Raphael and his pupils, by Sebastiano del Piombo, Sodoma, and Peruzzi himself. In 1580 it passed to the Farnese. Today it houses the Accademia dei Lincei (Lincei Academy) and the Gabinetto Nazionale delle Stampe (National Print Collection).

The Renaissance façade of the church of S. Pietro in Montorio on the Janiculum, built perhaps by the school of Bregno and also attributed to Meo del Caprina.

gesque, which links [the building] to the natural and almost idyllic spaces of the park' (Argan). So too are his other buildings in Rome, the Tempietto di S. Andrea in Via Flaminia, and the nearby Villa Giulia, on a grander scale, and more animated in its various parts (the courtyard with ambulatory, the nymphaeum), which today houses the National Museum of Etruscan Art; and lastly, his colonnades on the Capitol (to right and left of the Senators' Palace). Giacomo della Porta, architect and sculptor, midway between Mannerism and Baroque, also enriched Rome with severe buildings of plain design with a classical respect for proportions. To him and Fontana fell the task of completing Michelangelo's dome of St Peter's. His churches, S. Atanasio dei Greci, in particular the Madonna dei Monti, the façade of S. Luigi dei Francesi, the façade and cupola of the Gesù, his fountains and altars (a very ornate one is in the Trastevere church of S. Maria dell'Orto) all reflect his Lombard discipline.

Not last among the sixteenth-seventeenth-century architects who were

Bramante. Monte Asdruvaldo (Urbino) 1444 - Rome 1514.
The Tempietto in the courtyard adjoining the church of S. Pietro in Montorio.
It was among the first works of architecture by the artist in Rome (1502).

the most assiduous builders of Rome was Carlo Maderno, author of the façade of St Peter's and the extension of the nave, and also of some nobly conceived civil and religious buildings, among them Palazzo Mattei and the façade of S. Susanna, erected in 1603.

Many churches, palaces and museums in Rome offer a rich anthology of painting of the period after Raphael and Michelangelo and before the arrival of the Emilian artist Carracci and the Lombard Caravaggio. The 'manner', or that 'lucid and disquieting abstractness, that parade of inventions, subtleties, and whimsicalities, that extraordinary affair of odd, crazy, introverted humours' (Briganti) which united different artists in a homogeneous and by no means minor episode of European art in the sixteenth century and the particular period between the 'constellation of the great', as Giovio called it, and the Academy of the Carracci and Baroque, had its centre in Rome, after Florence and at the same time as Fontainebleau, and from there it spread throughout Europe. And it was right that it should be so, because Rome was the

place where the 'slender crest' (as Woelfflin has called it) of supreme
Classicism could most easily be crossed, in the examples there by
Raphael and Michelangelo; because there better than elsewhere the
worldly and intellectual game initiated by the Mannerist artists adapted
itself to the renewal of ideas, the demands of history and the discussion then arising as to the sacredness of certain principles. Both the
most faithful maintainers of the classical idea, Vasari, Giulio Romano,
Perin del Vaga, and Salviati, and the other artists, Pomarancio, the
Zuccari brothers, and Cavalier d'Arpino inundated Rome with their
painting in iridescent colours, varying in appearance and substance
but homogeneous in its general tone of elegant archaeological evocation, moved by those gestures, imperious yet improbable in the
languor they express, which were one of the most typical aspects of
Mannerist disquiet. The Logge and the last of the Stanze in the
Vatican had been the first practice-ground of the 'Manner'. The Sack
of Rome in 1527 had caused many artists to leave the city, but once
that unhappy event was past the influx resumed on a larger scale, and
not only from Florence and the rest of Italy but from more distant
countries like Flanders and Holland, so that in due time Rome was
full of 'Romanists' speaking different tongues but all of them interpreters of the same language in art. Everything that went on in painting

Antonio del Pollaiuolo. The Wolf nursing Romulus and Remus. *Bronze.*
*Palazzo dei Conservatori. Tradition says that the twins were added
to the famous Capitoline bronze by Pollaiuolo (or by his brother Piero) at the
end of the 15th century, shortly after Pope Sixtus IV
had made a gift of the sculpture to the Roman populace.*

as the century ran its course reflected that international mode — rather in the same way as the end of Gothic — mingling divers accents in a single speech.

There are innumerable examples of Mannerist painting in Rome. They range from isolated paintings in churches (for instance the *Deposition*, unfortunately damaged, of Daniele di Volterra, in the Trinità dei Monti) and in the museums (the Borghese, the Spada, the National Gallery of Ancient Art in Palazzo Barberini, the Gallery of the Accademia di S. Luca) to whole cycles of frescoes. The oratory of San Giovanni Decollato, annexed to the church of that name, is one of the most characteristic instances of the former category and perhaps the one that gives the visitor the best general idea of that period. It lies near the Arco degli Argentari (or money-changers), a curious little bastard monument of the third century, and near the outlet of the waters of the Cloaca Maxima. It was frescoed mainly by Salviati, but it also contains other paintings by Mannerists, Jacopino del Conte and Pirro Ligorio, while in the church there are works by Vasari and Pomarancio. No less unusual for its wealth of decoration is the later Oratorio del Gonfalone, near Via Giulia, frescoed in the last quarter of the sixteenth century by Federico Zuccari, Livio Agresti, Nebbia, and Raffaellino da Reggio (interesting concerts of old music are given in the Oratory). The visitor may come upon another cycle, curious for the crudity of the tortured representations, almost verging on expressionism, in the paleo-Christian church of S. Stefano Rotondo, on the Celio, where Pomarancio and others have painted a sadistic martyrology on the wall round the ambulatory.

Salviati was extremely prolific in Rome, for example in the Farnese and Sacchetti Palaces. In the latter, formerly Palazzo Ricci (No. 66, Via Giulia), the daring of the perspectives borders on surrealism. A tortuous winding staircase of light colouristic transparencies, in one of the frescoes of the salon on the first floor, goes beyond the metaphysical. The marble colours of the architecture in the background of the *Stories of David and Bathsheba* are 'extraordinary plays of intellect' (Briganti), to the point where the artist really puts himself in the place of the chief actor in all this comedy. Almost as if Ignatius Loyola and Giordano Bruno, the Counter-Reformation and freedom of conscience, had never happened or were not going to happen in modern society.

In contrast to the archetypes of Mannerism, by reason of the predominantly human and natural character of his painting, was Michelangelo Merisi da Caravaggio, the artist who set his mark more incisively on the art of painting in Rome in the seventeenth century. Indeed, Caravaggio, with his stylistic revolution, restored the city to the rank of an international centre of art more effectively than Mannerism had done. In fact, even before his death in 1610, many artists began once more to take the long journey to Rome from the countries of northern Europe to learn at first hand the great lesson of luminosity.

Caravaggio, like Buonarroti, came to Rome very young, perhaps only as a sixteen-year-old apprentice, in the train of the Bergamasque artist Simone Peterzano. He then went into another workshop and ate in the house of a 'Monsieur Insalata', a curial prelate who, in exchange for the lad's services, provided him with nothing but a diet of herbs, as the old biographer Giulio Mancini informs us. His other masters were a certain Lorenzo Siciliano, perhaps merely a humble picture-dealer, the Sienese Antiveduto Gramatica, Cavalier d'Arpino, and Prospero Orsi from Brescia, but there is no knowing what he learnt from them.

The young Merisi 'tried to stand on his own and did a few little pictures of himself drawn in the mirror', but he did not manage to sell them, and had to make do with the lodging provided for him by a second prelate, Cardinal del Monte, who, however, proved a better sustainer of his artistic merits.

Suddenly the fame began to spread of this penniless Lombard boy now in Rome, who wandered about among the taverns and wineshops, was restless and quarrelsome, ready with both tongue and sword, ardent and venturesome; and that fame went beyond Rome to reach his native region, the ears of Cardinal Federigo Borromeo in Milan, and

Piazza del Campidoglio. The broad staircase, flanked by the two marble groups of the Dioscuri, of the late imperial age, found in Pompey's Theatre and set up here in 1583, blends with the harmonious urban complex, the first in modern Rome, after a project of Michelangelo.
In the background, the Palazzo Senatorio (Senatorial Palace); the Palazzo dei Conservatori on the right and the Capitoline Museum on the left.

all Europe. Michelangelo Merisi then became, after the name of his birthplace, simply Caravaggio in every language.

Rome offers a longer list of his works than any other place in the world. It has some thirty of them, in churches, museums, and collections, nineteen of which are certainly by his hand. Together they constitute a complete itinerary through all his periods, from his early youth up to the eve of the ill-fated journey on which, steeped in sweat and fever, the artist died on a barren malarial heath by the Tyrrhenian Sea — like Raphael, only thirty-seven years old.

The Borghese Gallery alone has six of his pictures, of various periods.

The *Bacchino malato* and the *Boy with a Basket of Fruit* are the earliest, of around 1589-90. Both belonged to the Cavalier d'Arpino and went to the Borghese family in 1607, just when their famous collection was beginning to be formed.

The Palazzina which houses the Gallery and the magnificent park surrounding it were the product of a felicitous architectural plan for which the ideas and designs were provided by Flaminio Ponzio and the Flemish architect Jan van Santen, whose Romanized name was Giovanni Vasanzio.

Piazza del Campidoglio, the Senatorial Palace with Michelangelo's double staircase (c. 1550) and Giacomo della Porta's façade (1582). The elliptical court, which links the three architectural works of the piazza was constructed in the 20th century, and is based on a design by Michelangelo taken from old prints.

For Scipione Borghese, nephew of the Pope and with him creator of the collection, van Santen also built the palazzo opposite the Quirinal, on the remains of the Baths of Constantine, which later belonged to Cardinal Mazzarino and which is now the Palazzo Pallavicini-Rospigliosi. It includes the Casino dell'Aurora, so called from the fresco by Guido Reni on the ceiling, and the Pallavicini Gallery, with works by Rubens, van Dyck, Poussin, Lorenzo Lotto and many others. Van Santen also built, again with Ponzio, the new basilica of S. Sebastiano, beside the catacombs of S. Sebastiano.

Michelangelo. The Last Judgment. *Sistine Chapel. Michelangelo's titanic project for the Papal Chapel. It was executed between 1536 and 1541.*

The title of the *Bacchino malato* was first coined in 1927 by Roberto Longhi, and the name has stuck, with its appealing allusion to the painted figure 'made livid by malaria' (Della Pergola) which perhaps gives us a first self-portrait of the artist, lightened by the stupendous passage of the still-life, the crown of leaves, the grapes, the peaches, and the vine-leaves. The *Bacchino* and the *Boy with a Basket of Fruit* (in which the still-life becomes the luxuriant focal centre of the picture) are contemporaneous, both of the artist's youthful early period; contemporaneous, too, are his two other pictures in the Borghese, *St John the Baptist* and *David,* which according to a recent hypothesis of Longhi should both be dated after 1606 and assigned to the Naples period (the artist fled to Naples after a brawl in the playing-grounds below Villa Medici which involved him in a murder). The same subject of St John the Baptist reappears with some compositional variation in the *Youthful St John* in the Doria-Pamphilj Gallery (a replica is in the Pinacoteca Capitolina, and there are also other later copies in Rome); with its evident reflection of the nudes of the

Palazzo Farnese in the piazza of the same name. In the foreground, one of the twin fountains with the Farnese fleur de lys and the Egyptian granite basins, attributed to Vignola, but more probably by Rainaldi (1626). The façade of the Palazzo, begun by Antonio da Sangallo, had additions made to it by Michelangelo in 1546.

Sistine ceiling, it undoubtedly precedes the Borghese painting by some years.

Cardinal Scipione was certainly an experienced connoisseur of the art of his day — he was on friendly terms with all the major contemporary artists. Further proof of his expertise can be seen in his timely acquisition of the great altar-piece of the *Madonna of the Palafrenieri* when the Vatican refused it as being unsuitable: the Child so immodestly nude, plebeian women for St Anne and the Virgin!... The work was intended for the altar of the Palafrenieri in St Peter's. Instead, by 1613 the Cardinal had already acquired it; clearly he was not disturbed by the scandal provoked by the crude and violent immersion of the personages in the realities of life.

The picture suffered the same fate as the *Death of the Virgin* for the church of S. Maria della Scala in Trastevere, now in the Louvre; and had it not been for Rubens, who rescued it and sent it to Mantua, it might have been destroyed. The theory of the unsuitability of these pictures and their consequent refusal, which has been handed down by old chroniclers and biographers, has, it is true, been questioned by modern scholars (for example Friedländer), but it is in any case certain that Caravaggio provoked scandals both by his life and by his works; the former was chequered by all kinds of misdeeds, the latter too redolent of earthly matters. It seems likely that it was not so much the realism of his pictures that worried the patrons and other religious characters, but rather the licence that Caravaggio allowed himself in relation to the theological canons governing sacred representations: and then, too, that so-naturalistic realism of his scenes almost smelt of the pyre set up for Giordano Bruno in the Campo dei Fiori on 16 February 1600! Had not the Dominican heretic written that the divine presence identifies itself with natural reality, whose every moment is presided over by a living force which is 'consistency of the parts, which stretches the cartilages, hollows the arteries, intertwines the fibres, ramifies the nerves...'?

The *St Jerome* and a copy of the *Portrait of Paul V* (the original is still in Palazzo Borghese) conclude the series of Caravaggio paintings in the Borghese Gallery, which, however, also contains numerous other works from the master's circle.

Other early works of his are the *Fortune-teller* in the Pinacoteca Capitolina, the *Rest on the Flight into Egypt* and the *Magdalen* in the Doria-Pamphilj Gallery, and the *Narcissus* in the National Gallery of Ancient Art in Palazzo Corsini.

Michelangelo. The Pietà *(detail of the Christ).*
St Peter's Basilica.
The celebrated marble group was executed by the twenty-five-year-old artist for the French Cardinal Jean de Bilheres.

Michelangelo. The Pietà *(detail)*. *St Peter's Basilica. This is the only work signed by Michelangelo (on the ribbon on the Virgin's bosom) and the first of the four* Pietàs *sculptured by him.*

The confused and controversial existing records are of no help in unravelling the truth surrounding the central problem of Caravaggio's activity in Rome and of the great burden it must have been for him to undertake the paintings for the chapel which the French prelate Mathieu Cointrel, cardinal of Santo Stefano (known by the italianized name of Contarelli), dedicated to his patron saint Matthew; this chapel is in the national church of S. Luigi dei Francesi which he acquired in 1565, and which his heirs continued to embellish after his death. Caravaggio was the last of various artists who worked on the chapel, among them Cavalier d'Arpino, who painted its ceiling between 1597 and 1598. Caravaggio probably also began work there at the same time, and he finished in 1603, when the second version of *St Matthew and the Angel* was placed on the altar (the first version, formerly in Berlin but destroyed by bombing in 1945, had not met with approbation, for the same reason of alleged vulgarity as in the cases of the *Madonna of the Palafrenieri* and the *Death of the Virgin*). On each side of St Matthew, Caravaggio painted the two great pictures of the *Calling* and the *Martyrdom* of the saint, both of them subjected to numerous changes in the course of the work, which recent radiographic investigations by the Central Institute of Restoration have revealed. All three paintings herald the arrival of something quite new in religious art. The saints descend from the hagiographic pedestal on which they had been set for centuries and immerse themselves in everyday life, the life of the Roman taverns that the artist assiduously frequented, where people played dice and drank wine and shouted and quarrelled. The shafts of light are those that entered like a gust of wind into the dark rooms with their windows open to the sun; the gestures are the spontaneous ones of ordinary people; the tables, benches, objects and clothes are those of everyday life. This meant that

Raphael. A detail of the predella of The Coronation of the Virgin. *Vatican Pinacoteca, Room VIII. The central section with the* Epiphany. *The side sections show the* Annunciation *and the* Presentation in the Temple.

the story was told in a bolder, less inhibited way, like an actual event, not conveyed by allusion, analogy or allegorical metaphor — the very opposite, in fact, of a mystical vision such as a 'calling' and 'martyrdom' might have been. But a tinge of mystery remains in both, and precisely in the light effects, not because the lights come from mysterious sources but because in both cases they burst in with a supernatural force; indeed, they are the keys to a whole style and not merely of these particular compositions.

The papal treasurer, Tiberio Cerasi, commissioned the other great Roman works of Caravaggio, the *Conversion of Saul* and the *Crucifixion of St Peter,* which stand on both sides of Annibale Carracci's *Assumption* in the chapel which the prelate had destined for himself in S. Maria del Popolo. About these, at least, documents give us some precise details: the signature of the contract, on 24 September 1600, the price agreed upon (which was quite high) on 10 November of the following year.

In the pictures in S. Maria del Popolo, Caravaggio, who had previously

(above) Michelangelo.
The Delphic Sibyl. *Detail
of the Sistine Chapel
vault. It took the artist
four years from 1508 to
1512 to complete the
tremendous fresco
decoration commissioned by
Pope Julius II.*

(below) Michelangelo. The
Drunkenness of Noah.
*Detail of the Sistine Chapel
vault. This is the last
of nine biblical stories
which follow each other
along the centre of the
vault, but it was the first
to have been painted.*

Michelangelo. The Eritrean
Sibyl. *Detail of the Sistine
Chapel vault. Five on
each long wall, one on each
short wall, the Prophets
and the Sibyls are among
the most majestic figures of
the whole composition.*

experimented by painting the walls of a room black to try out the
effect of forms emerging from the shadow, 'shows himself master of
darkness and takes away from it just as much as is needed so as
not to diminish mentally his tragic, virile pessimism' (Longhi). In the
dim light of the Cerasi chapel, the two compositions elevate to a
gigantic scale the forms of the human beings, of that monumental
horse, of the chosen Saul and Peter and of their less consequential
companions. The Vatican *Deposition,* which followed soon after, also
employs this monumental scale, and the figures seem frozen in grief
as they go about their act of mercy, just as would the most ordinary
mortals in such a situation! It was painted between 1602 and 1604
for Pietro Vittrice, for an altar in the Chiesa Nuova, where it consequently stood in company with the triptych of Rubens, who made a
free copy of it (which is now in the Ottawa National Gallery).
For the chapel of the Cavalletti, a Bolognese family, in the church of
S. Agostino, Caravaggio painted the *Madonna of the Pilgrims* or
Madonna of Loreto, here too interpreting the devotional subject in
eminently human everyday terms.
Caravaggio, forced to flee after the Villa Medici affair, never had time
to return to Rome, to his cherished ways, to the Osteria del Moro
where he had thrown a plate of artichokes in the face of an impertinent
apprentice, to the Trinità dei Monti where he hurled stones at the
watchmen, to the racket games under the Muro Torto where, wounded
in the brawl of 29 May 1606, he had killed Ranuccio Tommasoni, the
man from Terni.
Only four years after that affair, on 18 July 1610, he died 'in want

Michelangelo. The Crucifixion of St Peter. *Fresco. Cappella Paolina (Pauline Chapel). Vatican. It is one of the two great works which decorate the chapel built by Pope Paul III Farnese.*

and uncared-for' at Porto Ercole, just when the papal pardon was on its way that would have reopened the gates of Rome to him.

At that date, the great Baroque adventure in Rome had not really begun. True, Caravaggio had introduced, along with his use of light effects, the new element of the representation of everyday, almost slice-of-life, experience — and light and space were to become fundamental motifs of Baroque. True, the great decoration of the Carracci brothers and the other artists of the Bologna Academy, Domenichino, Guido Reni, Guercino, and later Lanfranco, had opened up the ceilings of the interiors to an illusory space decked with skies, clouds, naked bodies and luxurious garments. True, the architecture of Fontana, Maderno, and Giacomo della Porta had initiated a new dialogue with urban space. But the cultural moment had not yet arrived when all three arts, painting, sculpture, and architecture, would express themselves in striking accord, uniting all three to provide a spectacle, a single magnificent spectacle, the new image of the city. The Pope who witnessed the birth of the century's new dimensions

◁

Raphael. Urbino 1483 - Rome 1520. The Coronation of the Virgin. *Vatican Pinacoteca, Room VIII. The great altarpiece with its predella was commissioned of the twenty-year-old artist by the Perugian Maddalena Oddi for the church of S. Francesco di Perugia. Originally painted on a panel, it was transferred to canvas in Paris, where it remained from 1797 to 1816.*

167

Michelangelo. The Conversion of Saul *(detail). Fresco. Pauline Chapel. Vatican. The two scenes seem to express the mystical exaltation felt by the artist in his old age.*

was the same Paul V Borghese who had begun the art collection and the villa. He was not the only Roman prince to participate in the city's renovation. The Colonnas, the Giustinianis, the Ludovisis, the Farneses, the Aldobrandinis — all the most illustrious families of Rome — surrounded their dwellings with wide green parks, and these dwellings were for the most part sumptuous palazzi, within the city or in its environs. But Paul V, who died in 1621, did not live to see the great Baroque transformation of the city which his successors, two other Roman princes, Urban VIII Barberini and Innocent X Pamphilj,

▷

St Peter's Basilica. The central nave. Majestic and enormous, the interior of the largest Christian temple presents the typical aspect of a Counter-Reformation church, of which this was the prototype. The first by three arches Maderno (1614) are in keeping with the original Michelangelesque design.

brought about by decisive personal intervention, imbued as they were with an awareness of the autonomous values of artistic expression. It was, in fact, during their pontificates that the greatest artists of the century undertook and carried out their work, which they — including the two protagonists, Bernini and Borromini — would designate as the new physiognomy of Rome.

Art historians have long debated the date of the birth of Baroque, if indeed a precise date can ever be assigned to a cultural change of this kind. As long as Baroque was still regarded as a continuation and a development of Mannerism, that date was assigned to the last or last two decades of the sixteenth century. Modern studies, however,

St Peter's Square. Bernini's extended colonnade (1656-67) is designed to hold the floods of visitors from all continents.

are more inclined to separate the two trends and therefore to wait until the third decade of the seventeenth century to identify finished work in the Baroque spirit: and this thesis seems to correspond more with what actually happened. In the first decades of the seventeenth century there had been time for a complex debate, the prelude to the stylistic revolution, to develop among treatise-writers, theoreticians, philosophers and craftsmen.

By emphasizing that the first signs of the Baroque ferment developed before the end of the sixteenth century, however, implicit credit was given to the idea of its natural derivation from Mannerism whereas from the beginning it was opposed to it. The second and more realistic

P. 172/173

St Peter's Square. At night, the jets of the two fountains, one by Maderno (1613), the other by Bernini (1675), vie with Michelangelo's cupola against Rome's night sky.

One of the gigantic fonts on the first pillar of the central nave of St Peter's Basilica. The putti were sculptured by Francesco Moderati, Carnacchini designed the whole, and Lirone modelled the marble drapery (1722-25). They were all commissioned by Pope Benedict XIII Orsini.

hypothesis, advanced by, among other scholars, Haskell, Briganti and Portoghesi, according to which the 'decisive outburst' of Baroque occurred around 1630, is confirmed, moreover, by the early architectural works of Gian Lorenzo Bernini (1598-1680): the *baldacchino* over the altar of the Confessio in the basilica of St Peter's and the alterations, carried out together with Borromini, to Palazzo Barberini, which Carlo Maderno had some years earlier begun.

The *baldacchino* was commissioned from Bernini by Urban VIII in July 1624 soon after he become Pope, but the work went on until 1633. There seems to be no doubt about the Pope's determining influence on the iconographic scheme of this immense object, which Bernini regarded as an enlarged processional canopy — so Argan writes — which a throng of the faithful might have carried to the tomb of the Apostle. The bees, suns and laurel branches of the Barberini coat-of-arms recur on the great ciborium, as if to assert the indelible link between the Roman family and the very heart of Christianity. The *baldacchino,* at Bernini's suggestion, was made from bronzes taken from the portico of the Pantheon, thereby provoking Pasquino's sardonic comment '*quod non fecerunt Barbari, fecerunt Barberini*' (what the barbarians didn't do, the Barberini did).

Even before the *baldacchino* was finished, Bernini had been nominated architect of the Vatican basilica by Urban VIII and had also been given the task of finishing the Barberini palazzo near the Quattro Fontane, for which Carlo Maderno had laid down the plan and begun the work. The palazzo is the key to the new style and at once reveals how Bernini intended to draw his inspiration not from Mannerism, which he had already advanced beyond, but from a new interpretation of Bramante's classicism, so that the front of the building was somewhat reminiscent of those exteriors that Julius II's architect loved to design with picturesque illusions of perspective, for example the courtyard of S. Damaso in the Vatican.

At the time of the *baldacchino* and Palazzo Barberini, Gian Lorenzo Bernini and Francesco Borromini used to exchange ideas and plans and work in collaboration. The antagonism between the two artists had not yet broken out; this was to express the fundamental contradiction — and it was the contradiction of the whole century — between two conceptions irrevocably opposed and yet complementary. In the *baldacchino* and in Palazzo Barberini their work went on contemporaneously; both continued to work in the Palazzo, and even at times respected Maderno's original conception, but their ideas inevitably diverged widely from the first builder's plan. Bernini is regarded as the undoubted author of the staircase in the square room on the left of the façade, the staircase leading to the National Gallery of Ancient Art (now unfortunately divided by an incumbent military club, into two sections, one here and one in Palazzo Corsini) while the elliptical staircase on the opposite side (now disfigured, like the Bernini staircase, by a lift) is attributed to Borromini. But the work

◁
(above) Michelangelo's cupola seen from the Vatican Gardens. The superb architectural work, created by Giacomo della Porta, after Michelangelo's designs, in 22 months (1588-89).

(below) Basilica of St Peter. The crossing. In the space under the immense cupola, Bernini set up for Urban VIII his bronze baldacchino *(1624-33), as high as the Palazzo Farnese, to cover the Papal altar. In the casting, the artist used bronze slabs taken from the* pronaos *of the Pantheon.*

of both artists went beyond this, even if it only affected certain parts of the building. Borromini, who had been assistant to Maderno and then to Bernini, was in a position of inferiority especially in relation to the latter, which was one of the causes of the deep dissension between the two artists. Besides the staircase, the elaboration of the main front of the palazzo and of the back, overlooking Via Barberini and visible from the piazza below (where an enormous advertising sign now outrages the view), is attributed with certainty to Bernini, and also 'the whole production of the internal decoration' (Portoghesi); whereas it is more difficult to assign to Borromini all the work that may in fact be his. Hempel noted the stylistic difference between the windows of the top storey on each side of the sham-loggia façade, so ornate and broken up by wings; and he rightly attributed the former to a design of Borromini's. Portoghesi extends this to the colonnades of the lower storey, the doors of the great salon with an allegorical fresco on the ceiling of the *Triumph of the Papacy and the Barberini,* painted by Pietro da Cortona between 1633 and 1639, and also to the back windows.

The question is an extremely complex one, for the birth and growth of this building, which combined the dual characteristics of a town palazzo and a suburban villa (it was originally isolated by vineyards and gardens on the side of the Quirinal), occurred precisely in the period of transition from one culture to another, and it was carried out by three artists who were profoundly different from each other. The 'collective intuition' that was Baroque (Portoghesi) nevertheless saw in this building the new historical prospects that the seventeenth century was proposing to European culture.

After the work on the palazzo, the paths of Bernini and Borromini separated; the dissension between the two artists broke out into open quarrel. There were endless stories and anecdotes about it, plentifully embroidered. It was, after all, the most notorious affair of the day in Rome.

Bernini concentrated on the works of sculpture and architecture in St Peter's: the statue of Longinus in the central crossing and the one of Constantine in the atrium; the tombs of Urban VIII and Alexander VII and the design for the tomb of Countess Matilda of Tuscany (beside the second pillar in the right aisle); the altar of the Chapel of the Sacrament; the marble decoration and floor of the part lengthened by Maderno so as to transform Michelangelo's plan into a Latin cross; and lastly that convulsive riot of sculptural forms that is the Cattedra of St Peter at the back of the apse, supported by the Doctors of the Latin Church, St Ambrose and St Augustine, and of the Greek Church, St Athanasius and St John Chrysostom. (Bernini's Cattedra encases a seat of wood and ivory which was traditionally regarded as the seat used by St Peter, but recent research has recognized it as being not of the apostolic time but Carolingian and possibly re-composed with earlier ivory decorations of 875, a gift from Charles the Bold to Pope John VIII).

Gian Lorenzo Bernini also brought into the urban spaces of Rome

P. 178/179
Piazza Navona. In this organized Baroque setting, the shape and dimensions of Domitian's Stadium are preserved. The church of S. Agnese in Agone at left. Borromini's concave church façade (1653-57), Bernini's Fountain of the Rivers in the centre of the piazza (1651) and two other minor fountains (1655 and 1873) with 16th-century basins.

Piazza Navona. Borromini's cupola for the church of S. Agnese and a detail of the Fountain of the Rivers (Nile, Ganges, Danube, Plata, which correspond to the four quarters of the world known in Bernini's time).

the bizarre gaiety of his fountains, each so different from the other. Nature and architecture seem to intermingle in them with the common intent of bringing a note of gaiety into city life, a decorative pause in the functional impulse of the town-planner. They are a refreshment for the passer-by, a welcome break in a piazza or at a street-corner, by reason not only of the water they furnish but their artistic quality. With their forthright plastic intention they gratify the modern taste for open-air sculpture set in places where life is at its busiest. Where they are no longer in scale with the surrounding buildings, as is the case with the Fontana del Tritone in Piazza Barberini today, they nevertheless maintain their aristocratic detachment as subtle plastic inventions. In Bernini's work, the fountains correspond to the artist's instinctive desire to move space, as he did when he designed the series of angels for his wonderful perforated balustrade on the bridge to Castel S. Angelo, which Matteo de Rossi set up for him.

The Fountain of the Barcaccia in Piazza di Spagna is not unanimously accepted as Bernini's (Baglione ascribes it to him, but Baldinucci attributes it to his father, Pietro Bernini). But there is no doubt about the others, the Fontana del Tritone in the centre of Piazza Barberini; the Fontana delle Api, now in the same Piazza at the beginning of Via Veneto (it was originally at the corner of Via Sistina), with the symbols of the Barberini arms on the simple, broad shell of travertine; the much restored fountain of Palazzo Antamoro in Via della Panetteria; and the Fontana del Bicchierone in the Villa d'Este

at Tivoli. (Cardinal Ippolito d'Este, son of Duke Alfonso di Ferrara and of Lucrezia Borgia, governor of Tivoli from 1550, patron of literature and the arts, friend of Cellini and Titian, and an ardent admirer of Palestrina's music and the poetry of Tasso and Ariosto, had this villa built for him by Pirro Ligorio and surrounded it by the famous whimsical fountains in the vast park, which was planned as a magnificent application of the formal or Italian garden principles, with a scenographic intermingling of waterfalls and jets, rocks, sculptures and other expedients to make artifice natural and nature artificial.)

S. Andrea al Quirinale. The façade. The church was commissioned of Bernini by Cardinal Camillo Pamphilj, nephew of Pope Innocent X.

◁

S. Andrea al Quirinale. The interior of the cupola. Bernini's imaginative architecture (1658-71) was decorated with stuccos by Antonio Raggi, the master's pupil and assistant.

183

But the place in Rome where Bernini designed one of the most romantic spots in the whole city, one of the rare ensembles that is still intact, which has no counterpart, and in which the relationship between everyday life and the image of a still-living past preserves a tangible meaning, is Piazza Navona; this is one of the places in Rome that is mesmerizing, captivating, seeming to be suspended in an abstract dimension. It is perhaps a fictitious life that goes on there, especially when, between Christmas and Epiphany, the perfect proportions of the piazza are violated by the booths of a popular fair, but also during the rest of the year, now that motor traffic has been banned, the sacred enclosure has become a haunt of hippies. And yet there are evenings when the Roman takes possession of it, savours the sharp scent of the *ponentino*, the west wind, accepts the tourist without assimilating him; it is something else that happens in the piazza of the Fontana di Trevi, whose spectacular background was set up by Niccolò Salvi in 1751, and the 'Ocean' group with its marine horses sculptured in 1762 by Bracci, where a coin thrown into the great basin is said to guarantee the traveller a second return to Rome. Bernini's work in Piazza Navona began in 1648, with the Fountain of the Four Rivers in the centre of the harmonious oval that corresponds to the ancient perimeter of Domitian's Stadium. It is perhaps due to the tradition of athletic contests in Domitian's circus that the piazza continued, especially in Baroque times, to be the place of popular festivals and assemblies (its present name derives, by phonetic corruption, from *agone*, a contest). In the Fountain of the Four Rivers (the figures represent the Nile, the Ganges, the Danube, and the Rio della Plata, and symbolize the four parts of the then-known world) Bernini, who was assisted by pupils on the sculptures, challenged the laws of statics and produced not only a demonstration of skill but also a quasi-ironical comment on that hyperbole inherent in the obelisk balanced on the hollow rocks with a void for its base, in the palms shaken in the wind, in the agitated poses of the rivers, in the restive animals, and the gushing water. Later on, Bernini enlarged and renovated the second fountain in the piazza, the so-called Fountain of the Moor, between the Palazzo Pamphilj and the church of S. Giacomo degli Spagnoli. The basin had been designed by Giacomo della Porta in 1574. Bernini sketched a design and made a model of the 'Moor' struggling with the dolphin, which was sculptured by a pupil, while other ornaments were added at the end of the nineteenth century, at the same time that the Fountain of Neptune was set symmetrically at the other end of the piazza and adorned with modern decorative sculptures deriving from the old basin of della Porta.

The Palazzo Pamphilj, beside the church of S. Agnese in Agone, which Innocent X had built by Girolamo Rainaldi (1644-50) and donated to his sister-in-law Olimpia, was a meeting-place of artists in the middle of the seventeenth century. Pietro da Cortona frescoed the ceiling of the great gallery with the *Stories of Aeneas*. Today the whole building is the seat of the Brazilian Embassy and houses Brazilian cultural and artistic exhibitions. Piazza Navona was the scene of a sharp dispute between Bernini and Borromini, for Borromini finished the church of

▷

Lucas Cranach the Elder. Cranach 1474 - Weimar 1553. Venus and Cupid. *Borghese Gallery. The 1531 date is not regarded as the actual one. The writing at the top reproduces verses of Theocritus, in Latin, on the subject of Venus and Cupid with a honeycomb.*

DVM·PVER·ALVEOLO·FVRATVR·MELLA·CVPI
DVRATI·DIGITVM·CVSPIDE·FIXIT·APIS·
SIC·ETIA·NOBIS·BREVIS·ET·PERITVRA·VOLVP
QVA·PETIMVS·TRISTI·MIXTA·DOLORE·NOC·

Antonello da Messina. Messina c. 1430 - Venice 1479. Portrait of a Man.
Borghese Gallery.
A painting of his last years (c. 1474-75),
it is the only work by the great Sicilian painter in Rome.

S. Agnese, begun by Girolamo and Carlo Rainaldi, altering it considerably, while respecting the Rainaldis' plan of a Greek cross. On the
façade, in particular, which overlooks Bernini's Fountain of the Rivers
and is in direct and immediate competition with it, Borromini applied
his bold architectonic vision, relating it to the oval shape of the piazza,
giving an explicit vertical echo of it in the concave movement of the
masses in the lower area (the dome and campanile were finished by
other architects after the dispute between Borromini and the principal
commissioner, Camillo Pamphilj, became acute).
The interior of S. Agnese in Agone is a fine museum of Roman Baroque
sculpture, which formed an important chapter in itself in the artistic
history of the seventeenth century.
Roman life was intense in those years. Artists came to the city where
so much new building was going on, they stayed there, and worked

Raphael, The Girl with the Unicorn *(detail), Borghese Gallery. Found in damaged condition, it was changed, towards the end of the 17th century, into a St Catherine. The overpainting was removed in 1932. It is dated to around 1505-6.*

for the pontiffs and the Roman princes. Christina of Sweden chose to live in what is today the Palazzo Corsini on the Lungara, and there she gathered together an important collection of works of art and received artists and men of letters, both Italian and foreign. When she made her solemn entry into Rome on 23 December 1655, having abjured Lutheranism for the Catholic religion, the recently-elected Pope Alexander VII Chigi was so delighted that he ordered Gian Lorenzo Bernini to embellish the Porta del Popolo, through which

P. 188/189

G. L. Bernini. Naples 1598 - Rome 1680. The Rape of Proserpina *(detail). Marble. Borghese Gallery. The subject of this youthful work was inspired by the famous story in Ovid's Metamorphoses.*

the Queen would pass to enter the centre of the city on her way to St Peter's.

Innocent X posed not only for Bernini and Algardi but also for a masterpiece by Diego Velasquez, the portrait now in the Doria-Pamphilj Gallery in the Corso, where Bernini's marble bust of him is also kept, together with many other incomparable works of all the schools of painting, sculptures, classical marbles, and sumptuous furnishings, which give the visitor an idea of the magnificence of those palaces of Baroque Rome in which cardinals, popes, sovereigns, ambassadors,

The Castel S. Angelo, or Hadrian's Mausoleum (A.D. 135-39) remains one of the most significant monuments of antiquity. The bridge,
Ponte Elio (after the Emperor Hadrian's first name), was constructed
by Demetrianus, the same architect who was responsible for the Mausoleum, and was enlarged, after a design
by Bernini, by new parapets and ten statues of angels.

artists, and the *beau monde* used to meet on festive occasions. The sixteenth-century courtyard of the Palazzo Doria-Pamphilj is surrounded on all four sides by a subtle interplay of arcades and perspectives of Bramantesque inspiration. The back of the building, articulated and severe, which forms two sides of the Piazza del Collegio Romano (so called from the Jesuit College which occupies one side of it, built in 1583-85 by Bartolomeo Ammanati), was designed by Antonio del Grande in 1659-61. The church of S. Maria in Via Lata, an ancient diaconate, frequently altered over the centuries and at that time the

chaplaincy of the Pamphilj, was rearranged internally by Cosimo Fansago and Fancelli and given a harmonious façade and campanile by Pietro da Cortona which are among the most finished examples of Baroque architecture in Rome. The contiguous rococo façade of the Palazzo on the Corso is almost the only example of that style in Rome; it was designed around 1734 by Gabriele Valvassori.

Bernini's subsequent architectonic work (after Piazza Navona, the Porta del Popolo, the restoration of S. Maria del Popolo beside it, the fountains, and the sculptures which will be described below) continued to have a profound effect on the physiognomy of Rome. His first plan for Piazza S. Pietro goes back to the same year, 1656, in which the artist began work on the Cattedra. Two or three fixed points were already established for the architectural systemization of the forecourt of the first Christian basilica in the world, which would receive the throng of pilgrims beneath the Loggia delle Benedizioni: the dome, Maderno's projecting façade, and the central obelisk set up by Fontana. From these three points Bernini set out to conceive the great oval with a quadruple colonnade, in which a third central arm was also envisaged, with two openings between the three blocks, from which the crowd could flow into the interior of the basilica to receive the full impact of its majestic spaciousness. But the third arm was never built, and in our own century, after the demolition of the old houses in the so-called 'spina dei Borghi', that unbelievable maelstrom that is Via della Conciliazione was created, having as its approaches at one end Bernini's august colonnade and at the other the uninspiring official artery.

The colonnade was the result of an extremely elaborate plan, of the most ingenious consideration of visual and scenographic effects, and also of a desire to preserve the relationship with the already existing structures — the basilica and the apostolic palaces — in reciprocal visibility, in the proportions, both actual and in illusory perspective, and in the connection with Maderno's façade: hence the eminently successful trapezoidal space in front of the basilica which unites the portico with the oval without breaking the spatial continuity but, rather, by inserting the one into the other naturally, by means of the two lateral bodies, the corridors. Of the simple geometrical principle which governs the definition of the oval space, all the elementary secrets have been made plain; the visitor even has pointed out to him by means of round slabs in the pavement of the piazza the two visual centres of the two semicircles; when one stands on these slabs, all four rows of columns seem to become one. The calculations of the radii of each semicircle are absolutely precise; even the distance between the two fountains (reconstructed by Bernini after Maderno's designs, in 1667 and 1677) correspond to these radii, so that the three intersections stand geometrically in relationship. But it is not only these relationships that give the space its solemn grandeur. The whole ensemble of Doric

◁

(above) Francesco Borromini. Bissone 1599 - Rome 1667. The cupola of the Church of S. Ivo. The work of construction on this daring complex lasted from 1642 to 1660.

(below) Palazzo Venezia (The Venetian Palace). The courtyard. The fountain showing Venice marrying the Sea, *in travertine, by Carlo Monaldi (1730), installed when the Palace housed the embassy of the Venetian Republic.*

columns forms incisively plastic volumes, given movement by the intense light and shade.

As the colonnade forms the solemn approach to the basilica, so the Scala Regia, which Bernini designed between 1663 and 1666, was the regal introduction to the papal residence. It joins directly, by three flights of steps, the right arm of the portico and the atrium of the basilica (at the end of which Bernini, with a subtle eye for psychological effect, placed the great equestrian monument of Constantine) with the vestibule of the Sistine Chapel. Beside the vestibule is the Cappella Paolina, where Michelangelo in 1550 painted his last pictorial work, the two dramatic frescoes of the *Conversion of St Paul* and the *Crucifixion of St Peter*. The Scala Regia, like the Sala Ducale (redecorated by Bernini with landscapes and putti), tackles in terms of great theatrical effect the problem of the approach to the apostolic palaces. The ingenious disposal of the various parts — steps, arches, columns, walls — the gradient of the ascent, which is gentle, uniform and easy, and the articulation of the light as it comes and goes, are the most evident qualities of this noble architecture.

The little oval church of S. Andrea al Quirinale (in the street flanking the palazzo) is another striking example of the whimsical architecture dear to Bernini, and was his last important work. Two other churches on a central plan, which Bernini built in the immediate neighbourhood of the city, resemble it; one at Ariccia, on the Via Appia, and the other at Castel Gondolfo, on Lake Albano, the summer residence of the Popes (the papal palace was built by Maderno for Urban VIII in 1629, but it was subsequently enlarged and rearranged). Free play of genius governs the architectonic solutions of S. Andrea al Quirinale: the little façade on classical lines is given plastic variety by the convex porch and the curious Baroque fantasy of the tympanum.

Some mention has already been made of Bernini's sculptural works but there are many more in Rome than have been noted. The Borghese Gallery alone has a splendid collection of them, equal in interest to its collection of Caravaggio's paintings.

Many other sculptures of Bernini's adorn the churches of Rome (among them S. Bibiana, S. Andrea delle Fratte, S. Maria del Popolo). The visitor will not miss the two most famous examples, fundamental testimonies of Baroque sculpture, the *Blessed Ludovica Albertoni*, at the last gasp on her deathbed, in the Trastevere church of S. Francesco a Ripa, and the *St Theresa* in her mystical swoon, in the Cornaro chapel in S. Maria della Vittoria. The *Blessed Ludovica Albertoni*, done when the artist was eighty, but entirely his own work, expresses the last tremulous pathos of the hand that carves at once with fury and with delicacy. The *St Theresa*, in its turn, a work of his full maturity (it was done between 1645 and 1652), is the fulcrum, one may say, of all the sculpture of the century, with its theatrical impetus — and in fact the marble group is the climax of an effective scenic background — with the movement of the figures in their sensual abandonment as if in consummation of love which the light suggestively intensifies and emphasizes.

Baroque sculpture as initiated by Bernini had a vast development in Rome throughout the seventeenth century and after. It had had its forerunners in such transitional sculptors between Mannerism and Baroque as Guglielmo della Porta, author of the monument to Paul III in the apse of St Peter's (the figure of Justice, originally nude, depicts the Pope's sister Giulia Farnese); Nicolas Cordier, of Lorraine, known in Rome as 'il Franciosino', with works in S. Maria sopra Minerva and S. Maria Maggiore; Christoforo Stati from Florence; the Lombard Stefano Maderno, whose *St Cecilia* of 1601 was mentioned earlier; and above all the Tuscan Francesco Mochi, whose most successful work is the fine marble group of the *Baptism of Christ* for S. Giovanni dei Fiorentini, today in the Museo di Roma in Palazzo Braschi, and Bernini's father as well, Pietro Bernini, whose *St John the Baptist* is in the church of S. Andrea della Valle.

A second leading figure was Alessandro Algardi from Bologna, who was educated at the Academy there, was three years older than Bernini and placed in opposition to him, even by contemporary historians, by reason of his more severe style; Algardi came to Rome when he was thirty years old, in 1625, after a sojourn at the Mantua court of the Gonzagas, and began by restoring and integrating damaged classical marbles, for example the *Hercules and the Hydra* in the Capitoline Museums, and transformed the Julius Cæsar, in collaboration with Bernini, into a monument to Carlo Barberini, brother of Urban VIII, for the Palazzo dei Conservatori (where his powerful bronze monument to Innocent X also is). But he soon gave proof — with the Hellenistic *Sleep* in marble in the Borghese Gallery — of his own qualities as a sculptor and designer. His monuments and marble altar-pieces (in St Peter's, the *St Leo's Meeting with Attila* on the left-hand altar in the apse) and his portrait-busts (he sometimes risked doing the same subjects as Bernini — Scipione Borghese and Innocent X), especially of his patrons the Pamphilj, of which the Doria-Pamphilj Gallery possesses

In the 16th-century courtyard of the Palazzo della Sapienza (Palace of Wisdom) ancient seat of the Roman University, Borromini constructed the church of S. Ivo, succeeding in blending the harmony of the Renaissance with his Baroque audacity.

a large collection, reveal how, though working at the height of the Baroque period, he was the 'creator of a style of great correctness and decorum' (Faldi), which is as much as to say a moderator of the extravagances of the Berninian frenzies. As has been pointed out, although the types of humanity portrayed by Algardi, visible in so many examples of his work preserved in Roman churches, included a good many members of the pontifical court and the most influential princely house of the time of Innocent X, that same house (the Pamphilj, to which the Pope also belonged) nevertheless did not disdain 'a less sublime, more everyday and approachable human species' (Faldi). Consequently the artistic testimony left to us by the sculptor considerably extends our knowledge of seventeenth-century tastes to the apex of the social pyramid as well as to the bourgeois milieu, men of letters and the intermediary classes, if not precisely to that poor and lowly humanity of the streets that Caravaggio had elevated to be universal protagonists of his art. It was the whole prolific band of Bernini followers, of various origins and extractions, who introduced into the Baroque trend, that had by then conquered the whole of Europe, the Roman message of Bernini and Borromini.

Rome in fact owes it to Francesco Borromini that its Baroque did not become worn out by excess. This architect from Lugano, with his restlessness and his touchy isolation, his obstinate severity and the lively controversy that he introduced into the Roman scene, gave the whole trend a more highly coloured character and more clearly defined

G. L. Bernini. The Blessed Ludovica Albertoni. *Marble. Church of S. Francesco a Ripa. Sculptured in 1674; echoes the theme of the mystic swoon of St Teresa in S. Maria della Vittoria.*

aims. Borromini, at bottom, was rather like Caravaggio: like the painter, he came from the north (he had his early training in Lombardy), had a difficult character, and was conscious of his gifts. It tortured him if a work of his did not correspond in execution to the design he had made for it (one of his first works, the Oratory of the Philippines, beside the Chiesa Nuova, provided a theme for his scrupulously detailed *Opus architectonicum,* 1648, published posthumously) and he seems a little, in this dissatisfaction and care for accurate accomplishment, like Caravaggio in his elaborations in S. Luigi dei Francesi. Borromini began and ended his career with the same work, San Carlino alle Quattro Fontane. He built the monastery when, after the separation from Bernini, he was in a position to take on a responsible work alone. The interior followed four years later, and the building of the façade of the church coincided with the year of his death — which was violent, for he killed himself after a night of anguish. Such were the bounds confining the long life and career of the most introverted and unsatisfied artist of seventeenth-century Europe.

Some thought him a little touched in the head, some quite mad. His contemporaries found him at least very queer, and this is why Borromini's architecture in Rome, like that of the Venetian Palladio, disconcerts the onlooker, because he is unable to find in it the spirit of the time in which it was born. Thinking of him in modern terms, he is an anti-conformist, in Italian terms of the 1970s, a *contestatore*

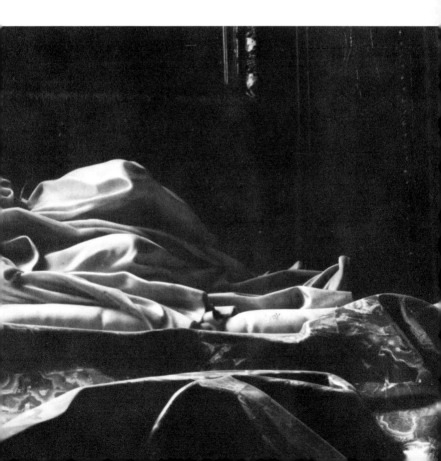

(one who is against everything). How many people, lifting their eyes above the roofs of Rome to the daring surprises of S. Ivo alla Sapienza or S. Andrea delle Fratte, will not ask themselves to what century this tortuous winding of stone into the sky can belong — to Baroque or to some later period, to Gothic or to the Catalonian Gaudí's time?

Borromini's work invests Baroque Rome with suggestions for the future. Invited by the patrician family of a Cardinal, who was his friend and patron, to work on their palazzo (Palazzo Spada in Piazza Capodiferro), the artist carried out, among other things, an essay in space-perspective of his own invention, a gallery of columns which appears to run its full length, but is only a *trompe l'œil* in a short corridor. It ends in another little courtyard, and the tiny statue in it, seen through Borromini's fake telescope, also seems to be of enormous dimensions, as in fact it would be if the proportions of the whole were real. When, on the death of Urban VIII and the temporary decline of Bernini's fortunes, Borromini assumed the role of Rome's first architect, his great commission, which was to reconstruct the Lateran basilica, followed rapidly; though it proved less daring than S. Ivo, less ambitious than S. Agnese in Agone, and less restless than the façade of San Carlo alle Quattro Fontane. While a visit to the courtyard of the Sapienza (in Corso Rinascimento) and to the church of S. Ivo which rises unexpectedly in it may offer the tourist a luminous and fantastic picture of Borromini's detachment from the canons of every kind of conformist architecture, a picture of what his contemporaries called his queerness, the sight of St John Lateran will seem grandiose, animated, and also full of light. The great interior continued to respect in every way the plan of the ancient basilica, not, of course, by Borromini's wish but by that of Pope Innocent X, with the result that, as a chronicler of the time wrote, 'the whole site did not give satisfaction' to the artist, but 'to people in general, it did'. The architect undertook many other works in Rome; but he left most of them half-done. His town-planning ideas, too, remained at the design stage. In old Trastevere, the unfinished church of S. Maria dei Sette Dolori (in Via Garibaldi, not far from the Porta Settimiana) gives an idea of his congenital restlessness. Nor can it be said that the crude structures of the façade, the plastic effect of the protruding mouldings that so singularly articulate the block, are less fascinating than a finished building like the Philippine oratory; or that they do not fully reveal the character, the genius and the irrational logic of the architect. Not far from the church is the entrance to the Bosco Parrasio. In that place, in the eighteenth century, the poets of the Arcadia used to meet, that Academy which from the end of the seventeenth century strove to oppose the crystallization and decline of Baroque just as Borromini had tried to do in his works.

Two other seventeenth-century architects, Pietro Berrettini da Cortona and Carlo Rainaldi, left a definite mark on the city, even though their works in it were few. The former was less talented as a painter than as an architect. He too worked on Palazzo Barberini but to what extent is uncertain. He nevertheless revealed a new

▷

Piazza della Minerva. The Egyptian Obelisk (6th century B.C.*), found in the nearby Iseo Campense, was designed by Bernini to go on the bizarre pedestal with an elephant; the work was carried out by a pupil, Ercole Ferrata, in 1667.*

The crossroads of the Quattro Fontane (Four Fountains) (at the intersection of the ancient via Felice with the stretch from the Quirinale to the Porta Pia) so called because of the four display fountains with the recumbent statues (1588-93) set in the bevelled corners.

spaciousness in the first big work he undertook, the church of SS. Luca e Martina near the Roman Forum, where he made use of classicist elements and even of elements deriving from Michelangelo. The church, near the Senate and isolated between two streets, is just opposite the Carcere Tulliano, known in the Middle Ages, when it was enlarged, as the Carcere Mamertino, in which tradition has it that St Peter was imprisoned. Its articulated and noble façade, compressed and dilated by its various elements, pilasters, a mixture of straight and curving lines, two storeys superimposed, and the luminous interior represent two very early stages of Baroque in Rome. Cortona's church was begun, in fact, when Bernini's *baldacchino* was being unveiled in St Peter's and Borromini was still an apprentice there, though already full of ideas.

Three or four other works of architecture in Rome, mostly collaborations on already existing buildings, exemplify Pietro da Cortona's lucid style. One of the most significant has already been mentioned: the façade, with Palladian echoes, and the campanile of S. Maria in Via Lata (an interesting view of the campanile can be enjoyed through the skylight of the cabinet in the Doria-Pamphilj Gallery which contains Velasquez's portrait of Innocent X). Another is the façade and portico of S. Maria della Pace, one of the most interesting and least

Church of the Gesù, in the piazza of the same name. The interior.
The vault, animated by the stuccos of the Berninesque
sculptor Antonio Raggi, was frescoed by the
Genoese Giovan Battista Gaulli, called il Baciccia (1672-85).

known complexes of buildings in Rome, where the new architectonic
forms involve not only the building itself but the whole corner, the
church and the opening of the narrow side-streets, like a theatre
opening on to a piazza where the only thing lacking is an auditorium
for the spectators. But let the visitor try to identify himself with the
theatrical audience and his reward will be the imaginary spectacle of
a sacramental drama by Calderón.

Carlo Rainaldi, on the other hand, took a more practical interest in
town-planning — he was responsible for the definite systematization of
the three streets converging on Piazza del Popolo, the Corso in the
centre and Via del Babuino and Via di Ripetta on each side, and for
the plan of the two churches at its end (completed by Matteo de Rossi
with the assistance of Bernini). But he also did other architectural
works of considerable importance, the noble façade of S. Andrea
della Valle and the whole construction of S. Maria in Campitelli (in
Piazza Campitelli), the plans and elevations being surprisingly novel.
Many others besides Cortona and Rainaldi helped in the building of
Baroque Rome. Their methods always aimed to achieve an architecture
at once scenographic and severe within the city's narrow streets, which
still form the links in a fabric that has become increasingly complex
with the passage of the centuries.

Rome in the seventeenth century was like Paris in our own century when Cubism established itself there, the city of an international school whose members flowed into it from every country in Europe. The greatest of them was undoubtedly Nicolas Poussin, and his art was mainly that of an interpreter of the classical idea of Rome. Poussin arrived there in 1624. 'You will see a young man who is the devil's own fury,' was the description that Cavalier Marino, the most widely imitated and revered of the seventeenth-century poets, gave of his friend when introducing him to Cardinal Francesco Barberini. Simone Vouet was already in Rome, and the two compatriots were intimate with a whole group of foreigners whose researches did not seem particularly to be directed at the ornate and archaeological Baroque of Pietro da Cortona or the lyrical and delicate-toned Baroque of Guido Reni or Domenichino's classicism or the ample and resounding magniloquence of Guercino. Their enthusiasm went further back, to the ideals of the sixteenth-century, to Raphael, Titian and to curiosity about the antique, about classical sculpture and the romantic scenarios of ruins. These were also the favourite backgrounds of Poussin, as the landscapes of the Roman Campagna were to be for

Basilica of S. Maria Maggiore. The rear façade, among the most majestic Baroque structures in Rome, the work of several hands: Flaminio Ponzio, Carlo Rainaldi (1673), Domenico Fontana.

(below) Basilica of S. Maria Maggiore. Ferdinando Fuga's façade was inserted in 1743-1750 between the twin palaces, the first, at right, of the 17th century, and the second contemporary with Fuga's addition.

Claude Lorrain. There are not many works of Poussin in Rome: in the Pinacoteca Capitolina a replica, or copy, of the *Triumph of Flora* now in the Louvre, in the Colonna Gallery and *Apollo and Daphne*, in the Pallavicini Gallery a *Love*, in the Museum of Castel S. Angelo

a replica of a *Bacchanal*, a free version of Titian (two similar troops of gambolling putti, certainly by him, of 1626, are in the Incisa della Rochetta, a private collection) and lastly, in the same room as Caravaggio's *Deposition* in the Pinacoteca Vaticana, the *Martyrdom of St Erasmus* (signed), which was originally on an altar in the right transept of St Peter's, where a copy now stands. More numerous in the galleries and patrician palazzi of Rome are the canvases of Gaspard Dughet, also known as 'le Guaspre Poussin', a brother-in-law and pupil of Nicolas, who learnt from him a love of the romantic Italian landscape, picturesque ruins and streams of water amid the green; and who also came under the influence of Claude Lorrain when he worked in Rome. Only a few works of Lorrain remain there, in the Doria-Pamphilj and Colonna Galleries.

The classical ideal of Poussin was also pursued by Italian painters: by the Roman Andrea Sacchi, a collaborator of Bernini (who was himself quite a good painter); by Carlo Maratta, from the Marche, who was a pupil of Poussin's and who carried to extremes the official rhetoric of Baroque painting; by Pietro Testa from Lucca and Pier Francesco Mola from the Ticino. Their works, fluent in design, vivid in colouring, and often bathed in golden light, are to be found in large numbers in Rome's churches, palazzi and museums, where the visitor will come upon them constantly, for their production was prolific. But there is another kind of Baroque painting, of wider decorative scope and often of gigantic proportions, which involves architecture in its vortices of figures and which constitutes the coloured paradise of the ceilings and vaults of buildings. It is the consequence of the Cortonesque exaltation in the Barberini and Pamphilj palaces, and also of the triumph of the religious and more acclamatory idea of the Counter-Reformation. Outstanding examples of it are the great frescoed ceilings of the churches of the Gesù (in Piazza Gesù) and of S. Ignazio, the former with the allegory of the *Adoration of the Name of Jesus*, painted by the Genoese Giovan Battista Gaulli, known as il Baciccia, and the latter with the *Gloria of St Ignatius and the Company of the Jesuits*, painted between 1684 and 1685 by the Trentino artist Andrea Pozzo, who was a theoretician of perspective. The 'dome' that rises above the central crossing of the church of S. Ignazio is only an optical effect: it is a simulated dome, painted illusionistically on the enormous horizontal canvas which rests on the circular plane of the ceiling. It was damaged by an explosion in a powder-magazine in 1891 and was then covered up by an awning, rediscovered a few years ago by Emilio Lavagnino and restored; now once again, with its mathematical precision of perspective, it gives the illusion of curving and soaring upwards. With these grandiose cycles and with such plays of effect the Order of the Jesuits, paladin of the religious revival, launched its inflammatory proclamation.

Even so brief an account of painting in Rome in the seventeenth century cannot be considered complete without at least a mention of the other great pictorial cycles that decorate houses and churches. A visit to the Casino Ludovisi (in Via Ludovisi, now Villa Boncompagni: special permit needed), where Guercino painted the luminous allegories of *Night* and *Dawn*, and a visit to the Cappella di S. Andrea, annexed to the church of S. Gregorio Magno on the Celio, where there are frescoes by Domenichino (whose great altar-piece of the *Communion of St Jerome*, in the Pinacoteca Vaticana, is among his masterpieces), and by Guido Reni, will give a good idea, together with the Carracci brothers (Farnese Gallery), of the other great contribution that Bolognese painters brought to the Roman scene. As for the Caravaggesque painters, who, though they did not form a school, represented in various stages a coherent development of the master's lessons of realism and luminosity, more examples of their work may be seen in Rome than anywhere else. The works of Orazio Gentileschi and his daughter Artemisia, Orazio Borgianni and Carlo Saraceni, Bartolomeo Manfredi, Serodine, Valentin, and Mattia Preti, to mention only the more important of them, germinate throughout the city in the galleries, churches and oratories, and in the Pinacoteca Vaticana. One seventeenth-century church can be taken as a typical example of the Baroque climate: S. Andrea della Valle on Corso Vittorio Emanuele. Padre Francesco Grimaldi and Giacomo della Porta provided the first designs for it in 1591, but in 1608 Carlo Maderno resumed work on it and in 1622-25 raised the elegant dome, the highest in Rome after that of St Peter's. Thirty years later Carlo Rainaldi began the façade, which has already been mentioned, with its noble elevation in travertine and its Corinthian columns and pilasters, a most effective plastic combination animated by lively chiaroscuro. The vast interior at once reveals the luxuriance of Baroque buildings, with its vivid luminosity and reflections of gold, the colouring of the frescoes on the ceiling, in the dome and in the apse, and the spacious

Carlo Rainaldi, Rome 1611-91. The façade of the Church of S. Andrea della Valle, in travertine (1655-65). It was built by the Roman architect with partial modification of initial designs by Maderno, who also designed the interior and the great cupola.

side-chapels rich in sculpture, frescoes and paintings of the period. And in fact we have assembled here a whole anthology of Baroque art with some of its major representatives. Giovanni Lanfranco, from Parma, painted, in competition with Domenichino, the great fresco of the *Glory of Paradise* in the dome. The *S. Andrea Avellino* on the altar of the right transept is also his. Domenichino, competing with the imposing *Paradise* of the dome, painted in its pendentives the four majestic Evangelists and three years later, in 1624, frescoed the choir and the apse with stories of the saint to whom the church is dedicated, *Virtue*, and the famous nudes of Michelangelesque derivation which are really the result of a *tour-de-force*. The three stories of the saint in the curve of the apse, on the other hand, were painted in 1650-51 by Mattia Preti, known as the Cavalier Calabrese for his membership the Order of Malta, who had come to Rome from his native Taverna in 1630 and was an active and leading exponent of the international circle of painters. He was a member of the Accademia dei Virtuosi of the Pantheon and in his early days experimented with both the Caravaggesque and the neo-Venetian styles. Works of his are also to

Basilica of S. Giovanni in Laterano (St John Lateran). The principal façade. by Alessandro Galilei who had won the competition set by Pope Clement XII, consists of one gigantic order. It was built between 1732 and 1735.

be found in the churches of S. Carlo ai Catinari and S. Giovanni Calibita as well as in the museums and galleries; but his fine fresco decorations in Palazzo Pamphilj at Valmontone (some 30 miles from Rome
on the Via Prenestina), badly damaged, are now almost completely
ruined, together with those of Grimaldi and Cozza, because of the
deplorable state of neglect of that once superb building.

The first chapel on the right in S. Andrea della Valle was built in 1670
by Carlo Fontana and has fine sculptures by Antonio Raggi (1675); in
the next, the Strozzi chapel, with tombs of some members of that
Tuscan family, built around 1616 possibly from a design by Giacomo
della Porta, there are curious bronze copies of Michelangelo's *Pietà*
and of the two lateral sculptures for the tomb of Julius II in S. Pietro
in Vincoli; and the architectonic design also has Michelangelesque
echoes. The two tombs at the end of the central nave form an exception
in this seventeenth-century atmosphere: they were brought there in
1614 from St Peter's and belong to the two Piccolomini Popes, Pius
II and Pius III, the first of around 1465, by Roman sculptors, and the
second on similar lines, of some forty years later. The seventeenth-
century anthology is resumed with some interesting sculpture in the
first chapel on the left: the already mentioned *St John the Baptist* of
Pietro Bernini, a *St Martha* by Mochi, a *St John the Evangelist* by
Bonvicino, and the *Magdalen* by Cristoforo Stati. The chapel was
established by Maffeo Barberini, the future Urban VIII, between 1604
and 1616, at a time of transition in artistic culture, and was built by
Matteo Castelli; hence the tendency towards pre-Baroque sculptors.

S. Andrea della Valle is certainly not the only example in which artistic
history of the seventeenth century and the perfect fusion of the arts,
painting, sculpture, architecture and the decorative arts, can be seen
united in a single building. Baroque was more totalitarian than any
other style, and when it adjusted itself to the antique it superimposed
itself on it, leaving no trace of it. It was, indeed, part of its own
spirit to involve all visible reality in the new sumptuous garb: it has
been rightly defined as 'a collective intuition' and a consequence of
this is that it left indelible marks upon the face of Rome.

On a more workaday plane, Baroque art also provided a lively reflection
of matters of ordinary life as well as of the solemn and official: for
example, in genre-painting, which, according to seventeenth-century
critics, Caravaggio had been the first to foreshadow, anticipating it
in his still-lifes and slices-of-life. The still-life has no particular connection with the history and profile of a city, but the other trend, of
representing popular scenes and customs, is of considerable importance
because, like the passion for 'views' in the nineteenth century, it
documents the period. The pedlars in the streets of Rome, the beggars
and gypsies in the shadow of the solemn monuments, the rustic dances
among the ruins were subjects dear to the trend of the socalled *Bamboccianti*, who took their name from the Dutch painter Pieter van
Laer, il Bamboccio, who was its founder. Michelangelo Cerquozzi, a
Roman, was perhaps its most robust producer, while Viviano Codazzi,
of Bergamasque origin, as the first creator of unexceptionable painted
and fantastic architectonic '*Quadrature*', opened the series which were
soon, in the absence of cameras, to delight the travellers of the Grand
Tour, who loved to bring back from their journey a visible reminder
of ancient and modern Rome in the form of a lively and faithful little
picture of ruins and rural melancholy, of a masquerade by Trajan's
Column or the market on the romantic Appian Way. The painters of
these subjects were mostly foreigners, Dutchmen like Karel Dujardin,

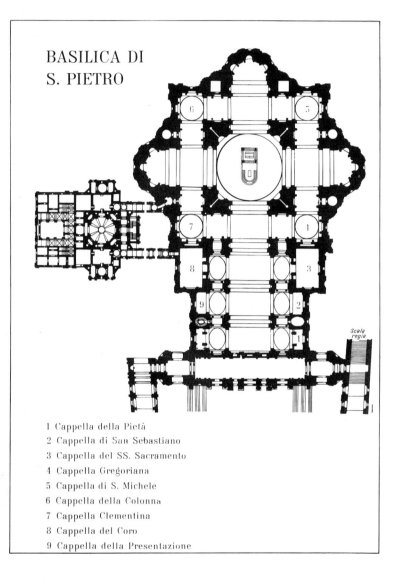

BASILICA DI
S. PIETRO

1 Cappella della Pietà
2 Cappella di San Sebastiano
3 Cappella del SS. Sacramento
4 Cappella Gregoriana
5 Cappella di S. Michele
6 Cappella della Colonna
7 Cappella Clementina
8 Cappella del Coro
9 Cappella della Presentazione

Theodor Helmbreker, Jacob van Staveren, and Hendrick Verschuring, and also Flemish like Michael Sweerts and Jan Miel; French like Le Nain, and Jean Michelin; or German like Johannes Lingelbach — all united in their great love of Rome. Museums and galleries contain a wide range of their works, which often help one to visualize the appearance of the city in the second half of the seventeenth century and the faces, dress and habits, not of princes and Popes, but of the humble genuine people of Rome.

The eighteenth century opened with famous displays of fireworks — the outward sign of the *joie de vivre* that was to characterize it. To that moment belongs the first painter who succeeded in 'painting the face of Rome in a natural way, without emphasis or adulation' (Lavagnino), the Dutchman Gaspar van Wittel, known as Gaspare Vanvitelli and also as 'Gaspare dagli occhiali' (Gaspare with the spectacles). He was 'the painter of *modern Rome*', as he has been called by Briganti, author

Michelangelo da Caravaggio. Caravaggio 1573 - Porto Ercole 1610.
The Madonna with the Serpent *(detail). Canvas. Borghese Gallery.*
The work was painted in 1605-06 for the altar of the Palafrenieri in the
Chapel of S. Anna in the Vatican, but was rejected as being too realistic.

of the principal book about him, in works which have the accuracy
of a miniature, the transparency of air, and the limpid colours of a
serene day in Rome itself. Among the many paintings by Vanvitelli
which have survived, the Roman views are the most numerous. The
artist came to the city in 1674, when he was not yet twenty, and
except for brief journeys he spent his whole life there. He always
looked at the nature and architectural development of the city from
an original standpoint of his own, with the result that his views of
Rome are poetic works rather than true portraits of the time. The
very large number of his paintings preserved in Palazzo Colonna and
those in the National Gallery of Ancient Art in Palazzo Corsini, the
Museo di Roma in Palazzo Braschi (which, being the City Museum, is
fullest documented), the Pinacoteca Capitolina and the Pallavicini
Gallery constitute a repertoire of at least fifty different 'points
of view', as Briganti has accurately indicated; a remarkable album of

Michelangelo da Caravaggio. Sick Bacchus. *Canvas. Borghese Gallery. Fairly youthful work, around 1589. The figure is probably a self-portrait.*

what Rome looked like in the first half of the eighteenth century. The city is reproduced in its precise physiognomy, the same, in those areas given over to antiquities which have not been changed by modern building, as we see it today. Vanvitelli used to seize on every occasion to record that aspect, the building transformations of Clement XI, excavations in progress, festivals, and scenes of daily life. Giovan Francesco Albani had ascended the pontifical throne, taking the name of Clement XI, in the year of the new century's birth. He concerned himself at once with adapting the city to the needs of the times, furthering learning and scientific research, reconstructing, and building — perhaps foreseeing that the Enlightenment was to lay the foundations of a new society. Giovan Paolo Pannini, from Piacenza, who spent fifty years in Rome from 1715 to 1765, and Rome's greatest engraver, the 'Venetian architect', as he liked to call himself, Giovanni Battista Piranesi, who came there at twenty and died there when sixty-eight, were also poetic interpreters of the real face of Rome, adding as well the other, more personal and imaginary aspect. Pannini represented Rome in a galaxy of colours and light, the papal and aristocratic city,

Michelangelo da Caravaggio. Youth with a basket of fruit. *Panel. Borghese Gallery. Contemporary with the painting of Bacchus, it shows the Lombard influences on the formation of the artist.*

but also the city of the people, with its streets thronged with crowds and processions and its luminous, minutely-described interiors. Piranesi saw it, drew it, and engraved it as splendid and dramatic, in a violent contrast of black and white more effective than any palette. Then there were painters who dreamt of it as a sacred and romantic place, in which ruins and moss, arches, stairways, porticos with immense fountains and mutilated sculptures recreate a lost atmosphere. Such was the Parisian Hubert Robert, who stayed in Rome from 1754 to 1765 and never ceased to be enchanted by it (a series of his paintings from the Cervinara bequest is displayed in the National Gallery of Ancient Art in Palazzo Barberini). Lastly, Canaletto was in Rome at least once and retained in his memory the sight of the imperial ruins (as witness his masterpieces at Windsor Castle).

If these are the happy images of a serene, unmoved Rome, the eighteenth-century reality was nevertheless rich in ferment. The century, as has been said, began with a great building boom, despite the Wars of Succession and the incipient conflict of ideas. Clement XI kept the city neutral in the European disputes and promoted types of building more suited to the popular needs as well as the reconstruction or completion of old basilicas (SS. Apostoli, St John Lateran). The category of buildings more suited to the real needs which social inequality — a few people were privileged and the mass impoverished — was increasingly thrusting into the foreground; these included public works, among them the great harbour of the Ripetta on the Tiber, a scenographic composition by Alessandro Specchi, now destroyed; the extensive Ospizio di San Michele on the Lungotevere a Ripa, built by Carlo Fontana and then by Fuga as a reformatory for vagrant boys,

The Trevi Fountain. The famous water-display was constructed by Niccolò Salvi between 1732 and 1751 and was finished in 1762 by Bracci, who also sculptured the group representing the Ocean. The other sculptures are works of various 18th-century artists - Filippo Valle, Bergondi, Grossi and others.

which it still was until a few years ago when dilapidation brought it near to collapse (it was acquired by the state in 1969 to be the headquarters of the Department of Antiquities and Fine Arts); the granaries at Termini; and the flight of steps from Piazza di Spagna to Trinità dei Monti, built by De Sanctis between 1723 and 1726 under Benedict XIII, who was also responsible for the spectacular and ingenious plan of Piazza di S. Ignazio in front of the Jesuit church. Filippo Raguzzini, from Benevento, was in charge of this work from 1727 to 1728, and he made it one of the most impressive places in the

city's centre. It was not appreciated by contemporaries: a historian of the period, Milizia, found the houses ridiculous, like great *canterani*, or chests-of-drawers. And since even in those days furniture was often spoken of by French names and the *canterano* was called a 'bureau', this complex of houses and streets acquired the italianized name of *Burrò* which is still retained in one street. Today, however, we can see very clearly how ingenious was its relation to the seventeenth-century church. In a recent graphic experiment, the application of a new method of surveying (1968), the Institute of Technical Architecture of the Politecnico in Turin very clearly reveals Raguzzini's superb sense of composition, which reproduced in the lines of the piazza the same geometrical elements that are inherent in the plan of the church itself. Another scenographic and imaginative creation of Raguzzini's is the foreground of the Trastevere Ospedale di S. Gallicano, carried out before the Piazza di S. Ignazio and possibly the testing-ground that decided the Pope to entrust that second task to him.

The eighteenth century was the century of music and the theatre. Handel was in Rome at its beginning, Mozart towards its end. Handel composed two oratorios there and had them performed; and he competed with Domenico Scarlatti at the harpsichord during a musical evening given by Cardinal Ottoboni in the Palazzo della Cancelleria but the Italian won. Mozart heard Gabrieli's *Miserere* in the Sistine Chapel and repeated it from memory at a musical evening soon after. Pietro Metastasio, the greatest theatrical poet of the day, was born in

Colossal statue of the Ocean, popularly called Marforio, one of the so-called 'talking statues', like Pasquino and Madama Lucrezia, to which the populace used to attach notes with salacious witticisms, almost always of political import. Capitoline Museum, courtyard.

Rome. The choir of the Sistine Chapel, which was endowed with special privileges, sang the polyphonic works of Palestrina and the great composers of every nation, while the Collegio dei Musici di S. Cecilia performed sacred and secular music, cantatas and operas. Both these institutions still exist today, with the same prerogatives, the Sistine Chapel concentrating on sacred polyphonic music and the Accademia di S. Cecilia, which descends from the Congregazione dei Musici established in 1584, on instrumental and symphonic works, though at present they have no auditorium of their own in Rome.

On 13 January 1732 the Teatro Argentina, in Piazza Argentina, was inaugurated with a performance of *Berenice* by Domenico Sarro. The theatre (now radically restored; the façade dates from 1830) was commissioned by Duke Giuseppe Sforza Cesarini and built by the architect Marchese Theodoli. Antonio Vivaldi was in Rome three times and two of his operas were performed there. Niccolò Jommelli was Maestro of the Cappella Giulia in St Peter's and his *Astianatte* was performed at the Argentina in 1741. There was no school of scenography in Rome as there was in Venice and Turin, but Filippo Juvarra prepared scenery for Cardinal Ottoboni's theatre and was the most important of the men concerned in the various theatres then functioning and now transformed or vanished: the Capranica, the Alibert, the Tordinona, and the Valle. Francesco Bibiena, Pietro Gonzaga, and Alessandro Mauro, scenographers from Bologna, Milan, and Venice, also came occasionally to Rome. Well-known painters such as Pannini and Pier

Leone Ghezzi, who was a witty caricaturist, also worked for the theatre, but more frequently for festival scenes. Ghezzi designed the scenes for a cantata on a text of Metastasio's with music by Vinci, performed in the courtyard of Palazzo Altemps on the occasion of the French Dauphin's birth on 26 November 1729. The architects Fuga, Specchi, Salvi and Valvassori also designed decorations for public festivals and for the firework displays then much in fashion. Spectacles and carnivals were held in the most famous palazzi as well as in the piazzas, and Piazza Navona's carnival was the most popular of all.

On 8 December 1733 Clement XII laid the foundation stone of the main façade of the basilica of St John Lateran, the commission for which had been won by the Florentine Alessandro Galilei, competing against Luigi Vanvitelli, son of Gaspare, who also entered. The jury included distinguished painters, among them Pannini and Sebastiano Conca, *principe* of the Accademia di S. Luca. A competition also resolved the thorny problem of the great spectacle for the Fontana di Trevi. It was won by Nicola Salvi, but he left the work unfinished at his death. The decorative scene was not inaugurated until 1762, after Giovanni Pannini had resumed the work and many sculptors had collaborated on the statues. A terracotta model of the *Ocean* figure by Pietro Bracci is in the Museo del Palazzo di Venezia, and also the model of *Abundance* by Filippo Valle, while the original model of the fountain, in wood and terracotta, is in the Museo di Roma in Palazzo Braschi.

In 1730 Clement XII appointed Ferdinando Fuga pontifical architect. The Palazzo della Consulta in Piazza del Quirinale was the Florentine architect's first important work, almost contemporary with the rebuilding of the Chiesa dell'Orazione e Morte in Via Giulia, where winged skulls serve as unusual corbels of the façade, but they are the only concession to the picturesque in this orderly and solid building. Next came the general renovation of the Palazzo Riario on the Lungara, where Queen Christina of Sweden had lived; it had been acquired by Cardinal Neri Corsini, nephew of the Pope, and was to be known in future as Palazzo Corsini. The elegant façade (finished later, around 1750) with its dual colour rhythm, luminous staircase and sumptuous interior (which now houses, as indicated, the seventeenth and eighteenth century sections of the National Gallery of Ancient Art) constitute one of the most notable examples of eighteenth-century civil architecture in Rome.

Fuga prepared many designs, often for the façades of unfinished buildings and they always brought a new splendour to the city's profile, quite different from the style of post-Baroque architecture, which had become superficial and capricious. The coffee-house or 'Retreat' which he built in the Quirinal gardens between 1741 and 1744, with interior decorations by Costanzi and Van Bloemen and with two fine Pannini paintings of views of the Piazza del Quirinale and Piazza di S. Maria

◁
Piazza di Spagna. The Barcaccia Fountain (detail) of Gian Lorenzo Bernini or by his father Pietro (1627-29). In the background the Church of the Trinità dei Monti (Trinity of the Mountains) begun by the order of Louis XII of France in 1502 and consecrated in 1585.
Between the church and the piazza unrolls the theatrically effective Scalinata (The Spanish Steps) in travertine
by Francesco de Sanctis, built between 1732 and 1736.

Pietro da Cortona. Cortona 1596 - Rome 1669. The façade of the Church of S. Maria in via Lata, adjoining Palazzo Doria Pamphilj on the Corso, and erected between 1658 and 1662, which is among the most characteristic of Roman Baroque structures.

Maggiore, was an ingenious piece of work which nevertheless maintained his usual nobility of design and careful plan. Sureness of touch distinguishes the works of Ferdinando Fuga, which are always animated by rational and consistent forms, simple structures, articulated proportions, and a careful calculation of their relationship with their surroundings. The rich collection of some eighty of his designs in the Gabinetto Nazionale delle Stampe at the Farnesina demonstrates the development of his style, the finest in the architectural history of Rome after the great Baroque era, to which Fuga both succeeded and reacted. With the sculptors of the Fontana di Trevi and a few others, with Fuga's architecture, typical of the Enlightenment, and the more traditional style of such architects as Carlo Marchionni, designer of the Villa Albani, the Portuguese Manoel Rodriguez dos Santos, who built in Via Condotti (now one of the busiest streets in the city) the church and monastery of the Trinità degli Spagnoli, and Giuseppe Sardi, architect of the animated façade of the church of the Maddalena; with some visiting painters like the Frenchman Subleyras, the Neapolitan Conca, the Apulian Giaquinto, Batoni from Lucca, and the Roman painter Marco Benefial, who produced pictures and decorations alternating between the courtly or sentimental and the classicist — with all these artists, the Baroque era in Rome reached its epilogue. The classicist experiments of the Bohemian painter and theoretician Anton Raphael Mengs, imbued with the aesthetic precepts of Winckelmann (who was in

Carlo Rainaldi. Rome 1611-1691. The façade of the Church of S. Maria in Campitelli was built by Alexander VII between 1662 and 1667 as a thanksgiving offering at the end of the plague of 1656. It is the Roman architect's masterpiece.

Rome in 1755), and the few successful efforts, after an unfortunate start, of the other architect of the Enlightenment, Luigi Vanvitelli, did not belong to that era; nor did Piranesi's sole architectural work, though his engravings had borne such romantic testimony to it. Before speaking of that noble work, the unexpected conclusion to an era begun so long before, a few words must be said about the distribution of urban boundaries which took place in Rome in the first half of the eighteenth century, when Charles de Brosses could say that 'though large, it did not seem at all like a capital' (*Lettres familières*, 1739). On 18 May 1743, Benedict XIV, the Pope who presumed to 'make Rome the model of all the cities', had instructed Bernardino Bernardini, prior of the heads of the *rioni* (known in Rome as *Caporioni*), to trace the precise confines of the fourteen *rioni* of the city established by Sixtus V. In less than a year the work was done and Giovan Battista Nolli, who collaborated in it, registered the division in his *Plan of Rome* published in 1748, the most exact plan that had hitherto appeared, drawn iconographically instead of in perspective, orientated to the north, showing all the monumental edifices more exactly than in the previous plan of Bufalini, and also provided with an index and clear captions. As a result of this division, 220 marble street nameplates were placed on the confines of each *rione*, with their respective names and coats-of-arms: most of them can still be seen *in situ*. The two largest, first and last in the series, were those at the Quirinal and at Castel S. Angelo. The fourteen *rioni* of the historic centre of Rome, after more than 220 years and an extension of the city far beyond their perimeter, are still the same, with the same confines.

Like most of the important artists we have mentioned, Giovan Battista Piranesi too was in Rome by the time he was twenty. He arrived there in 1740 as a draughtsman in the suite of the ambassador of the Venetian Republic to Benedict XIV. He lodged with the Sicilian Giuseppe Vasi (who in those years was engraving a fine album of views of Rome), and was in close relations with the scenographers and the English and French scholars who had their centre between Piazza di Spagna and Trinità dei Monti, where he also lived, with antiquarian culture, with the illuminist philosophers (Calvesi mentions his links with G.B. Vico, author of the *Scienza nuova*), and even with Freemasonry. He was an engraver, an architect and a painter (the *Perspective* in the Accademia di S. Luca has recently been attributed to him), and a most unusual and individual artist, of whom Focillon could say that he 'revealed to his contemporaries the beauty of the Roman ruins and something more'; and of his work he said that it appeared 'to the eyes of his public not like the clear and logical result of previous efforts, but like a revelation.'

The jewel that is his only work of architecture, the church of S. Maria del Priorato on the Aventine, is indeed a revelation. The visitor is prepared for it by the evocative surroundings, unreal as an engraving seen through a stereoscope, that enclose, on the last bastion of the hill, the Piazza dei Cavalieri di Malta, which he also designed. On two sides, obelisks, pillars, trophies and dark cypresses rise alternating skywards; on the third side that completes it (for the entry from Via S. Sabina is merely its approach), a continuous low wall leads to the majestic gateway of the Villa. The illusion pervading this scene also includes a picturesque detail. If you put your eye to the keyhole of the door leading into the Knights' Priory you will see framed at the end of an avenue of trees the dome of St Peter's more than a mile away. The church is set back in the garden, its clear, harmonious outlines as incisive as the lines bitten by acids on the copper plate of an engraving. It recalls the antique, but the decorative fantasy is something quite new — it approaches the style of the Englishman Robert Adam, who was in fact associated with Piranesi both by friendship and by work; it suggests a different sort of elegance from that hitherto produced in a building by a simple façade with pilasters and a pediment. The interior, which a little recalls Borromini's daring ventures, is invaded by a restless light that flickers over the white blocks, the smooth walls, the audacious apparatus of the altar, the abstract lines pregnant with elaborate details. It was the Venetian Cardinal Giovan Battista Rezzonico who ordered Piranesi to build the magic piazza, the villa, and the church of the Roman priorate of the Knights of Malta, in 1765; and four years later Piranesi dedicated to him the series of engravings on the *Diverse maniere di adornare i camini* (The different ways of decorating fireplaces). The original plates of the hundreds of engravings by Piranesi are preserved in the Calcografia Nazionale in Via della Stamperia. The series is almost complete. It was bought back in 1839 by Gregory XIV from Paris, where the artist's son Francesco had taken it in 1800 and sold it to the publishers Firmin Didot.

With his group of buildings on the Aventine, Piranesi had satisfied his greatest wish and endowed Rome with an original *ensemble* that was the forerunner of new things in town-planning. And with his engravings, as Focillon says, 'since he could not build the city of which

The Aqua Felice Fountain in the Piazza San Bernardo. Left, the Church of S. Maria della Vittoria containing Bernini's The Ecstasy of St Teresa. The fountain, built for Sixtus V (Felice Peretti) was the first architectural fountain in Rome (1585-87) and was the work of G. B. della Porta and other sculptors. The façade of S. Maria della Vittoria is by Maderno (1608-20).

he dreamed, he set down on copper its terrifying proportions, seeking its architectonic models in a past that seemed to him in every way the exemplar of the majesty.'

The Capital

'We believe', wrote Napoleon in his *Memoirs*, 'that Rome, though it has not all the qualities to be desired, is undoubtedly the capital that the Italians will choose one day.' He had known it as the capital of the Papal State and also, for a short time, of a compromise republic. But mindful, as he said, of the political and geographical entity of Italy, despite its subdivision into so many monarchies, and of the spiritual weight of Rome's history and its ancient memories, the Emperor declared that it offered 'more suitable resources for the needs of a great capital than any other city in the world,' not to mention 'the fascination and nobility of its name.'

The century following the Enlightenment, which witnessed the practical consolidation of technical and scientific advances, had been preceded by dramatic events in Rome. On 28 December 1797 a French general was killed in a popular uprising in Trastevere. Joseph Bonaparte, brother of the Emperor and Ambassador of France to Pius IV, left the city without waiting for the Curia's apologies, and the incident soon came to be regarded as an act of war. In the following February General Louis Alexandre Berthier, future Marshal of France, occupied Rome after going through a form of negotiations with the patriots and in the name of the Directory proclaimed from the Capitol the Roman Republic and the end of the temporal power of the Papacy. Pope Pius VI Braschi was forced to flee and died in exile. The official portrait that Pompeo Batoni did of him in 1775 is in the Museo di Roma in Palazzo Braschi, the palazzo that the Pope's nephews had had built by Cosimo Morelli in 1792; it was the last of the Roman palazzi of papal families. The Republic did not last long: involved in revolutions and reactions, it came to an end on 30 September 1799 when Neapolitan insurgents occupied the city. In the following July Pius VII, elected in Venice after a long conclave, entered Rome by the Porta del Popolo amid triumphal decorations set up by the nobility and sighs of relief from the people. Jacobinism had never gone down well in Rome. The first gas lamps were lit in the streets by way of celebration.

A sculptor and an architect were present at these dramatic events but not involved in them, each in his way intent on following his own line. The sculptor was the Venetian Antonio Canova, who had first come to Rome in 1779, as a very young man, needless to say, like so many other artists eager to get there; he definitely established himself there in the following year. The architect was a Roman, Giuseppe Valadier, and the best architect of his day.

The neo-classicists' love for the antique had in it a deep vein of melancholy. Rome, which together with Paris was the main centre of neoclassicism, saw it affirmed in the aesthetic ideals of Canova, the last Italian artist of European repute until modern times. Like David in Paris, he opposed eighteenth-century empiricism by the poetics of the sublime rather than by the imitation of the ancients proclaimed by Winckelmann. Rome offers an extensive panorama of his work, which he began in 1782 with the monument to Clement XIV in the church of the SS. Apostoli. In this first group of statuary the style he was to adopt was already apparent. For the composition Canova went back to Bernini and Algardi, but he loaded its various parts with symbolism, moulding the forms in a sublime perfection—the absolute of finish— from which sentiment was intentionally excluded.

There are three works of Canova's in St Peter's: the tombs of Clement XIII Rezzonico and of the last Stuarts (in which the genii of death beside the pillar reverse their torches to symbolize the dying life of a dynasty at its end) and the *Pius VI* kneeling before the altar of the Confessio, which was the artist's last work, left unfinished at his death (it was completed by Adamo Tadolini). Another bust of Pius VI is in the new wing of the Museo Chiaramonti in the Vatican, where also, in the Cortile del Belvedere, is the perfect *Perseus* (the two *Pugilists*, Damoxenus and Creugas, on each side are also by Canova), who seems itching to enter the lists with the nearby *Apollo* of Leochares.

The famous (and rightly so) statue of *Pauline Borghese* in the attitude of the conquering Venus, in the Borghese Gallery, has been linked

▷

(above) The Villa Albani today Torlonia, in via Salaria,
At the end of the garden is the villa, built between 1743 and 1763
by Carlo Marchionni for Cardinal Alessandro Albani.

(below) Tivoli. Villa d'Este. The Oval Fountain. The villa and park, with
its fanciful water games was built in 1550 by Pirro Ligorio for
Cardinal Ippolito d'Este, governor of Tivoli and a patron of arts and letters.

with the literary precedent of one of Foscolo's *Lettere di Jacopo Ortis,* where the sudden romantic appearance of a woman is described. Pauline Bonaparte, sister of Napoleon, married the Roman Prince Camillo Borghese. The sculpture, which was finished in 1808, was at first in Turin. After the fall of Napoleon, Borghese transferred it to his palazzo in Rome, from which it went to the villa and was at first placed in surroundings (the Sala di Paride, dismantled in 1889) with neo-classical decorations, where it constituted the focal point in a most fitting setting (Faldi). Canova himself, it seems, devised the now-discarded apparatus at the base of the sculpture which made it rotate. Many others of Canova's works can be seen in churches and museums in Rome: tomb-monuments in San Marco and in S. Antonio dei Portoghesi, plaster casts in the Gallery of the Accademia di S. Luca, among them a *Self-Portrait* (the original is in the Galleria Comunale d'Arte Moderna), busts in the Capitol, and, lastly, the colossal *Hercules and Lycas* in marble in the Galleria Nazionale d'Arte Moderna, where also is the model for the monument to Vittorio Alfieri in Santa Croce in Florence.

Giuseppe Valadier contributed appreciably towards illuminating the last urbanistic horizon in a Rome that still belonged more to the past than the present. He was not ambitious, and carried out no projects that involved asserting the political views of their commissioners. He was prudent and perhaps also timid, being first and foremost what would be called today a professional, with no bees in his bonnet. In Rome, amid revolts and the ups and downs of government, it was no longer a case of taking into account the current political or religious power; the thing to be done, rather, was to create a fabric linking up with the monuments of the past, a functional organization for the sumptuous sporadic building activity that was in constant contrast with the humble character of the ordinary houses. This was precisely what was involved in the transformation of Piazza del Popolo, the last great town-planning undertaking to be completed in Rome before the unification of Italy: the combination of existing buildings and natural surroundings in a new spaciousness, taking into account the uneven heights of the urban framework. The spectacular result can still be admired today. The period when Valadier was working (he died in 1839) would but for him have been, architecturally speaking, one of the dullest in the city's whole history. In addition to Piazza del Popolo, for which the first plans, frequently changed as the work progressed, go back to 1784 (they are documented in Feoli's engravings of 1794, which Valadier dedicated to Pius VI, in the Museo di Roma), the architect was concerned in many works of urban and architectonic transformation, in which he always took account of Rome's most outstanding characteristic, that of the Baroque city. He restored numerous ancient and modern monuments: on the Velia, the monastery annexed to the church of S. Francesca Romana, the Ponte Milvio over the Tiber, and the church of S. Lorenzo in Damaso (transformed in the second half of the nineteenth century); he added the two clocks to the façade of St Peter's, and himself built many façades, sober in style and sometimes Palladian in inspiration, for example that of the church of S. Rocco (once chapel of the ancient confraternity of innkeepers and bargees of the river port of the Ripetta) at the end of Piazza Augusto Imperatore, and the façades of the Teatro Valle and the churches of S. Pantaleo and SS. Apostoli. He also built the small palazzo which houses the Calcografia Nazionale, and the Casina Valadier on the Pincio, the great park and gardens which proved the most difficult undertaking of the period and was badly help up during the French occupation. Valadier nevertheless welcomed quite a number of the ideas put forward by Napoleonic architects and town-planners, 'the arrangement of rectilinear avenues' (Hoffmann), the terrace overlooking Piazza del Popolo (from which a wonderful panorama of the city unfolds) which was included in a first plan by Berthauld and Gisors, and other general suggestions, so that in the end the Pincio resulted in a 'new and most successful compromise' between the traditional Roman garden and the French landscape garden, arranged on neo-classical lines. The size of the park was in any case something new; with its ample stretches of green and its wide avenues, it already belonged to the future ideas of urban spaciousness.

The terrace of the Pincio seen from the Piazza del Popolo. The monumental complex of the piazza in combination with the Pincio on high was a masterpiece of neoclassic urban design constructed by the Roman architect Giuseppe Valadier between 1784 and 1820.

The French, the English and the Germans, and their archaeologists, poets and artists, still continued to visit Rome and the Roman Campagna. They met in the evenings in the Caffè Greco in Via Condotti, which has retained practically intact the decoration of that period. Some wished to be buried in Rome. The Protestant (strictly speaking non-Catholic) cemetery by Monte Testaccio, near the Pyramid of Caius Cestius, preserves their remains, and many of the graves were the work of foreign artists of the period. German artists still came to Rome after the days of Winckelmann and Mengs. The *Parnassus* that Mengs painted on the ceiling of the gallery of Villa Albani, with Raphaelesque reminiscences, was widely renowned. Among eighteenth-century artists, Philipp Hackert painted beautiful views of the Campagna and the surroundings of Rome (some are in the Galleria Nazionale d'Arte Antica), while Angelica Kauffmann left some of her delicate portraits there (and in the Gallery of the Accademia di S. Luca). A group of German painters (Overbeck, Veit, Koch, Führich, and Julius Schnorr von Carolsfeld) decorated with frescoes the rooms of the Casino Massimo, at the Lateran, with scenes inspired by the poems of Dante, Tasso, and Ariosto, and some of them also left works in Roman churches and in the Vatican. Veit frescoed some lunettes in the Museo Chiaramonti, Seitz painted in the Galleria dei Candelabri and also at Trinità dei Monti, Schadow at S. Andrea delle Fratte; a canvas by Koch is in the Aula delle Benedizioni in the Vatican. In the quiet of the cemetery, by the Pyramid, Keats rests, and Trelawney buried Shelley's heart there; and they have their Roman memorial in the Keats-Shelley house in Piazza di Spagna, in which Keats died in 1821. The painter Hans von Marées is also buried in the cemetery, in a tomb carved by Arthur Volkmann.

Among English artists, Wilson and Reynolds visited Rome; and Sir Thomas Lawrence was there and stayed in the Quirinal to do portraits of Pius VII and his Secretary of State, Cardinal Consalvi, for the Waterloo Chamber at Windsor. Turner came to Rome in 1819 when he was forty-four years old, after waiting for years to reach that longed-for goal.

The Museo di Roma has a large collection of views of Rome and the Campagna by foreign artists, especially as a result of recent donations and purchases. It has none, however, by one of the most poetical interpreters of the city, Jean-Baptiste-Camille Corot, the last of the classic landscape-painters. Nor is there anything by Jean Dominique Ingres, who spent twenty-one years of his life there and was director of the French Academy in Villa Medici from 1835 to 1841.

Two Italian artists, the eminently Roman Bartolomeo Pinelli (1781-1835), chiefly a designer and engraver, and Ippolito Caffi (1809-66), from Belluno, dedicated their main activity to views of Rome, and a large number of their works can be seen in the city museums. Pinelli worked with a verve that recalls the vernacular poetry of the great nineteenth-century Roman dialect poet Giuseppe Gioacchino Belli (1791-1863), who in his pungent sonnets gave a tragic-comic picture of stagnating Roman life on the eve of Italy's unification. Caffi, on the other hand, sympathetically immersed himself in Roman life and painted it with a pictorial vision derived from the Venetian tradition. The watercolours of the Roman Ettore Roesler Franz (1852-1907), in the Galleria Comunale d'Arte Moderna, with his views of the Tiber, also constitute a remarkable record of aspects of Rome that have now completely vanished. The name of Roesler Franz, the modest water-

*The Monument to Victor Emmanuel II in Piazza Venezia, also called
The Vittoriano, in Brescian limestone, erected between
1885 and 1911 by Giuseppe Sacconi with the collaboration of various
academic sculptors.*

colour painter, is indeed indelibly linked with those views of a
'vanished Rome' which he was just in time to seize upon before the
pickaxes came to destroy its picturesque lineaments.

Nothing much happened in Rome between Valadier's transformations
and the entry of the troops at Porta Pia on 20 September 1870
which heralded the unification of Italy. In 1856 the first railway line
from Rome was opened: it connected the city with Frascati, 15
miles away! In 1863 the first railway station was built at Termini and
soon aftwards the first stretch of the Via Nazionale was opened.
The Italian troops led by General Cadorna entered the city on 20
September 1870 after having opened up a breach with their artillery
beside the gateway, Porta Pia, which Michelangelo had embellished.
It was not a bloodless entry: twenty soldiers of the papal troops fell,
as against sixty-two Italians, and there were 150 wounded. However,
the temporal power of the Papacy was definitely ended and Rome
was the capital of Italy. The dream of Garibaldi, Mazzini and Cavour
had become a reality. The plebiscite, in a Rome of something under
200,000 inhabitants, produced only forty-six negative votes. Pius IX
refused to accept the guarantees offered him, in other words the
law assuring him of inviolability and sovereign authority, and regarded
himself as a prisoner in the Vatican. His successors continued to do
so until 1929. On 27 November 1871 Parliament opened. On that
day the third existence of Rome began.

The story of the city in the hundred years that have passed since then belongs to the history of building, town-planning, political and civil affairs and social transformations; it belongs much less to the history of art which had motivated it almost exclusively for eighteen centuries, from the century of Augustus to the time of Canova and Valadier.

No masterpieces were erected, no ingenious architectural solution discovered in that period. A few up-to-date constructions based on the use of ferro-concrete appeared, isolated cases amid the bourgeois eclecticism which governed the conception of all the buildings bordering the streets opened up at that time, Via Nazionale and Via Cavour, Viale Trastevere and the Corso Vittorio Emanuele, Via Veneto and the Passeggiata Archeologica. From the town-planning point of view, some broadly-conceived works were undertaken, such as the systematization of the Tiber banks and the roads along them, but the buildings that arose beside them completely destroyed their appearance. Outlets for traffic were opened up, such as the tunnel under the Quirinal and some big piazzas like Piazza dell'Esedra or Piazza della Repubblica, which in 1885 was adorned with the pompous Fountain of the Naiads by the Sicilian sculptor Mario Rutelli. New districts were gradually added to the Sistine plan, and featureless, uninspired buildings encroached upon the fields and gardens. Nor was there any particular architectural quality about the prestige buildings erected for public functions or cultural purposes, such as the Palazzo di Giustizia of Calderini (1889-1910), the enlargement of the Palazzo di Montecitorio in Piazza del Parlamento by Ernesto Basile (1903-25), in which one can discern a slight reflection of Art Nouveau, as one also can in the villino built by the same architect for the Florio family in Via Piemonte, and in the villa of the architect Ettore Ximenes in Piazza Galeno, the Palazzo delle Esposizioni in Via Nazionale, designed by Pio Piacentini (1878-82), the Galleria Nazionale d'Arte Moderna of Bazzani (1911) at Valle Giulia, and, lastly, the *Vittoriano,* the monument to Victor Emmanuel II and shrine of the Unknown Soldier. The monument was inaugurated in 1911 on the occasion of the International Exhibition, for which the Palazzo delle Belle Arti, or National Gallery of Modern Art, was also built (it was expanded by Bazzani in 1933). The author of the *Vittoriano* was the architect Giuseppe Sacconi, winner of a national competition. Work on it had been begun in 1885.

If Fascism had carried out all the demolitions that it planned, the face of Rome today would have been even more disfigured than it is. Of the town-planning ventures carried out during the two decades 1922-43, the creation of the new quarter known as EUR (Esposizione Universale Roma), planned for the international exhibition which was to have been held in Rome in 1942 and which was prevented by the war, is certainly the least offensive. It developed out of a town-planning operation already proposed in 1928, at the time of the opening of Via del Mare which, setting out from Piazza Venezia and following the route of the Teatro di Marcello and the Forum Boarium, was to go in the direction of Ostia, and also out of a plan to expand the city in that direction which had been discussed at a congress of the Institute of Roman Studies in the same year. The original nucleus consists of that kind of cardboard architecture which was the special pride of Fascist builders, where columns become cylinders without base or capitals, spaces are simply cut-out outlines, and masses are completely non-existent though massive, as in the

Giacomo Manzù. Bergamo 1908. Two details of the Door of Death,
(Porta della Morte), one of the side doors of the Basilica of St Peter's.
The bronze portals contain images of the pontificate of John XXIII (left).
The artist worked on the project from 1949 to 1964,
when the doors, after long controversy, were finally installed.

Palazzo della Civiltà del Lavoro which the Romans call the 'Colosseum squared'. But in the last twenty years the EUR district has seen the rise of a more professional kind of architecture, good harbingers of which are the two office-buildings by the architect Luigi Moretti, already distinguished for his successful constructions, especially the Palazzina del Girasole in Viale Bruno Buozzi of 1948-50. The airy cap-like vault built in 1938 by Adalberto Libera in the Palazzo dei Congressi, the first of its kind in Italy, is another landmark in the development of this no longer remote suburban quarter. By comparison, the complex rhetoric of the Foro Italico, with its statues and its lack of relationship between masses and their surroundings, though possibly inoffensive, was no credit to either the commissioners or the executants. Luigi Moretti and Adalberto Libera built the successful 'Villaggio Olimpico' for the Olympic Games held in Rome in 1960. Pier Luigi Nervi, together with other architects and architectural engineers, extended over it the daring viaduct which leads to the entrance into the city from the two consular highways, the Via Cassia and the Via Flaminia. The confluence of those two roads, which is now known as Corso Francia, leads in turn into the city by the fly-over built, even before the Olympic Games, by Riccardo Morandi, who is, with Pier Luigi Nervi, one of the greatest technicians of modern architectural engineering. He also built the Alitalia hangars (of 1965 and 1970) at the Leonardo da Vinci airport of Fiumicino, which are remarkable for their ingenious structural solutions, daring design, and aesthetic effect, with a system of ties for the flat roofing, achieved, in the more recent of the two buildings, by means of daring tensile structure. The same characteristics enhance another work of Morandi's, the great structure at the bend of the Tiber, in prestressed concrete, which connects with the autostrada from Fiumicino airport to the city, and at the threshold of Rome, on the ancient river itself, provides a dramatic link between the past and the future.

Rome is indebted to Pier Luigi Nervi for some important and widely-admired architectural works: the Palazzetto dello Sport, built in 1957 with the collaboration of Annibale Vitellozzi, the Stadio Flaminio of two years later, the Palazzo dello Sport at the EUR, built in 1960 on the already existing site planned by Marcello Piacentini, the Officina Carte Valori (Mint) in Largo Bastia, in the Tuscolano quarter, of 1968, and the new Hall for Papal Audiences in the Vatican, of 1964-70, capable of accommodating 20,000 people, about half the number the Colosseum used to hold.

The Palazzetto dello Sport, in the area between Viale Tiziano and the Stadium, was also, like the larger Palazzo dello Sport, built for the Olympic Games of 1960. Circular in plan, with a dome and spherical cap imposed on a circle of thirty-six Y-shaped struts bent according to the tangent at the curve in the plane of impost, it is one of the key buildings of contemporary architecture exemplifying structural calculation as an element of form. The Vatican Hall, commissioned from Nervi by Pope Paul VI, where the comparison it had to encounter was a good deal more intimidating, also postulates, with its undulating roof and the subtle flexibility of its structures, the same relationship between technique and form.

In much the same way and still in that same area, a modern contribution in the sphere of painting and sculpture comes from the works of Giorgio de Chirico, Giorgio Morandi, Filippo de Pisis, Mario Sironi,

Pier Luigi Nervi. Sondrio 1891. The Palazzetto dello Sport, near the Viale Tiziano, was constructed in 1957 with the assistance of the architect Annibale Vitellozzi, and can accommodate 15,000 spectators.

Arturo Martini and other contemporary artists, foreign as well as Italian, in the most recent room of the Pinacoteca Vaticana. And in the same way, too, Giacomo Manzù's Porta della Morte ('Door of Death') stands beside Filarete's doors at the entrance to St Peter's. Painting and sculpture in Rome during the present century have, like architecture, gone through a period of arrested development, followed by a lively revival since the Second World War. Amedeo Modigliani, who is represented by two good works in the Galleria Nazionale d'Arte Moderna, had no links with Rome either before or after he went to Paris in 1906. At that time the painters in the forefront in Rome were Giacomo Balla and Gino Severini, both of them signatories, with Boccioni, Carrà and Russolo, of the Futurist painters' Manifesto of 1910. Thereafter Paris became the international centre for art and the best Italian artists emigrated to it. In Rome, except for exhibitions of the Futurist group in 1913 and 1914, the occasional presence by some important international artist, including Picasso in 1917, and performances at the Teatro Costanti, as the Teatro dell'Opera was then called, by Diaghilev's Russian Ballet (it was during that visit that the idea of the Picasso-Massine-Satie-Cocteau Cubist ballet *Parade* was born), there were few memorable artistic events. Nor were there in the subsequent years, except for the Roman School of painters which, around 1929-30, brought together artists of repute such as Scipione Bonichi, known as Scipione, Mafai and Antonietta Raphaël (their works are in the Galleria Nazionale d'Arte Moderna, in the room dedicated to that important movement), for during the Fascist period art became

for many artists merely a vacuous homage to the rhetorical concepts of the regime. Few pictorial works linked with architecture survive from that period, perhaps only Gino Severini's great mosaic in the hall of the Palazzo dei Congressi at the EUR. But the revival of the arts after the Second World War was in inverse proportion to the lethargy and cultural isolation of the two preceding decades. Rome has today some of the best artists in Italy, both of the middle and the younger generations. Afro, Burri, Capogrossi and Guttuso have their studios there. Manzù lives in a village not far from the city, at Ardea, and a museum dedicated to his works has recently been established near his studio. Other artists, Cagli, Scialoja, Turcato, Sadun, Scordia, Dorazio, Accardi, live and work there. One of the best Italian contemporary sculptors, Ettore Colla, lived in Rome until his death in 1968. The sculptors Consagra, Franchina and, of a younger generation, Mario Ceroli, to mention only a few, live and work in Rome. Arnaldo Pomodoro, whose studio is in Milan, is the author of the great sphere of gilded bronze that stands in the forecourt of the Ministry of Foreign Affairs at the Farnesina, after having been in the Italian pavilion at Expo '67 in Montreal.

The Galleria Nazionale d'Arte Moderna has a representative collection of twentieth-century art, recently improved by new acquisitions, though it still lacks works of some basic movements and artists. It is only in the last twenty years that Rome has become once more a living city in the sphere of art. There is a constant flurry of exhibitions, debates, and cultural meetings; Roman artists frequent Piazza del Popolo as they do Greenwich Village in New York, and foreign artists linger there too, happy to plunge into the friendly, cordial atmosphere characteristic of social relationships in Rome. The foreign artists especially love Trastevere, the old quarters, the places where modern life with its clamorous demands has not yet assailed the once peaceful character of the city. Alexander Calder in 1968 produced a memorable show at the Teatro dell'Opera, *Work in Progress*, with his mobiles, and with electronic music by Castiglioni, Clementi and Maderna, which in its quality and *avant-garde* character recalled the show that Balla created in 1917 for Diaghilev's Ballets Russes with Stravinsky's *Feux d'artifices*. The presence in Rome of many foreign academies and schools of art, with resident artists from all countries of the world, makes cultural cross-fertilization even easier than it would in any case be in these days of rapid communications and mass media. Thus side by side with the relics of the past, of which the preceding pages have given a profile in all-too-summary fashion, Rome today presents a cultural life in tune with the needs of the times and with the enlarged dimension of human curiosity. Rome, for Romans and non-Romans alike, for hurried visitors and for the artists and poets who decide to settle there, is, as it was in the past for Fouquet and Valentin, for Vanvitelli and Keats, for Turner and Corot and so many others, a subtle poison.

The city, it is true, still lacks an organic plan which will allow it to develop in a way suited to the function of a modern capital and to the fascination and nobility of its name so frankly acknowledged by Bonaparte. Architects and town-planners are right to lament this static

▷

One of the evocative fountains of Rome, near Santa Sabina on the Aventine. The mask was taken from the Campo Vaccino; the granite basin is Egyptian.

situation and to do all they can by words and deeds to remedy it. Rome nevertheless remains, above all, a city that makes itself beloved. To declare one's love for stones, streets and skies may seem rhetorical. It is impossible to love these inert things in the same way that in a human being one loves the body and mind, the thoughts and actions,

Antonio Canova. Possagno 1757 - Venice 1822. Pauline Borghese. Marble. Borghese Gallery. The neoclassic work of sculpture (1808) shows Napoleon's sister, who married the Roman Prince Camillo Borghese, in the pose of a triumphant Venus.

the ways of happiness or suffering. Yet Rome is, by reason both of its native and its acquired characteristics, something that is loved or hated exactly like a person. And if the fleeting visitor has no such strong feelings about it, it is always at least a love affair whose memory it is hard to forget.

◁
*One of the Villa Borghese
fountains. The largest and most
agreeable of the Roman parks was
created at the beginning of the
17th century by Cardinal Scipione
Borghese and altered and enlarged
in the succeeding centuries.*

*(above) Villa Borghese, a detail
of the fountain. Trees, paths
small buildings and fountains make
the park a relatively tranquil
oasis in the jostling traffic of
the city.*

P. 238/239
Map of Rome.

P. 240
*The Piazza dell'Esedra (now
known as Piazza della Repubblica)
with Rutelli's Fountain of the
Naiads in the centre, (1885-1914).
At right the austere façade of the
Church of St. Maria degli Angeli,
which Michelangelo created from
a hall of the Bath of Diocletian
The piazza itself repeats in its
curve and its amplitude the
structure of the earlier great exedra
of the baths.*

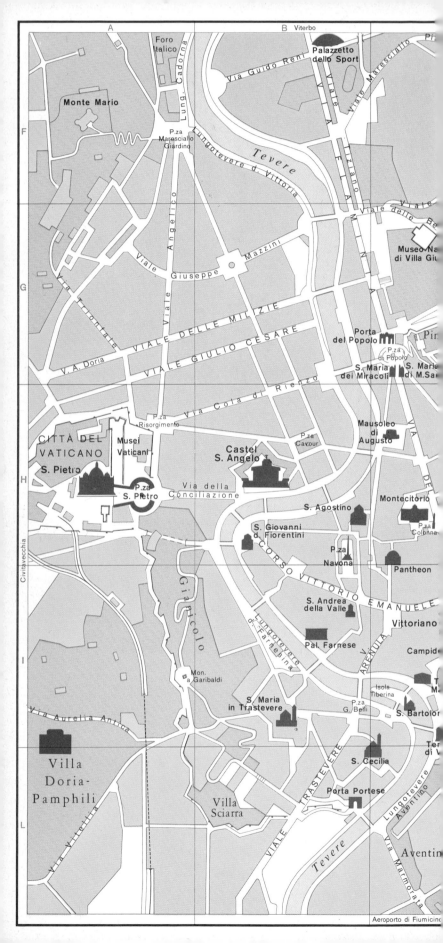

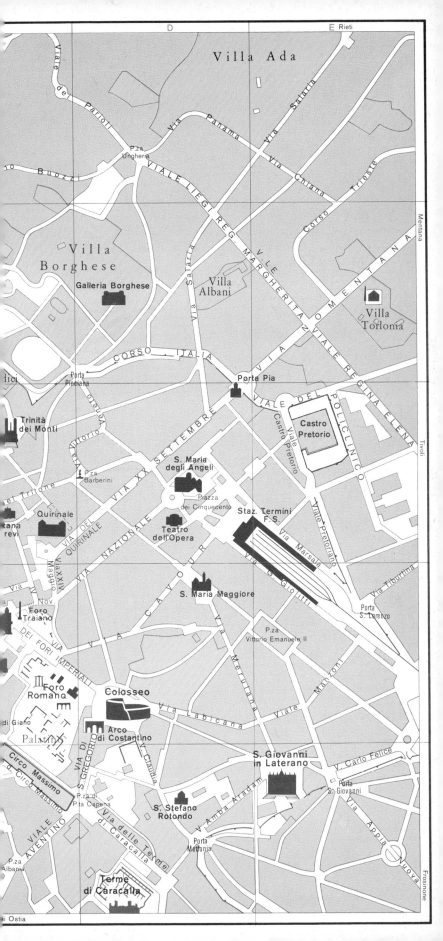

Place names in the main text take the English form. For the convenience of readers who are visiting Rome, place names in the Appendices take the Italian form.

Antiquarium del Foro and Antiquarium del Palatino
Piazza S. Maria Nova, 53. Open daily from 9 to 1, Sundays included. State property.

The Antiquarium del Foro was set up at the beginning of this century by the archaeologist Giacomo Boni. The collection of archaeological finds from the Roman Forum (the prehistoric cemetery, the Temple of Vesta, the fountain of Juturna, and the Basilica Emilia) is laid out in the ground floor rooms, the cloister, and some of the upper rooms of the convent of S. Maria Nova. There is a small epigraphic collection. The Antiquarium del Palatino was assembled in 1870 from objects excavated in the Napoleonic era in the Orti Farnesiani. It was re-arranged in 1920. Of special interest among the excavations on the Palatine are the pre-historic finds on the Cermalus, the graffiti from the Paedagogium, sculptures and frescoes from the Casa dei Grifi, the Aula Isiaca and the Schola praeconum.

Biblioteca e Archivio dell'Accademia di S. Luca (CH)
Via della Stamperia.
Contains about 2,000 volumes and a larger number of documents and autographs. The Biblioteca Romana Sarti is attached to it, with over 30,000 volumes specializing in architecture and fine arts. Entry on request. 220, 224.

Biblioteca Alessandrina
Città Universitaria. Palazzo del Rettorato.
Founded by Alexander VI and opened in 1670, it was transferred from the Sapienza in 1935. It is the university library.

Biblioteca Americana (DH)
Via Veneto 62 b.
Open from 10 to 1, and from 4 to 7.30. Closed Saturdays.

Biblioteca Angelica (BH)
Piazza di S. Agostino.
Founded in 1614 by an Augustinian friar, it passed to the state in 1873. It specializes in literature and philology. Open weekdays 8.30-1.30.

Biblioteca Apostolica Vaticana (AH)
Vatican City.
Founded by Nicholas V. Its present building was designed by Domenico Fontana. It contains about 60,000 codices, 7,000 incunabula, a million printed volumes, and illuminated mss. Entrance to readers only. Open weekdays 10 to 1.30. 88, 112 ff.

Biblioteca Britannica (DH)
Via Quattro Fontane, 20.
Open from 10 to 1, and 4.30 to 7. Closed on Saturday afternoons and during the month of August.

Biblioteca del Burcardo (CI)
Via del Sudario, 44.
A specialist collection on theatre history and theatre arts. A theatrical museum is attached. Entry on request.

Biblioteca Casanatense (CH)
Via di S. Ignazio, 52.
It specializes in church history, and contains printed volumes and illuminated manuscripts. Open weekdays from 8.30 to 1.30.

Biblioteca Corsiniana (BI)
Palazzo Corsini.
Founded in 1754, it has a valuable collection of manuscripts, autographs and incunabula. It is attached to the Accademia Nazionale dei Lincei (*q.v.*) together with the Biblioteca dell'Accademia, and the Biblioteca della Fondazione Caetani which specializes in Moslem civilization.

Biblioteca Hertziana (CH)
Via Gregoriana, 28-31.
A library of art history, specializing in Italian art, and open to readers on weekdays, morning and afternoon.

Biblioteca dell'Istituto Archeologico Germanico (DG)
Via Sardegna, 79.
Specializes in archaeology and art history. Open 9 to 1, and 4 to 8. Closed on Saturday afternoons from 15 July to 15 September.

Biblioteca dell'Istituto Nazionale di Archeologia e Storia dell'Arte (CI)
Palazzo Venezia. Piazza Venezia, 3.
Entrance to art history students only.

Biblioteca Lancisiana (AH)
Borgo S. Spirito, 3.
Founded in 1711 by the famous physician Lancisi. It specializes in the history of medicine, and is open to doctors on weekdays from 9 to 12.

Biblioteca Nazionale Centrale (EH)
Castro Pretorio.
It is in process of being transferred from its original site in the Collegio Romano, where it was founded in 1877. It is the best general library in Rome.

Biblioteca Vallicelliana (BH)
Oratory of St Philip Neri, Piazza della Chiesa Nuova.

Founded in 1581. It specializes in Roman history and church history, and has manuscripts dating from the 7th century. It contains the oldest Roman missal. The same building houses the Biblioteca della Società Romana di Storia patria, and the Biblioteca dell'Istituto Storico Italiano per il Medioevo.

Calcografia Nazionale
Via della Stamperia, 6. Open on weekdays from 9 to 1. Closed on Sundays and feast days.
Founded as the Calcografia Camerale Romana in 1738 by Clement XII, it was transferred in 1837 to the present building, designed for it by Valadier. It became state property in 1870. With its 20,000 engraved plates, it is the largest collection of its kind in the world. There are 1,432 plates by Piranesi alone. The original nucleus of the collection consists of material from the Casa de' Rossi, and to this were added further sets of considerable importance, such as the plates by Canova, Marcantonio Raimondi, and the Roman painter-engraver Bartolomeo Pinelli (1781-1825), whose speciality was Roman traditions and costumes. 220, 224.

Gabinetto Nazionale delle Stampe
Via della Lungara, 230 (in the Farnesina). The reference room is open on weekdays only, 8.30 to 1.30. Parts of the collection are often on view.
This owes its origins to Cardinal Neri Corsini, who made an outstanding collection of drawings and prints in the first half of the seventeenth century, with the help of Giuseppe Bottari. The collection was donated by Prince Tommaso Corsini in 1882, together with the library to the Accademia dei Lincei. In 1940 it was set up as an independent foundation. It contains a very large number of engravings by Italian and foreign masters, from the 15th century to the present day. Artists of the 16th to the 19th centuries are particularly well represented. The collection of drawings, less extensive than that of the engravings, has some works of very high quality, especially by Tuscan artists of the late 16th century, and Romans of the 17th century. 218.

Galleria dell'Accademia Nazionale di San Luca
Piazza dell'Accademia di S. Luca, 7. Open on Mondays, Wednesdays and Fridays from 10 to 1.
This collection was started in the 17th century near the church of S. Luca nei Fori Imperiali with bequests from members of the Accademia. It was transferred to the Palazzo Carpegna (where it occupies eight rooms) when the via dell'Impero was laid out and the building was demolished. It has some notable works. Among the Italians, there is a fragment of a fresco by Raphael with a little putto, and works by Bassano, Reni, Guercino, Maratta, Piazzetta, Vanvitelli and Canova. Foreign painters represented are Rubens, Van Dyck, Clodion, and Vernet. 153, 223, 226.

Galleria Colonna
Palazzo Colonna, Piazza SS. Apostoli. The entrance is at the back of the building, via della Pilotta, 17. It is privately owned, and is open on Saturdays from 9 to 1.
Begun in 1702, although Cardinal Girolamo Colonna already had the magnificent gallery designed by Antonio del Grande in 1654 to house the family collection. There are some 15th-century works of fine quality (Stefano da Verona, Vivarini, and Flemish artists), a notable group of the Venetian cinquecento (Tintoretto, Palma), and works by Florentine Mannerists. The most outstanding part of the collection is the collection of 17th-century paintings by the chief artists, both Italian and foreign, who worked in Rome. A typical example of a patrician Roman gallery in the quality of the works and of their setting. 204, 209.

Galleria Doria Pamphilj
Palazzo Pamphilj on the Corso. Entrance in Piazza del Collegio Romano, 1 A. Open on Tuesdays, Fridays, Saturdays and Sundays, from 10 to 1. Privately owned.
This is the most important collection to be still in the possession of the family which began it. It dates back to the time of Innocent X, when the Pamphilj family were at the height of their prosperity, and its growth was helped by connections with the Aldobrandini and Doria families. The first group of works was collected by Olimpia Maidalchini, sister-in-law of Innocent X, in her palace in piazza Navona, and it was through him that they came into this gallery, which is arranged around a sixteenth-century court of honour. The private apartments may also be visited, and these contain the rest of the collection of paintings, the original furnishings (17th and 18th centuries), tapestries and objets d'art. There are very fine works by Memling, Gossaert, Filippo Lippi, Pesellino, Giovanni di Paolo, Raphael, Titian, Lorenzo Lotto, Parmigianino, Caravaggio, Velasquez, Guercino, and Carracci. There

is some important sculpture, especially of the Baroque. The collection in its magnificent surroundings gives a very clear idea of the kind of establishment kept up by the Roman nobility in the 17th century. 158, 191, 196, 201, 204.

Galleria Nazionale d'Arte Antica

This is divided into two parts, one in the Palazzo Barberini, with its entrance in via Quattro Fontane 13, and the other in the Palazzo Corsini, via della Lungara 10. Both are open on weekdays, the first from 9 to 4, the second from 9 to 2. On Sundays and feast days they are open from 9 to 1. The first is closed on Mondays, and the second on Tuesdays.

In the Palazzo Barberini, which was acquired by the state in 1949, the paintings are of the 12th to the 16th centuries. There is some sculpture, including the portrait of Urban VIII Barberini by Bernini. There are paintings by Simone Martini, Lippi, Angelico, the famous Fornarina of Raphael, works of the Venetian school of the 16th century of the Tuscan Mannerists, and of Flemish artists (including the portrait of Erasmus of Rotterdam by Quentin Matsys). A recent addition to this collection is a series of good French works of the 18th century, donated by the Duke of Cervinara. The rest of the palace is occupied by a military club. The mezzanine over the *piano nobile* is in process of being laid out as a museum of decorative arts. The palace also houses temporarily the Istituto di Numismatica and the Odescalchi Armoury, which has been acquired by the state. On the top floor of the right wing of the building, the Ente Premi Roma organizes exhibitions of modern art.

The paintings on view in the Palazzo Corsini are the 17th- and 18th-century works which it has not yet been possible to arrange in the Palazzo Barberini. Most of these belong to the original collection of Cardinal Neri Corsini (*see* Gabinetto Nazionale delle Stampe), and they became state property in 1883, together with the palace. Other paintings were added from the Torlonia collection and the Monte di Pietà. The Gallery was inaugurated in 1895. The collection is one of the most representative of Italian painting in the 17th and 18th centuries, but there are also fine works by Flemish, French and Dutch artists.

The question of uniting all these works under one roof has often been raised, but has yet to be resolved. 153, 162, 177, 209, 211, 217, 226.

Galleria Nazionale d'Arte Moderna

Viale delle Belle Arti, 131. Open weekdays from 9 to 2, Sundays and feast days from 9.30 to 1.30. Closed Mondays.

The first Italian gallery of modern art came into being at the Rome Exhibition of 1881. It was originally arranged in the Palazzo delle Esposizioni in via Nazionale, and comprised a number of state acquisitions. In 1915 it was transferred to its present site, built for the purpose by Cesare Bazzani in the eclectic and rather exaggerated taste of the time. Italian painting of the 19th century is well represented, but 20th-century art less so. There is a notable absence of works by some of the more important artists, including the Futurists. It must be admitted that the gallery was started with a rather unfortunate critical outlook. This has, however, gradually been remedied to some extent in recent years, and the collection does give some idea of contemporary trends, particularly in Italian art. 223, 228, 231 ff.

Galleria Spada

Palazzo Spada, Piazza Capodiferro, 3. State property. Open on weekdays from 9.30 to 4, and Sundays and feast days from 10 to 1. Closed Mondays.

The palace was built by Giulio Merisi for the Spada family in the mid-16th century. The gallery contains a collection of paintings begun by Cardinal Bernardino Spada in the 17th century, and since added to by his heirs. The paintings are hung in the Baroque style, as interior decoration rather than exhibition. There are works by Titian, Rubens, and the major Caravaggesque painters who worked in Rome, also some classical sculpture. 149, 153.

Istituto Centrale del Restauro

Piazza San Francesco di Paola, 9. Transferring to the S. Michele building. Lungotevere a Ripa.

Together with the Centre International pour la Conservation et la Restauration des Biens Culturels, via Cavour, 256, this constitutes the most up-to-date centre in Italy for the preservation and restoration of works of art. Not normally open to the public, it can be visited on application to the directors. There is also a school of restoration. 163.

Keats-Shelley Memorial House

Piazza di Spagna, 26, 2nd floor*. It can be visited on request.

It is here that John Keats stayed, and where he died on 23 February 1821. There is a fine collection of books, prints, drawings, sculptures

* US 3rd floor.

and other relics of the Keats and Shelley circle (Byron, Leigh Hunt, etc.). 226.

Museo dell'Alto Medioevo
Viale Lincoln, 1, EUR. Open daily from 9.30 to 1.30. Closed on Mondays. State property.
This museum is of recent foundation, and contains the basis of a collection of early medieval works, especially fragments of sculpture and architectural decoration mainly from central Italy and dating from the seventh to the eleventh centuries.

Museo Barracco
Corso Vittorio Emanuele, 168 (in the Piccola "Farnesina" ai Baullari). Open on weekdays from 9 to 2, and on Tuesdays and Thursdays also from 5 to 8. Sundays from 9 to 1. Closed on Mondays. Local government property.
This museum gets its name from Senator Giovanni Barracco, who bequeathed it to the city of Rome in 1902. It was transferred to its present site in 1948. It contains Egyptian, Assyrian, Etruscan, Greek and Roman sculpture. 36, 132.

Museo e Galleria Borghese
Villa Borghese. Open weekdays from 9.30 to 4, Sundays and feast days from 9.30 to 1. It is owned by the state.
The villa was built in 1613 by Cardinal Scipione Borghese to house the collection that he was in process of making. The architects were Flaminio Ponzio and Jan Van Santen. Later additions to the collection came from the Aldobrandini and the Salviati, and already in the 17th century it was one of the major collections of Europe. Marcantonio Borghese had the inside of the villa re-decorated at the end of the 18th century in the neo-classical style, and he added to the collection an important group of classical sculptures that were excavated in Rome by Gavin Hamilton, the Scottish sculptor and antiquarian. Some of these, however, were ceded to France in 1815. Camillo Borghese acquired Correggio's *Danae* in Paris in 1823. The statue of his wife, Pauline Bonaparte, is by Canova. In 1833 the whole collection was arranged in the villa. Before that date, part of it was housed in the Palazzo Borghese. The museum and gallery were acquired by the state in 1902.
Canova's *Pauline* and the famous groups of Bernini are among the sculptures to be seen on the ground floor, a collection which includes classical and Baroque works. Among the paintings, which are arranged in eleven rooms on the first floor, are outstanding works by Antonello da Messina, Correggio, Lotto, Raphael's *Deposition* and Titian's so-called *Sacred and Profane Love.* (Panofsky's researches have proved the title to be a mistaken one.) There are also works by Caravaggio and Bernini. It is a world-famous collection of masterpieces. 36, 118, 131, 153, 159, 162, 194, 222.

Musei Capitolini
Piazza del Campidoglio. Open weekdays from 9 to 2, Tuesdays and Thursdays also from 5 to 8, Saturdays also from 9 to 11.30 p.m. Sundays 9 to 1. Closed Mondays.
These are the Museo Capitolino, the Museo del Palazzo dei Conservatori (with the Appartamento del Palazzo dei Conservatori, the Museo Nuovo and the Braccio Nuovo), the Pinacoteca Capitolina, the Galleria Lapidaria, the Protomoteca and the Medagliere. They are housed in two buildings at right angles to the Palazzo Senatorio.
The original nucleus, which is in fact the oldest public collection in the world, goes back to 1471. It began with Sixtus IV's gift to the Roman people of some outstanding classical bronzes, including the Capitoline she-wolf. Further additions came with such bequests as that of Cardinal Alessandro Albani's collection, and as a result of archaeological excavations in the city.
The Museo Capitolino was opened to the public by Clement XII in 1734. It contains some very famous sculptures, such as the *Capitoline Venus*, the *Satyr* of Praxiteles discovered at the Villa Adriana, and the *Dying Gaul.* There is a small Egyptian collection, a series of Greek and Roman portraits, and a collection of exhibits relating to the oriental cults practised in Rome during the first centuries of the Empire. There are also epigraphical collections.
The Museo del Palazzo dei Conservatori was opened in 1876. In the rooms of the Appartamento dei Conservatori are frescoes by Cavalier d'Arpino, Jacopo Ripanda, and Tommaso Laureti, and sculpture by Bernini and Algardi. Etruscan and Roman bronzes include the *Capitoline she-wolf*, the *Spinario,* and the *Esquiline Venus.* The Castellani collection consists of Greek and Etruscan vases. The marbles of the Fasti Capitolini are important sources of Roman history. The museum was enlarged in 1925 with a new wing in the Palazzo Caffarelli, the Museo Nuovo Capitolino. This contains

classical sculpture arranged in chronological sequence. In 1950 the Braccio Nuovo was added, to contain recent archaeological discoveries, and in 1957 the Galleria Lapidaria. The Pinacoteca Capitolina, also in the Palazzo dei Conservatori, was founded in 1749 by Benedict XIV, and subsequently benefited from the Pio, the Sacchetti, and various other bequests. It contains paintings of the 14th, 15th and 16th centuries, and has a rich collection of works by Roman and Bolognese painters of the 17th century. The most outstanding pictures are those of Giovanni Bellini, Titian and Veronese, *Romulus and Remus suckled by the Wolf* of Rubens, portraits by van Dyck and Velasquez, and works by Caravaggio. Among the paintings of the Bolognese school, Guercino's altarpiece, the *Burial of Santa Petronilla,* is an outstanding achievement of the Baroque. It once hung in St Peter's.

The Protomoteca, restored in 1950, contains a collection of busts of famous men. It was begun in 1820 by Pius VII. There are two works by Canova in the collection. Both the Protomoteca and the Medagliere can be visited on request. 36, 145, 195, 204, 207.

Museo della Civiltà Romana
Piazza G. Agnelli, EUR. Open on weekdays from 9 to 2, and on Tuesdays and Thursdays also from 5 to 8. Sundays from 9 to 1. The museum is local government property.
This is essentially a documentary museum for the study of Roman civilization. Of particular interest to visitors is the large reconstruction of ancient Rome, which gives a clear idea of what the city looked like at the time of the Roman Empire.

Museo Napoleonico
Via Zanardelli, on the corner of Piazza di Ponte Umberto. Open weekdays from 9 to 2, and on Tuesdays and Thursdays also from 5 to 8. Sundays 9 to 1. Closed on Mondays. Local government property.
It was donated to the Roman commune in 1927 by count Giuseppe Primoli, son of Carlotta Bonaparte. It contains pictures, statues, drawings and various relics of the Bonaparte family. The princes of Canino (the Roman line of the family) are especially represented, as is also the period of the Bonapartes' stay in Rome. The most notable portraits are those by David, Gérard, Fabre, Canova and Carpeau. In this connection it may be noted that Napoleon's mother, Letizia Ramolino, lived in the Palazzo Bonaparte after

his fall from power, until her death in 1836. This palace is today the Palazzo Misciatelli, and stands at the corner of Piazza Venezia and the Corso.

Museo Nazionale d'Arte Orientale
Palazzo Brancaccio, via Merulana, 248. Open weekdays from 9 to 1, Sundays and feast days from 10 to 1. Closed Tuesdays. State property.
This museum was opened in 1958 to exhibit archaeological finds of the Istituto Italiano per il Medio ed Estremo Oriente. Since that date, the collection has been enlarged, notably with finds made by the Istituto in Pakistan. There are sections on the art of Iran, China, India, Tibet, Nepal, and Siam.

Museo Nazionale delle Arti e Tradizioni Popolari
Piazza Marconi, 8, EUR. Open daily from 9 to 2. Closed on Mondays. It is owned by the state.
Lamberto Loria started up a private ethnographical museum in Florence in 1906. It was later transferred to the Villa d'Este and in 1953 it was removed to its present site, enlarged and re-arranged. It deals with the folklore, traditions and popular arts of every part of Italy. It is organized according to subjects: the seasons, daily life, household affairs, popular art, traditions (dancing, music and singing), popular religious beliefs. There is a library and a centre for recording data.

Museo Nazionale di Castel S. Angelo
Lungotevere Castello. Open weekdays 9.30 to 4, Sundays and feast days from 9.30 to 1. Closed Mondays. It is owned by the state.
The original Hadrianeum was built for the Emperor Hadrian, possibly by the architect Demetrianus, between AD 135 and 139. In the Middle Ages it became a fortress and prison. During the Renaissance further ramparts were added to it. In 1925 it became a museum, the building itself being of considerable interest, quite apart from its collection of paintings, sculptures, historical armory, etc.

Museo Nazionale Etrusco di Villa Giulia
Piazzale di Villa Giulia, 9. Open weekdays from 10 to 4, Sundays and feast days from 10 to 1. Closed on Mondays. It is owned by the state.
This suburban villa, built by Vignola, Ammannati and Vasari for Julius III, contains the most important Etruscan collection in the world. It is also the most up-to-date from the point of view of arrangement, which is the work of Franco Minissi

(1960). There are outstanding works of Etruscan pottery, the Apollo of Veio, sarcophagi from Cerveteri and Tarquinia, sculpture, bronzes, furniture, and terracottas, paintings and objects from burial grounds, including the *Cista Ficoroni*. 36, 150.

Museo Nazionale Romano
Piazza della Repubblica. Open weekdays from 9.30 to 3, Sundays and feast days from 9 to 1. Closed Mondays. State property
Founded in 1870 and opened in 1889, this was Rome's first national museum of classical art when the city became the capital of Italy. It occupies halls in the Baths of Diocletian, and parts of the Carthusian monastery.
The collection was enlarged by bequests, notably from the Ludovisi, and archaeological finds. Today it is one of the most important archaeological museums in the world. Some of the most famous works of classical statuary are to be found here: the *Ludovisi Throne* (a magnificent Ionic relief of the fifth century BC, the *Dying Niobid* of the same period, the *Discobolus* (copied from Myron), the *Venus of Cyrene,* and the *Girl of Anzio*. There is a fine collection of paintings, mosaics, and stuccos from Roman buildings, also terracottas, grave objects, glass and jewellery. Especially noteworthy is the 'Aspasios jasper', showing the profile of Athena Parthenos by Phidias. 32, 36, 38.

Museo Numismatico
Via 20 Settembre. Open weekdays only, from 10 to 2. The collection is owned by the state, and is housed in the same building as the Mint.
Founded in 1958, it contains all the medallions of the popes from Martin V (1417) to the present pontiff. This collection was begun by Pius VII and some of the exhibits are of considerable value (including some of Cellini's work). There is a complete set of Italian coins from 1861 to the present day, and a collection of wax moulds by Benedetto Pistrucci, who was engraver to the English Mint and designed the sterling currency. There is also a collection of over 100,000 coins donated to the state by Vittorio Emanuele III of Savoy in 1946. These dates from the fall of the Roman Empire to the present day, and are on exhibition upon request in the Palazzo Barberini, Istituto di Numismatica, but notice must be given in advance.

Museo del Palazzo di Venezia
Piazza Venezia. Temporary entrance in via del Plebiscito. Open on weekdays from 9 to 2, Sundays and feast days from 9 to 1. Closed Mondays. State property.
The palace belonged to Austria from 1797 (Treaty of Campoformio) until 1916. In 1921 it was opened with an exhibition of medieval and Renaissance works from Castel S. Angelo. The collection has increased during the last fifty years. The palace was used by Mussolini as his headquarters, and his office was the Sala del Mappamondo. In 1944 the palace was again opened to the public. The collection is in process of re-arrangement. Among the more important works are tapestries from Tournai (*Judith and Holofernes, c.* 1520) and Brussels (*Last Judgment, c.* 1510, one of a series of the Seven Capital Sins, of which other examples are in the Louvre and the Metropolitan). Also a Byzantine ebony marriage casket of the 10th or 11th century, paintings by Giuseppe M. Crespi, the Romanèsque sculpture of the *Madonna di Acuto* and other works from Alba Fucense. There is a fine collection of bronzes; sketches in terracotta by Sansovino, Bernini, and Algardi; a group of minor arts. 78, 217.

Museo Preistorico Etnografico « Luigi Pigorini »
Via Lincoln, 1, EUR. In process of re-arrangement. It is owned by the state.
Founded in 1875 in the Collegio Romano (in via del Collegio Romano), it has recently been transferred to this new site. It is one of the major institutions of its kind in Europe, containing a variety of collections of prehistoric and ethnographic interest, with special reference to Italy, from the palaeolithic period to the first iron age, arranged in geographical order. The prehistoric section dealing with Latium is of especial interest.

Museo di Roma
Palazzo Braschi (entrance in Piazza S. Pantaleo, 10). Open on weekdays from 9 to 2, Tuesdays and Thursdays also from 5 to 8. Sundays 9 to 1. Closed Mondays. Local government property.
Transferred to its present site in 1952, this museum occupies the three floors of the palace built by relatives of Pius VI after 1791. It contains a large quantity of pictures, sculpture, drawings and other things that throw light on the history, traditions, topography and daily life of Rome, from the Middle Ages to the present day. Of special interest is the documentary section dealing with Rome as it was before the demolitions and modern developments began entitled 'Roma sparita', comprising drawings, prints and paintings. 195, 209, 217, 221, 226.

Musei Vaticani

Entrance in viale dei Musei Vaticani. Open weekdays from 9 to 2. Closed on Sundays and feast days.
The complex includes the Pinacoteca Vaticana and the various Musei di Antichità, the Museo Gregoriano Egizio, the Museo Pio Clementino, the Museo Chiaramonti, the Galleria dei Candelabri, the Museo Gregoriano Etrusco, the Museo Profano della Biblioteca which gives onto the long gallery of the Biblioteca Apostolica Vaticana, the Museo Sacro (which gives access to the Borgia Apartment, the Sistine Chapel, the *Stanze* and *Logge* of Raphael, and finally the Galleria delle Carte geografiche e degli Arazzi).
A complex of this size, containing as it does so much that is of the highest value in western art and civilization, requires more than the cursory visit many tourists make. The Pinacoteca Vaticana alone comprises seventeen rooms, and contains paintings dating from the eleventh century to the present day. The earliest work is the *Last Judgment,* signed by the Roman Benedictine painters Giovanni and Nicola. Present-day painters include Rouault, Villon, and Zadkine. Every school of the intervening periods is represented. The Museo Gregoriano Egizio, founded by Gregory XVI, is a small collection of fine works, including the granite statue of Tewe, Queen of Egypt and mother of Ramses II, *c.* 1280 BC.
The Museo Pio Clementino owes its name to its two principal benefactors, Clement XIV and Pius VI, and is rich in sculpture. It contains the porphyry sarcophagi of Helena and Constantia, the mother and daughter of Constantine the Great, and the superb classical and modern sculptures of the Belvedere.
The Museo Chiaramonti takes its title from Pius VII Chiaramonti and consists of three sections: the museum itself, the Galleria Lapidaria, and the Braccio Nuovo. This latter is also rich in classical works, and includes the *Augustus of Prima Porta* (so-called from Livia's villa in that place), the Hellenistic *Nile* (whose companion statue is the *Tiber* in the Louvre), discovered in 1513 at S. Maria sopra Minerva.
The long Galleria dei Candelabri (about 265 feet) takes its name from the pairs of splendid marble candelabra in the arcades.
The Museo Gregoriano Etrusco, founded in 1837 by Gregory XVI, contains the famous Regolini-Galassi tomb found at Cerveteri in 1836 in a remarkable state of preservation. Also

the Mars of Todi and other Etruscan, Greek, Italic and Assyrian works. The Biblioteca Apostolica Vaticana (*see* p. 241), founded by Nicholas V and enlarged by Sixtus IV, could be called the very heart of western culture on account of its unrivalled collection of manuscripts (many of them illuminated), records and documents. The Museo Sacro offers what is almost a complete panorama of minor Christian arts. It includes one of the best preserved paintings of antiquity, the *Aldobrandini Wedding,* which depicts the marriage of Alexander the Great to Roxana.
The Borgia Apartment, the Sistine Chapel, the *Stanze* and *Logge* of Raphael have been discussed at length (pp. 103-6, 110, 118-30). These are a positive treasure-house, containing much of the finest work of the Renaissance artists. The Galleria delle Carte geografiche contains maps of Italy, painted by the Perugian Antonio Danti, under the guidance of his brother Egnazio, the famous cosmographer.
The Galleria degli Arazzi gets its name from the tapestries by Raphael which originally hung there. (These are now in the Pinacoteca Vaticana.) The present series of tapestries in the gallery are based on cartoons by Raphael's pupils, but woven, as were Raphael's, in the workshop of Pieter van Aelst of Brussels. 18, 30, 36, 112, 204 ff.

Museo della via Ostiense

Porta S. Paolo, Piazza di Porta S. Paolo o Piazzale Ostiense. Open daily from 9 to 1. Closed Mondays. State property.
This collection was begun in 1954, to illustrate the history and monuments of the via Ostiense, the link between the city of Rome and its port and trading centre. It contains sculpture, inscriptions and architectural fragments, plans and models.

In the vicinity of Rome there are other museums (antique, medieval and modern collections) which may be mentioned here. Among the collections of ancient works, most notable are those at Cerveteri, Formia, Minturno, Ostia, Palestrina, Sperlonga (containing a recently-discovered Hellenistic Polyphemus group), Tarquinia (where the famous Etruscan tombs may also be visited), Villa Adriana at Tivoli, and Veio.
Medieval collections are to be seen at the diocesan museums at Orte, Gaeta and Rieti, the civic museum of Viterbo (for Sebastiano del Piombo's magnificent *Pietà*), and the national museum of Villa d'Este at Tivoli.

Historic Buildings and Churches

Accademia Musicale di S. Cecilia (CH) *Via Vittoria.* A concert hall is attached to the Academy. 215.

Accademia Nazionale dei Lincei (BI) *Palazzo Corsini, via della Lungara.* Founded in 1603 by Federico Cesi, it takes its name from the lynx on its coat of arms. An institute for higher studies, with two libraries attached to it. 134.

Aqueducts *Campagna romana.* A series of arcades for bringing water into the city, begun by Appius Claudius in 312 BC. They create an impressive approach to Rome from the south. 12, *14*.

Ara Pacis Augustae (CH) *Piazza Augusto Imperatore.* Erected by Augustus between 13 and 9 BC to celebrate the peace which followed his expeditions into Spain and Gaul. Fragments of it were first discovered in the 15th century under the Palazzo Fiano on the Corso, and it was finally reconstructed in 1938. 15, 16, 18.

Arch of Constantine (DI) *Via dei Trionfi.* Erected in AD 315 to celebrate Constantine's victory over Maxentius at the Milvian bridge. Restored in 1804. The sculptures and reliefs on it were taken from monuments of early periods (Trajan, Hadrian and Marcus Aurelius). 23, 35, 36, *92, 94.*

'Arch of Janus' (CI) *Via del Velabro.* Possibly erected in the age of Constantine, it incorporates materials of an earlier date. Its original top structure is missing. 10, 36, *57.*

Arch of Septimius Severus (CI) *Roman Forum.* Erected in AD 203 on the tenth anniversary of the accession of Septimius Severus, to celebrate his own triumphs and those of his sons, Caracalla and Geta, over the Parthians, Arabs and Adiabenes of Assyria. 26, 34, *38.*

Arch of Titus (CI) *Roman Forum.* Erected in the time of Domitian, or possibly of Trajan, to celebrate the victories of Vespasian and Titus, which culminated in the destruction of Jerusalem (AD 70). Restored by Valadier in 1821. 26, 34, *75, 78.*

Aventine (CL) One of the seven hills of Rome. 11, 200.

Basilica of Constantine (CI) (also known as the **Basilica of Maxentius,** and **Basilica Nova**) *Roman Forum.* Begun by Maxentius (AD 306-12) and completed by Constantine after his victory at the Milvian bridge. It was used for the administration of justice and various kinds of transaction. One of its columns is now in Piazza S. Maria Maggiore. Ruined by the inadequacy of its foundations and subsequent earthquakes (9th century). 26, 27, 36, *37,* 78 .

Basilica Emilia (CI) *Roman Forum.* The original basilica was founded in 179 BC by the censors M. Emilius Lepidus and M. Fulvius Nobilior, and embellished by M. Emilius Paulus, the consul in 78 BC. Later destroyed by fire. Restored in the Augustan age, it was again destroyed, possibly in the 5th century during the sack of Rome by Alaric. 26, *34.*

Basilica Julia (CI) *Roman Forum.* Erected by Julius Caesar (55-44 BC) and completed by Augustus. It was used for the administration of justice, and for sessions of the tribunal of the Centumviri. Destroyed by fire, it was restored by Diocletian, and again in the 4th century. 14, 19 ff, 26, *31, 33.*

Basilica di Porta Maggiore (EI) *Piazzale di Porta Maggiore. Entrance in via Prenestina, 17.* Underground sanctuary of the first century AD used by oriental religious sects. Discovered in 1916. 44.

Basilica Ulpia (CI) *Forum of Trajan.* Partially excavated, it was originally divided into five aisles by four colonnades, with two exedrae on the short sides. 27, 28, 33.

Baths of Caracalla (DL) *Via Terme di Caracalla.* The building was begun in 206 by Septimius Severus, opened nine years later by his son Antoninus Caracalla, completed by Heliogabalus and Alexander Severus, and restored by Aurelian. The baths were extremely beneficial and their architecture was magnificent. The ruins are used for operatic performances in the summer months. 32.

Baths of Diocletian (DH) *Piazza della Repubblica.* These were the most magnificent baths in Rome, covering an area from what is now the Piazza S. Bernardo to halfway down the via 20 Settembre, from via del Viminale to Piazza dei Cinquecento, and from via Volturno to via Torino. They were built between AD 298 and 306 and there was sufficient room for 3,000 people. The chief exedra corresponded to the modern one put up by Koch in the Piazza della

Repubblica. Part of the building is used by the Museo Nazionale Romano, and another part of it was laid out by Michelangelo as the church of S. Maria degli Angeli. Other parts are still visible in the circular halls of the church of S. Bernardo and the church in via del Viminale, also the octagonal hall which is now the Planetario. Other fragments remain, on ground level and beneath it. 32, 36, 57, 145, 149.

Baths of Septimius Severus (CI) Built next to Domitian's stadium and hippodrome, they were restored by Septimius Severus. The impressive supporting structure is the part best preserved today. 26.

Bosco Parrasio (BI) *Via Garibaldi.* In the 17th century, a rendezvous for poets of the Accademia dell'Arcadia. 198.

Caffè Greco (CH) *Via Condotti.* Opened in 1760 by a Greek (hence the name) it used to be very much frequented by Italian and foreign artists and men of letters. Its original décor is still almost intact. 225.

Campidoglio (CI)

Campo marzio (CH)

Capitol (CI) now called **Campidoglio.** 9-15, 26, 36, 62, 108, 136 ff, 145, 148.

Capitoline she-wolf, *see* **Lupa capitolina.**

Carcer Mamertinus (now the church of **S. Pietro in Carcere**) (CI) *At the foot of the Campidoglio.* Of the two superimposed buildings, the upper trapezoid structure is the Carcer Mamertinus, and is of the 1st century. The lower part, the Tullianum, is of the 4th century. 200.

Casa dei Cavalieri di Rodi (CI) *Over the forum of Augustus.* It was originally the Roman priory of the knights of St John of Jerusalem, and later of the knights of Rhodes and of Malta. Built at the end of the 12th century, it was rebuilt between 1467 and 1470.

Casa dei Crescenzi (CI) *Via del Teatro di Marcello.* A rare example of a private house of the Middle Ages, it dates back to the 12th century. Materials taken from buildings of the classical era were used in its construction. 62.

Casa dei Mattei (BI) *Piazza in Piscinula.* Although totally restored, it still retains some of its original features of the 14th and 15th centuries. 64.

Casino Ludovisi (CH) *Via Ludovisi.* Permission to see Guercino's fresco of Aurora is granted to students. 204.

Casino Massimo (EL) *Via Matteo Boiardo, 16 (Laterano).* The casino is all that is left of the Villa Giustiniani-Massimo. It was decorated in the 19th century by German painters, with scenes from Dante, Tasso and Ariosto.

Casino dei Quattro Venti (AL) *Villa Doria Pamphilj on the Janiculum, also known as Villa Belrespiro.* It was built in 1650 by Alessandro Algardi for Camillo Pamphilj. It was acquired by the State in 1970 for a museum of Baroque painting and sculpture.

Casina Valadier (CG) *Pincio.* Built by Valadier in the neo-classical style, it is now used as a restaurant. 224.

Castel S. Angelo, or **Mausoleum of Hadrian** (BH). The project was conceived by the Emperor Hadrian, and the architect may have been Demetrianus. The building was begun in 135 and finished in 139 under Antoninus Pius. It was used as a prison by Theodoric, and later became a fortress and a gallows. The central keep was built under Benedict XI (1033-44), the curtain under Alexander VI, and the loggia under Julius II. It houses the Museo Nazionale di Castel S. Angelo (*q.v.*). Michelangelo built a small chapel for Leo X (Medici) on one of the ramparts. 16, *62,* 83, 145, 183, *190,* 204, 219.

Catacombs of the Cimitero Maggiore *Via Asmara, 41.* 49.

Catacombs of Commodilla *Via delle Sette Chiese, 42.* 49.

Catacombs of Domitilla *Via Ardeatina, 41.* 48.

Catacombs of the Jews *Via Labicana* (DI). 49.
Villa Torlonia (not accessible)
Vigna di S. Sebastiano
Via Appia Antica

Catacombs of Priscilla *Via Salaria.* 49.

Catacombs of S. Calixtus *Via Appia Antica.* 49, 58.

Catacombs of SS. Marcellinus and Peter *Via Labicana.* (DI). 49.

Catacombs of S. Sebastiano *Via Appia Antica.* 49, 160.

Celian hill (CI) One of the seven hills of Rome. 10, 154, 204.

Cermalus One of the three hills on which, together with the Palatine proper and the Velian hill, the buildings of the Palatine were laid out. On Cermalus the remains of an ancient village (*pagus*) have been discovered.

Circus Maximus (CL) *Between the Palatine and the Aventine.* Tradition claims that it was founded by king Tarquinius Priscus on the spot where the rape of the Sabine women occurred. However, the walls cannot have been built before the second century BC. It was restored and enlarged during the Empire. It fell into ruin after AD 549.

Città Leonina (AH) The area within the walls encircling the Vatican, which were put up in the time of Leo IV. They have often been destroyed and restored. 62.

Cloaca Maxima (CI) This went down from Argiletum, between the Esquiline and the Quirinal, across the Forum to the Tiber. The arch over its outlet is still visible beneath Ponte Rotto. It is of the second century BC. 12, 153.

Collegio dei Musici This is the old name for the Accademia Nazionale di Musica di S. Cecilia (*q.v.*).

Collegio Romano (CH) *Piazza Collegio Romano.* Built in 1583 for Gregory XIII by Bartolomeo Ammannati, or possibly by the Jesuit Giuseppe Valeriani.

Colosseum (DI) Also called the Flavian Amphitheatre. 14, 16, 23, 27, 28, 30, 35, *45*, 48, 92.

Column of Antoninus (CH) *Piazza Colonna.* It has been misnamed thus since 1589. In fact it is the column begun in AD 176 to celebrate the victory of Marcus Aurelius over the Marcomanni, the Quadi and the Sarmati. It was completed in 193. 33, *78*, *81*, *101*, 137 ff, 144, 148.

Column of Marcus Aurelius (*see* **Column of Antoninus**).

Curia (CI) *Roman Forum.* Founded, according to tradition, by king Tullus Ostilius, and rebuilt *c.* 80 BC by Sulla, and later by Caesar and Diocletian. It was here that the Roman Senate used to meet. In the 7th century it was transformed into a church. Restored between 1883 and 1937. 12, *13*, 14, 26, *27*.

Domus Aurea (Golden House) (DI) *Entrance in the Parco Oppio.* Nero's residence, built after the fire of AD 64 and destroyed soon after his death. Trajan built his baths on the ruins of it, and it is still possible to distinguish fragments of the Domus Aurea under what is left of the baths. The best preserved parts of it are a long corridor, a series of great rooms, the entrance to a crypt, and the hall of the gilded roof. There are important remains of painted and stucco decoration of Nero's period. The

decoration of grottoes of the Domus Aurea were greatly admired by artists of the Renaissance. It was in this locality that the Laocoön (now in the Vatican Museum) was unearthed. 26, 28, 32, 38, *40*, 110, 129.

Esquiline (DI) One of the seven hills of Rome. The basilica of S. Maria Maggiore (*q.v.*) is built on that part of it called the Colle Cispio. On one of its slopes stands the church of S. Martino ai Monti (*q.v.*). 11, 52, *55*, 147.

Farnesina (BI) *Entrance in Via della Lungara.* This villa was built for the banker Agostini Chigi by Baldassarre Peruzzi (1508-11). It was decorated by Peruzzi, Raphael, Sebastiano del Piombo, Giulio Romano, Sodoma, and other pupils of Raphael. It is the perfect example of a Renaissance residence. It is now occupied by the Gabinetto Nazionale delle Stampe (*q.v.*) and certain departments of the Accademia dei Lincei (*q.v.*). 131 ff, *148*, 218, 232.

Fontana dell'Acqua Felice (DH) *Piazza S. Bernardo alle Terme.* Erected between 1585 and 1587 under Sixtus V by Domenico Fontana, this is the first fountain in Rome to have been put in an architectural setting. The reliefs on the upper part are by Flaminio Vacca and Giovanni Battista della Porta. The Moses in the centre is by Leonardo Sormani and Prospero da Brescia. The lions are copies of Egyptian originals, now in the Vatican. 221.

Fontana delle Api (DH) *At the bottom of Via Veneto, on the right-hand side.* Designed by Bernini (1644), it was originally on the corner of the piazza, by Via Sistina. 182.

Fontana del Bicchierone Designed by G.L. Bernini for the Villa d'Este at Tivoli. The attribution is, however, disputed. 183.

Fontana delle Naiadi (DH) *Piazza della Repubblica (also called Piazza Esedra).* Designed by Mario Rutelli (1885). The sculptures were added in 1901 and 1914. 228.

Fontana del Palazzo Antamoro (CH) *Via della Panetteria.* Designed by Bernini, but alterations have spoiled it. 183.

Fontana di Trevi (CH) *Piazza di Trevi.* Perhaps the best-known Roman fountain, and much visited by tourists. Built by Niccolò Salvi in 1732-51, and completed by Bracci in 1762 at the time of Clement XIII. The main group of sculptures is by Bracci, and the rest, including the reliefs, are by Filippo Valle, Andrea Bergondi, G.B. Grossi, and other 18th-century artists. 184, *212*, 217 ff.

Fontana del Tritone (DH) *Piazza Barberini.* A work of Bernini (1632-37) bearing the arms of the Barberini family. 181, 182, 184.

Foro Italico (AF) *Villa Farnesina.* Sports-ground constructed during the Fascist era, and subsequently enlarged. It contains the Stadio dei Marmi, the Stadio Olimpico, a swimming pool and a concert hall used by the RAI. 229.

Forum of Augustus (CI) *Via dei Fori Imperiali.* The temple of Mars Ultor originally stood here. 10, 14, 28.

Forum Boarium (CI) This is today the Piazza Bocca della Verità. It contains various Roman and medieval monuments. 9, 10, 36, 57, 228.

Forum of Caesar (CI) *Via dei Fori Imperiali.* 26, 27.

Forum of Nerva (CI) (also known as the **Transitorium**) *Via dei Fori Imperiali.* 27.

Forum Pacis (CI) (or **Forum of Vespasian**) *Via dei Fori Imperiali.* 27, 28.

Forum Romanum (Roman Forum) (CI) *Entrance in Via dei Fori Imperiali.* The best view of the forum is from the terrace of the Palazzo Senatorio on the Capitol. It provides the most evocative over-all view of the monuments of ancient Rome. 10, 13-15, 19-22, 22, 25, 26-7, 34, 82, 200.

Forum Ulpium (CI) *Via dei Fori Imperiali.* Built by Trajan and designed by Apollodorus of Damascus. 27.

Gesù (CI) *Piazza del Gesù.* This is the prototype of the Baroque churches of the Jesuits. Built between 1565 and 1578, it was designed by Vignola and Della Porta. The frescoes on the ceiling are by Baciccia. The right transept altar is by Pietro da Cortona (1678), and the altar-piece is by Batoni. The chapel of S. Ignazio is by Andrea Pozzo (1696-1700), paintings by Carlo Maratta and Federico Zuccari, sculpture by A. Raggi and F. Vacca. 149, 151, *201, 204.*

Gianicolo *see* **Janiculum.**

Isola Tiberina (CI) It is connected to the river banks by two bridges. The Ponte Fabricio, also called Ponte ai quattro Capi, is the oldest bridge in Rome. It was built by the consul Lucius Fabricius in 62 BC. The Ponte Cestio was put up in 46 BC but rebuilt in 1892. On the island are the churches of S. Bartolomeo and S. Giovanni Calibita, the hospital of the Fatebenefratelli, and the Caetani tower, formerly known as the Pierleoni tower. Recent research would suggest that it was on this island that the city of Rome first began to take shape. 15, *18*, 26.

Janiculum (AI) A hill in Rome, incorporated into the city at the time of the kings. It contains a number of important monuments. 11.

Lapis Niger (CI) *Forum Romanum.* Discovered in 1899, it was thought to be the tomb of Romulus. It probably marks the place which was sacred to the memory of Romulus already at the time of Julius Caesar.

Lateran Baptistry (EL) (also called **S. Giovanni in Fonte**) *Piazza S. Giovanni in Laterano.* Built by Constantine, re-modelled under Sixtus III in the first half of the 5th century, and by Urban VIII in 1637. Paintings and frescoes by Sacchi, Camassei, Gimignani, Cavalier d'Arpino and Maratta. In the adjacent chapels are early Christian mosaics, sculptures, and paintings by Reni and Sassoferrato. 56.

Lateran Palace, *see* **Palazzo Lateranense.**

Lupa capitolina (CI) *Musei Capitolini.* The wolf is a bronze of the 5th century BC and the two twins were added by Antonio, or possibly Piero del Pollaiuolo. *9, 108.*

Maddalena (CH) *Piazza Maddalena.* The architects were Fontana and De Rossi. The rococo façade is the work of Giuseppe Sardi. There is a fine 15th-century wood carving of the Magdalen, and paintings by Baciccia and Sebastiano Conca. 218.

Madonna dei Monti (DI) *Via dei Serpenti.* Giacomo della Porta's masterpiece. It contains 17th-century stuccoes and frescoes. 150.

Mamertine Prison, *see* **Carcer Mamertinus.**

Mausoleum of Augustus (CH) *Piazza Augusto Imperatore.* The burial place of Augustus and of members of the family of Julius and Claudius. After a long period of neglect and considerable alterations made in the Middle Ages and at later dates, it was finally restored in 1926. 16.

Mausoleum of Hadrian, *see* **Castel S. Angelo.**

Mint, *see* **Officina Carte-Valori.**

Monument to Eugene IV (BH) In the refectory at the church of S. Salvatore in Lauro. Built by Isaia da Pisa (1447) for St Peter's basilica, where it originally stood. A typical 15th-century Roman monument. 106.

Officina Carte-Valori *Largo Bastia, near via Tuscolana.* Built by Pier Luigi Nervi, decorated by contemporary artists, including Mario Ceroli. 230.

Oratorio dei Filippini (BH) *Piazza della Chiesa Nuova.* Next to the church of S. Maria in Vallicella (also called Chiesa Nuova). Built by Borromini between 1637 and 1650 with a typical concave brickwork façade. There are some ingenious ideas in the internal structure, especially in the two courtyards, the oval room, and the great staircase. 197, 198.

Oratorio del Gonfalone (BI) (correct title **S. Lucia del Gonfalone**) *Via Oratorio del Gonfalone, near via Giulia.* The façade has two orders, the upper one Baroque, and the lower one 16th-century. The decoration of the interior is in the Mannerist style, with frescoes by Federico Zuccari, Livio Agresti, Cesare Nebbia and Raffaellino da Reggio. Concerts are held in this building. 153.

Oratorio Mariano (DI) Connected to the church of S. Pudenziana (*q.v.*). Built between 1073 and 1085, it has some interesting frescoes. 73.

Ospedale di S. Gallicano *Via di S. Gallicano.* Built in 1722 by Filippo Raguzzini in a somewhat fanciful style. 214.

Ospizio di S. Michele (BL) *Lungotevere a Ripa.* Imposing architecture of Carlo Fontana, with later additions by Fuga. 212.

Palatine (CI) This is the hill that preserves the oldest memories of Rome; 50 metres above sea level, and 40 metres above the level of the Forum, its shape is trapezoid and its longest side is the one facing the Circus Maximus. It is in fact composed of three hills, the Palatine, the Cermalus and the Velia, but they were connected by buildings even before the Empire. There are still traces of prehistoric huts and other ruins of the 9th and 8th centuries BC. These were discovered in 1907 and 1949, in the vicinity of the Temple of the Magna Mater and the house of Livia. The Palatine was the Emperor's residence. 9, 10, 23, 26, 27, *28*, 83.

Palazzetto dello Sport (BF) *Near viale Tiziano.* Built in 1957 by Pier Luigi Nervi, in collaboration with the architect Annibale Vitellozzi. It holds 5,000 spectators, and is used for boxing tournaments. 229, *230*.

Palazzetto Zuccari (CH) *On the corner of via Sistina and via Gregoriana.* It gets its name from Federico Zuccari who built it as an Academy of Painting. Loggia facing Trinità dei Monti was added in 1711, possibly by Filippo Juvarra. It was once the residence of Maria Casimira Sobiesky, queen of Poland. It is now occupied by the Biblioteca Hertziana (*q.v.*).

Palazzina del Girasole (CF) *Viale Bruno Buozzi.* Built by Luigi Moretti between 1948 and 1950. One of the best examples of contemporary architecture in Rome. 229.

Palazzo Altemps (BH) *Via S. Apollinare.* Built in 1537 for Girolamo Riario, possibly by Peruzzi. It was completely altered by Martino Longhi il Vecchio. It has a simple façade, an elegant belvedere decorated with small obelisks, and a courtyard with loggias. It is occupied by the Spanish seminary. 217.

Palazzo Barberini (DH) *Via Quattro Fontane.* Begun in 1625 by Carlo Maderno, with the collaboration of Borromini. In 1633, G. Lorenzo Bernini was also working on the project. It is now occupied by the Galleria Nazionale d'Arte Antica, for which purpose it was acquired by the state in 1949. At the moment it is not possible to exhibit the whole collection, as the building is also used by other organizations. 130, 153, 198, 211.

Palazzo Braschi (BI) *Piazza S. Pantaleo.* Built after 1792 in neo-cinquecento style by Cosimo Morelli for relatives of Pius VI Braschi. It is the last of the Roman palaces to be built by a great papal family. It is now used by the Museo di Roma (*q.v.*). It is built on a trapezoid plan, and the main façade looks on to the via Pasquino. 195, 209, 217, 222.

Palazzo Cenci (CI) *On Monte Cenci.* A complex of buildings of different periods, occupying the site of the old residence of the Crescenzi. The earliest buildings are of the 16th century. It is a picturesque ensemble with a small 12th-century church dedicated to St Thomas, which was rebuilt in the 16th century. It was here that a painted cross was found, which has been attributed to the young Giotto.

Palazzo Cenci Bolognetti (CI) (formerly **Palazzo Petroni**) *Piazza del Gesù.* The façade is by Ferdinando Fuga. It is owned by the Università di Roma.

Palazzo Chigi (CH) *Piazza Colonna.* Begun by Carlo Maderno for the Aldobrandini family. Giacomo della Porta may have contributed to the design. It was completed by Felice della Greca. It came into the possession of the Chigi family in 1659. Since 1961 it has been occupied by the Consiglio dei Ministri. The façade is severe, but there is a fine Baroque courtyard. There are some magnificently decorated rooms but these are not open to the public. 148.

Palazzo Colonna (CH) *Piazza SS. Apostoli.* It dates back to Martin V Colonna (1417-31) but was rebuilt in 1730. The courtyard is large, and the doorways of monumental proportion. The Galleria Colonna (*q.v.*) occupies the part laid out by Antonio del Grande (1650-65). It was opened in 1703. 86, 209.

Palazzo Corsini (BI) *Via della Lungara.* On this spot Cardinal Riario, a nephew of Sixtus IV, built his residence in the 15th century. It was here that Christina of Sweden lived in the 17th century and founded the Academy which became the Arcadia. Entirely rebuilt by Ferdinando Fuga for the Corsini family between 1732 and 1736. Joseph Bonaparte lived here at the end of the 18th century. It was acquired by the state in 1883. It houses a section of the Galleria Nazionale di Arte antica (*q.v.*) and the Accademia dei Lincei. 88, 135, 162, 177, 187, 209, 217.

Palazzo dei Congressi, EUR. Built by Adalberto Libera in 1938. The central part is covered by a daring cross-vault resting on the four corners. 229, 232.

Palazzo dei Conservatori (CI) *Piazza del Campidoglio.* Built by Giacomo della Porta in 1568 to Michelangelo's design. The interior is particularly fine, and is decorated with magnificent works of art of various periods. The Sale dei Conservatori are used by the Comune di Roma. These give onto the Museo del Palazzo dei Conservatori. The Pinacoteca Capitolina is on the second floor*. 36, 74, 144, 195.

Palazzo del Quirinale (CH) *Piazza del Quirinale.* Designed as a summer residence for the popes, it was begun under Gregory XIII in 1574. Architects involved in the building were Mascherino, Domenico Fontana (who designed the courtyard and porticoes), Flaminio Ponzio, Carlo Maderno (who built the main doorway and the Cappella Paolina), Bernini and Fuga. It was occupied by the popes from 1592 to 1870, when it passed to the State. It is now used by the President of the Republic. Some of the apartments are open to the public. Among the frescoes and paintings are works by Melozzo da Forlì (from the church of SS. Apostoli),

Lanfranco, Saraceni, and Reni. Some of the tapestries are after cartoons of Jordaens, and there is some fine furniture. There are also large gardens within the palace.

Palazzo della Cancelleria (BI) *Piazza della Cancelleria.* Built between 1489 and 1517 originally for Cardinal Scarampo Mezzarota. It was then acquired by Cardinal Raffaele Riario to house his valuable collection of classical works, which is now in the Vatican. It has elegant façade and a great courtyard of pleasing design. Frescoes by Vasari, Perin del Vaga and Salviati. The church of S. Lorenzo in Damaso (*q.v.*) is built into it. 30, 88, *147*, 214.

Palazzo della Civiltà del Lavoro, EUR. Built in 1938 by Guerrini, La Padula and Romano. The plan is square, with six orders of arcades on each side, making a total of 216. 229.

Palazzo della Consulta (CH) *Piazza del Quirinale.* Built by Ferdinando Fuga under Clement XII (1732-34) for the Tribunale della Sacra Consulta. Now occupied by the Corte Costituzionale. 217.

Palazzo delle Esposizioni (DH) *Via Nazionale.* Erected in 1878-82 and designed by Pio Piacentini for art exhibitions. It houses the Galleria Comunale d'Arte moderna. 228.

Palazzo dello Sport, EUR. Built 1960 by Pier Luigi Nervi and Marcello Piacentini. Nervi is responsible for the powerful structure of the building, which is one of his best. It holds 15,000 spectators. It used for theatrical as well as sporting events, also for congresses.

Palazzo di Giustizia (BH) *Piazza Cavour.* Built between 1889 and 1910 by Guglielmo Calderini. The offices had to be evacuated in 1970 on account of serious structural damage. 228.

Palazzo di Montecitorio (CH) *Piazza di Montecitorio.* Begun in 1650 by Bernini for Innocent X, and completed in 1694 by Carlo Fontana. Since 1871 it has been the seat of the Camera dei Deputati. Enlarged between 1903 and 1925 by Ernesto Basile who built the hall with the allegorical frieze by Sartorio, and the back of the building in Piazza del Parlamento. 228.

Palazzo Doria Pamphilj (CI) *On the Corso.* Founded by the cardinals of the old diaconia di S. Maria in via Lata in the 15th century. The Della Rovere family built their residence here, and later the Aldobrandini and the Pamphilj, whose line merged into

* US third floor.

the Doria family. The rococo façade on the Corso was put up by Gabriele Valvassori in 1734. The façade on via del Plebiscito is by Paolo Aureli (1643) and the one on the Piazza del Collegio Romano is by Antonio del Grande. The façade on via della Gatta and piazza Grazioli is of the 19th century. There is a fine 16th century courtyard after the style of Bramante with a portico and open gallery. The palace houses the Galleria Doria Pamphilj (q.v.). 86, 191 ff.

Palazzo Farnese (BI) *Piazza Farnese.* Begun by Antonio da Sangallo il Giovane in 1514 for Cardinal Alessandro Farnese, later Paul III. Continued by Michelangelo in 1546, and completed by Giacomo della Porta. The entrance hall, and the main and side façades are by Antonio da Sangallo. The great cornice and the central balcony are by Michelangelo, also the second and third orders of the courtyard. Giacomo della Porta designed the back of the building, facing on via Giulia. Frescoes by Annibale and Agostino Carracci, Domenichino and Lanfranco. It is one of the great settings of Renaissance art, and is now the French Embassy. 30, 145, 149, 153, *159.*

Palazzo Fiano (or **Almagià**) (CH) *On the Corso, between via in Lucina and Piazza S. Lorenzo in Lucina.* Built on the ruins of the Ara Pacis Augustae (q.v.), fragments of which were discovered in the 15th century. It was rebuilt in the 19th century. 18.

Palazzo Lateranense (EL) *Piazza S. Giovanni in Laterano.* The Lateran was the residence of the popes from the time of Constantine until the move to Avignon. The present building was designed by Domenico Fontana for Sixtus V in 1586. The Lateran Museum has now been transferred to the Vatican. 34, 137, 226.

Palazzo Odescalchi (CH) *Piazza SS. Apostoli.* This palace has belonged to the Colonna, the Ludovisi and the Chigi families. Designed by Bernini and begun in 1664, it was continued by Nicola Salvi and Luigi Vanvitelli in 1750. The courtyard and portico, *c.* 1623, are by Carlo Maderno. It contains the Odescalchi collection, which is not open to the public. The side facing the Corso is modern.

Palazzo Pallavicini-Rospigliosi (CH) *Via 24 maggio.* Built for Scipione Borghese by Giovanni Vasanzio between 1611 and 1616 on the ruins of the Baths of Constantine. It belonged to Cardinal Mazarin. The Casino Pallavicini in the precincts has a ceiling fresco of Aurora painted by Guido Reni in 1614. Paintings by Antonio Tempesti and Paolo Brill. The palace contains the Galleria Pallavicini, which is not normally open to the public but permission is granted to students. It is a fine collection in which various European schools are represented. In the garden there is a loggia with frescoes by Gentileschi and Tassi, and a *Teatro d'acqua* probably designed by Vasanzio. 159, 204, 209.

Palazzo Pamphilj (BH) *Piazza Navona.* Built between 1644 and 1650 by Girolamo Rainaldi for Innocent X, who presented it to his sister-in-law, Olimpia Maidalchini. There is a large fresco of Turnus and Aeneas painted by Pietro da Cortona between 1651 and 1654. The palace is now the Brazilian Embassy and can be visited on request. 184 ff., 207.

Palazzo Ricci (BI) *Piazza de' Ricci.* The façade is attributed to Nanni di Baccio Bigio. There are traces of designs for decoration by Maturino da Firenze and Polidoro da Caravaggio. 148, 155.

Palazzo Sacchetti (BI) *Via Giulia, 66.* Built *c.* 1555 by Nanni di Baccio Bigio for Cardinal Ricci di Montepulciano with a fine garden courtyard with sculptures, and a frescoed room on the first floor* by Francesco Salviati. 154.

Palazzo Salviati (CI) *Corso 271, near Piazza Venezia.* Baroque façade of 1691, designed by Carlo Rainaldi. Built by the Duke of Nevers, nephew of Cardinal Mazarin. Acquired by Louis XV for the French Academy, which was later moved to the Villa Medici. It has belonged at different times to the Grand Duke of Tuscany, Louis Bonaparte, and the Salviati and Aldobrandini families. It is now used by the Banco di Sicilia.

Palazzo Sforza Cesarini (BI) *Piazza Sforza Cesarini.* Built by Alexander VI Borgia between 1460 and 1465. Considerably altered in 1888 by Pio Piacentini. The remains of the 15th-century courtyard are visible in the entrance hall. 88.

Palazzo Spada (BI) *Piazza Capodiferro.* Built *c.* 1540 by Giulio Merisi for Cardinal Girolamo Capo di Ferro. Later it passed to Cardinal Spada. Stuccoes by Giulio Mazzoni on the façade and in the courtyard, which also contains antique sculpture. Borromini built alongside the courtyard a row of columns to give the impression of a gallery. The building is occupied by the Galleria Spada and the Consiglio di Stato. 149, 198.

* US second floor.

Palazzo Venezia (CI) *Piazza Venezia.* Begun in 1455 by Cardinal Pietro Barbo (later Paul II) and completed by his nephew, Marco Barbo. It was original called the Palazzo di San Marco. It was a papal residence until 1564, when it passed to the Venetian Republic. It was occupied by the Venetian ambassadors and by the titular cardinal of the nearby basilica of S. Marco. It belonged to Austria from 1797 to 1916. It is now used as a museum. The architect is unknown. 30, 86, *146, 193.*

Pantheon (CH) *Piazza Pantheon.* Erected in 27 BC by Marcus Agrippa, son-in-law of Augustus, when he was Consul for the third time, as the Latin inscription on the pediment tells us. The inscription dates from the reconstruction under Hadrian, the building having burned down at the time of Domitian. Restored also by Septimius Severus and Caracalla. It is the best preserved of all our classical monuments. Originally dedicated to the seven planetary gods, in AD 609 Boniface IV consecrated the building as S. Maria ad Martyres. It was restored in various ways during the Renaissance, and in the Baroque period the bronze plates of the portico were removed and used for the baldacchino in St Peter's. This gave rise to the pasquinade: 'Quod non fecerunt Barbari, fecerunt Barberini'. The Pantheon consists of a single cell built on a circular plan, and a pronaos with sixteen monolithic granite columns surmounted by a triangular pediment. The interior is harmoniously proportioned with a vast coffered dome open to the sky in the centre. There are a number of works of art in the building, and tombs of artists (Raphael, Peruzzi, Taddeo Zuccari, Perin del Vaga, Flaminio Vacca) and kings of Italy. There is an important collection of records in the Accademia dei Virtuosi del Pantheon adjoining the building. 15, 16, *28,* 53, 56, 130, 177, 206.

Piazza Barberini (DH) Bernini's Fontana del Tritone is in the centre of the piazza, and his Fontana delle Api at the entrance to the via Veneto. The back of the Palazzo Barberini is visible on the south side. 181, 182.

Piazza Campitelli (CI) The church of S. Maria in Campitelli, Rainaldi's masterpiece, is on one side, and on the other the palazzi Spinola and Capizucchi, both built by Giacomo della Porta. He also designed the fountain on the way to via Montanara, where the Palazzetto di Flaminio Ponzio has been reconstructed. This was built in 1600 in somewhat whimsical style. 201.

Piazza Colonna (CH) The traditional centre of Rome. The column of Marcus Aurelius (*q.v.*) stands in the centre, surmounted by a bronze statue of St Paul. On the north side is the Palazzo Chigi, on the east side the Galleria Colonna, and to the south the chiesetta di S. Maria della Pietà (1735) the façade of which is by Valvassori. On the west side is the Palazzo Wedekind (1735), built by Pietro Camporese il Giovane. The fountain in the centre, recently installed, was built by Giacomo della Porta in 1575.

Piazza dei Cavalieri di Malta (CL) *On the Aventine.* A remarkable urban lay-out designed by G. B. Piranesi. The piazza gives access to a garden, in which stands the church of S. Maria del Priorato, also designed by Piranesi. 220.

Piazza del Collegio Romano (CH) The north façade of the Palazzo Doria Pamphilj overlooks two sides of the piazza. The Collegio Romano stands opposite. At the other corner stands the 17th-century church of S. Marta with the building alongside it which used to be a convent, both designed by Valadier. 191.

Piazza del Popolo (CG) An urban lay-out of Giuseppe Valadier, the first project of which is of 1784, although it was already determined by the surrounding Baroque architecture. It continues to the end of Via del Babuino, Via del Corso, and Via di Ripetta, and includes the twin churches of S. Maria di Montesanto and S. Maria dei Miracoli. The Porta del Popolo stands on the north side (façade by Bernini) with the church of S. Maria del Popolo alongside. The Flaminian obelisk was installed in the centre of the piazza by Domenico Fontana at the orders of Sixtus V in 1589. It came from Heliopolis during the reign of Augustus, and was destined for the Circus Maximus. The base of the obelisk, with the basins and the lions, is also by Valadier (1823). 148, 201, 223, 225, 232.

Piazza del Quirinale (CH) Open to one side on a wide panorama of the city, and dominated on the north-west by the Palazzo del Quirinale. Fuga's Palazzo della Consulta stands opposite, followed by the Palazzo Pallavicini-Rospigliosi. The colossal *Dioscuri* in the centre are Roman copies of Greek originals of the 5th-century BC. They stand beside an obelisk that was once in the Mausoleum of Augustus. 148, 217.

Piazza dell'Esedra (DH) now known as **Piazza della Repubblica** The exedra was constructed by Gaetano Koch after 1870, following the form of Diocletian's baths. In the centre is the Fontana delle Naiadi of Rutelli (1885) which utilizes the Acqua Marcia. The church of S. Maria degli Angeli (*q.v.*) stands opposite the piazza. 228, *237*.

Piazza di S. Maria in Trastevere (BI) Centre of the working-class quarter. The fountain is by Carlo Fontana, who is also responsible for the portico of the basilica of S. Maria in Trastevere, which has 13th-century mosaics on the upper part of the façade. Near the church is the 17th-century Palazzo di S. Callisto. *113*.

Piazza Navona (BH) This piazza faithfully preserves the outline of Domitian's Stadium. It is one of the most essentially Baroque localities in Rome. In the centre stands Bernini's Fontana dei Fiumi. The other two fountains are the Fontana del Moro, designed by Giovanni Antonio Mari in 1655 on a sketch by Bernini, and the Fontana del Nettuno, modelled on its companion in 1873, and incorporating a basin by Giacomo della Porta. On the west side is the church of S. Agnese in Agone, a name which reminds us of the games which took place in the stadium, and which has been corrupted into 'Navona'. The church was begun by Girolamo and Carlo Rainaldi, and completed by Borromini. Rainaldi was also the architect of the Palazzo Pamphilj alongside the church. On the south side of the piazza are the Palazzi Lancellotti and Braschi. Opposite Palazzo Pamphilj is S. Maria della Concezione, with its Renaissance façade. 64, *180-81*, 184, 186, 193, 217.

Piazza Pasquino (BI) So-called from the mutilated Hellenistic statue called Pasquino by the townsfolk. Pasquino was in fact a hunchbacked tailor who worked in this locality in the 15th century and was famous for his sharp and scurrilous wit. It was the custom to post satirical writings on the statue, on political and social questions, so that Pasquino became the most famous of the 'talking statues'.

Piazza S. Ignazio (CH) On one side is the imposing façade of the church of S. Ignazio, built by the Jesuit Orazio Grassi, possibly on designs by Algardi. Filippo Raguzzini designed the lay-out of the other side of the square in 1727. 213.

Piazza S. Marco (CI) It takes its name from the basilica that faces it,

at right angles with the Palazzetto Venezia. On the corner there is a somewhat disfigured marble bust of a woman, known as Madama Lucrezia. This is another of the 'talking statues'.

Piazza S. Pietro (AH) 62, 113, 147. 193.

Piazza SS. Apostoli (CI) This contains the church of the SS. Apostoli, the front of the Palazzo Colonna, and facing it the Palazzo Odescalchi with its long façade, begun by Bernini and enlarged by Salvi and Vanvitelli.

Piazza Venezia (CI) Dominated by the aggressively white monument to Vittorio Emanuele (*q.v.*), it has the severe and noble façade of the Palazzo Venezia on its west side. Facing it is a rather cold imitation of it, the Palazzo delle Assicurazioni Generali, built in 1911, on the site originally occupied by the Palazzo Torlonia. On the side of the Palazzo delle Assicurazioni is a tablet commemorating the house, now demolished, where Michelangelo died on 18 February 1564. On the left corner, between the piazza and the Corso, stands the Palazzo Bonaparte, built by Giovanni Antonio de' Rossi in 1660. It was here that Napoleon's mother, Letizia Ramolino, lived. 13, 27 ff., 86, *145*, 228.

Pincio (CG) *Approached through the Villa Borghese, or from Trinità dei Monti.* This large public park was laid out by Valadier and French gardener-architects between 1809 and 1814. It was originally the site of villas and gardens belonging to a number of families, including the Pinci—thus the name. The Casina Valadier is now a restaurant. From the terrace of the Pincio one has a view of the city comparable to those from the Janiculum and Monte Mario. 147, 149, 224 ff., *225*.

Ponte Milvio (also called **Ponte Mollo**) *Piazzale Ponte Milvio.* This is the ancient Pons Milvius, reconstructed by the censor Marcus Emilius Scaurus in the 2nd century BC and restored in the 15th century by Nicholas V, who had the tower added. Valadier worked on it in 1805, and it was partially destroyed by Garibaldi in 1849. In 1850 it was restored by Pius IX. The four central arcades are of the original structure. Not far from this bridge, at the 'saxa rubra' (13 km. along the via Flaminia), Constantine won his victory over Maxentius in 312 ('in hoc signo vinces'), which meant the triumph of Christianity. 36, 148, 224.

Porta del Popolo (CG) *Piazza del Popolo.* The old Flaminian gate, of which the outside façade was reconstructed in the time of Pius IV (1562-65) and decorated with sculptures by Francesco Mochi (1638). The inner façade was done by Bernini in 1655, in honour of the arrival of Christina of Sweden, as the inscription points out. The side arches were opened up in 1879. 190, 193, 221.

Porta Pia (DH) *At the far end of via 20 Settembre.* Erected by order of Pius IV, this is Michelangelo's last architectural work (1561-64). The upper part, already damaged at the end of the 16th century and later struck by lightning, was rebuilt in 1853 by Virginio Vespignani, who is also responsible for the façade on via Nomentana. 145, 226.

Porta S. Paolo *Piazzale Ostiense.* This is the old Porta Ostiense. The part facing the city dates back to the time of Aurelian (3rd century). The aedicule is medieval. The other side of it is of the time of Honorius (5th century). The Museo della via Ostiense (*q.v.*) is housed here, and shows the history of the via Ostiense and the port of Rome. At this point there is a very well preserved portion of the Aurelian wall. 30, 149.

Porta S. Sebastiano *Via di Porta S. Sebastiano.* The old Porta Appia was rebuilt in the 5th century, and restored in the 6th with two crenellated towers. It is preceded by a triumphal arch, called the arch of Drusus but in fact of the 2nd century. The Porta S. Sebastiano houses the interesting Museo delle Mura romane. A little further on is the rampart built by Antonio da Sangallo il Giovane, and the Aurelian wall. *111*, 149.

Porta Settimiana (BI) *Via della Lungara.* Opened by Alexander VI, on the site of an old postern gate of the Aurelian wall. 198.

Portico of Octavia (CI) *Via Portico di Ottavia.* Erected by Quintus Metellus in 149 BC, it was rebuilt by Augustus in 23 BC, and dedicated to his sister Octavia. It was later restored by Septimius Severus and Caracalla. There are still traces of a public walk which had a double row of columns and statuary, temples and libraries. The remains of the building now form the atrium of the church of S. Angelo in Pescheria (8th century, but restored). Within the portico is the old Jewish quarter, still mainly occupied by the Jewish community who have their synagogue nearby. 16.

Porto di Ripetta (BG) This was originally on the bank of the Tiber, beneath the Palazzo Borghese: It was built by Alessandro Specchi for Clement XI, but it was demolished after 1870. The modern ramps and steps near ponte Matteotti give a slight idea of what it must have looked like.

Pyramid of Caius Cestius *Outside Porta S. Paolo, near a long stretch of the Aurelian wall.* It is a funeral monument to the Praetor Caius Cestius Epulo, who died in 12 BC. The revetment is of lunense marble and the base is of travertine. The inscription on it records the fact that it was built in 330 days. 30, 226.

Roman Forum, *see* **Forum Romanum.**

S. Agnese in Agone (BH) *Piazza Navona.* Begun by G. and C. Rainaldi in 1652, it was completed by Borromini, Antonio del Grande and G.M. Baratta in 1657. Frescoes by Ciro Ferri in the dome and by Baciccia on the walls. Large marble reliefs on the seven altars by Ferrata, Raggi, Cafà, Campi, etc. In the crypt there is a relief by Algardi which was his last work. 184, 186, 198.

S. Agnese fuori le Mura (EG) *Via Nomentana.* Built in 342 by Constantia, the daughter of Constantine, over the catacombs of the saint. Rebuilt in the 7th, 8th, 9th and 11th centuries. The mosaic in the apse is of the time of Honorius I (625-38) and is one of the finest examples of Byzantine art in Rome. It shows St Agnes with the Popes Symmachus and Honorius (with a model of the church). Sculptures by Bregno and Cordier (?). 57.

S. Agostino (BH) *Piazza S. Agostino.* Built by Giacomo da Pietrasanta (1479-83). The interior was re-modelled by Vanvitelli in 1760, and decorated by Gagliardi in 1856. The marble sculpture of the Madonna del Parto is by Jacopo Sansovino (1521). Fresco of the prophet Isaiah by Raphael (1512). *Madonna dei Pellegrini* by Caravaggio (1605). High altar by Bernini. Other works by Andrea Sansovino, Guercino, Lanfranco, Cafà, Ferrata, Isaia da Pisa, A. Gramatica, etc. 132, 166.

S. Andrea delle Fratte (CH) In the 15th century this was the national church of the Scots. Completely rebuilt in 1612 by Gaspare Guerra, it was continued from 1653 to 1655 by Borromini, who is responsible for the apse, the cupola, and the elegant campanile. The façade is 19th century. Sculptures by Bernini (two angels at the sides of the apse), Bracci,

Queirolo (1752), and paintings by Cozza, Lazzaro Baldi, W. Schadow, etc. Next to the church, there is the house (12 via della Mercede) where Bernini lived and died. There is an inscription and a bust on the front of the house. 194, 198, 226.

S. Andrea al Quirinale (CH) Built by G.L. Bernini for Camillo Pamphilj, 1658-71. Paintings by Baciccia, Maratta, Giacinto Brandi, and Borgognone. Sculptures by Raggi. *183*, 194.

S. Andrea della Valle (BI) *Piazza S. Andrea della Valle.* Begun in 1581 by G. della Porta and P. Francesco Grimaldi, it was taken over by Maderno in 1608, who erected the dome (1622-25). Rainaldi built the façade (1655-65). See p. 207 for a description of the sumptuous Baroque interior, which is rich in works of art. 195, 201, *205*, 206 ff.

S. Antonio dei Portoghesi (CH) *Via dei Portoghesi.* The national church of the Portuguese, begun by Martino Longhi il Giovane, continued by Rainaldi, and completed by Cristoforo Schor in 1695. Paintings by Antoniazzo Romano (15th century and Giacinto Calandrucci (1646-1707). Sculptures by Bracci and Canova (Souza monument, 1806-08). 223.

S. Atanasio dei Greci (CH) *Via del Babuino* (a street famous for its antique shops). Greek catholic church. The twin campanili and façade are by Giacomo della Porta (1580-83). 150.

S. Benedetto in Piscinula (BI) *Piazza in Piscinula, Trastevere.* Paintings and frescoes of the 13th to 16th centuries. A small Romanesque campanile and the saint's vaulted cell are attached. 64.

S. Carlo alle Quattro Fontane (DH) (also known as **S. Carlino**) *Via del Quirinale.* Borromini's masterpiece, built in 1638. The façade was added in 1667. Sculptures by Raggi on the porch. The cloister is attached to the church. There is a painting by Borgianni in the sacristy. 197.

S. Carlo ai Catinari (CI) *Piazza Cairoli.* Built by Rosati and Soria (1612-38), it has a fine Baroque cupola. Frescoes by Domenichino, Reni, Gemignani, Gregorio and Mattia Preti, and Gherardi. Paintings by Sacchi, Lanfranco, Pietro da Cortona. Also a bronze crucifix by Algardi. 207.

S. Cecilia in Trastevere (CL) *Piazza S. Cecilia in Trastevere.* The old basilica was built before the 5th century, and has often been restored and transformed, so that the interior

is now a collection of varied styles. There is a large atrium with an antique basin in the centre. The façade and monumental front are by Fuga (1725). 49, 58, 74, 78, 86, *120*, *128*.

S. Cesareo *Via Appia Antica.* An Early Christian building, re-modelled at the end of the 16th century, possibly by Giacomo della Porta. Third-century mosaic floor in the crypt. Frescoes, mosaics and Cosmatesque sculpture. The apse contains paintings by Cavalier d'Arpino.

S. Clemente (DI) *Piazza S. Clemente (Laterano).* Two churches, an upper and a lower, of the 12th and 5th centuries respectively. Important medieval frescoes (8th - 12th centuries) in the lower church. Twelfth-century mosaic of the triumph of the cross in the upper church; also frescoes of the 14th century. The Cappella di S. Caterina contains frescoes by Masolino and Masaccio. Paintings by Sassoferrato, Pier Leone Ghezzi and Conca, and Renaissance sculpture. 59, 73, 80-81.

S. Costanza (EG) *Near via Nomentana.* Originally the imperial mausoleum for Constantine's daughters, it was turned into a church in the 13th century. Fifth-century mosaics in the ambulatory. There is a copy of the original porphyry sarcophagus, now in the Vatican. 56.

S. Eligio degli Orefici (BI) *Via di S. Eligio.* Designed by Raphael, and built in 1509. Façade by Flaminio Ponzio (1602). The interior is of great architectural interest and there are frescoes of the 17th century. 112.

S. Francesco a Ripa (BL) *Piazza S. Francesco d'Assisi, Trastevere.* A 13th-century foundation, it was rebuilt by Matteo de Rossi (1682-89). Paintings by Salviati, Vouet, Baciccia. Sculptures by Bernini (*Beata Ludovica Albertoni*), Rusconi, Ferrata and Mazzuoli. In the adjoining Santuario di S. Francesco there is a painting of the 13th century. 194.

S. Francesca Romana (DI) (also known as **S. Maria Nova,** as opposed to S. Maria Antiqua) *Near the basilica of Maxentius.* Of medieval origin, with a mosaic in the apse *c.* 1160. Façade by Carlo Lombardi (1615). An icon, which was discovered beneath the 12th-century icon on the high altar, is kept in the sacristy. Paintings and sculptures of the 17th and 18th centuries. Tomb of Gentile da Fabriano. Romanesque campanile. The monastery attached to the church was restored by Valadier. *38*, 64, 224.

S. Giacomo degli Spagnoli (or Our Lady of the Sacred Heart) (BH) *Piazza Navona.* Renaissance façade (contemporary sculpture by Paolo Taccone). In the interior, 15th-century choir. Chapel after a design by Antonio da Sangallo the Younger. 184.

S. Giorgio in Velabro (CH) *Piazza Bocca della Verità.* On a paleo-Christian foundation, reconstructed in the 7th century, restored in 1926. Velabrum is the point in the river where, according to legend, the Wolf nursed Romulus and Remus. Twelfth-century bell-tower. Medieval frescoes and sculptures in the interior. 35, 64.

S. Giovanni Calibita (CI) On the island in the Tiber, connected with the Hospital of the Fatebenefratelli, 1640-1711. Frescoes and canvases by Corrado Giaquinto. A painting by Mattia Preti. 207.

S. Giovanni Decollato (CI) *Via S. Giovanni Decollato.* Connected with the Oratorio della Confraternita della Misericordia for the assistance of those condemned to death. Completed in 1552. Paintings by Vasari and Pomarancio. Manneristic frescoes in the Oratorio (Salviati, Jacopino dal Conte — one of his altarpieces, with *The Deposition,* on the altar — Pirro Ligorio and Battista Franco). 153.

S. Giovanni dei Fiorentini (BH) *Near the Lungotevere dei Fiorentini.* National church of the Florentines, erected by Leo X. Architects Jacopo Sansovino, Antonio da Sangallo the Younger, Giacomo della Porta, Maderno (*c.* 1515-1614). Façade by Galilei (1734) with sculpture by Valle and Bracci. Michelangelo also designed projects for the church. Borromini collaborated on the interior; he and Maderno are buried there. Numerous works of art: paintings by Santi di Tito, Cigoli, Lanfranco, sculpture by Michelangelo (?) and the Baroque artists Bernini, E. Ferrata and A. Raggi, and a funerary monument by Fuga. 136, 145, 195.

S. Giovanni in Laterano (St John Lateran) (EL) *Piazza di S. Giovanni.* One of the four patriarchal basilicas and cathedral of Rome. First built in the time of Constantine, it has often been damaged and restored. Completely rebuilt by Borromini in 1650. The façade on piazzale di porta S. Giovanni is by Galilei, and the one on piazza S. Giovanni is by Fontana. The bronze doors are from the Curia in the Roman Forum. 4th-century pavement, 16th-century ceiling, stuccoes by Algardi, medieval, Renaissance and Baroque sculpture, and many paintings, including a Giot-

tesque fragment. 12th-century cloister. The chapels contain works of art of many different periods. 26, 52, 54, 73 ff., 80, 149, 198, *206*, 212, 217.

S. Giovanni a Porta Latina *Via S. Giovanni a Porta Latina.* On a paleo-Christian foundation (5th-century); rebuilt and expanded in the Middle Ages. Important frescoes, *c.* 1191, in the central nave; others in the apse. Polychrome marble pavement also of the 12th century. Romanesque bell-tower. 73.

S. Gregorio Magno (DL) *Piazza S. Gregorio (on the Celian hill).* Founded in the early Middle Ages, and renovated in the 17th and 18th centuries by G.B. Soria and Francesco Ferrari. The façade is by Soria. In the atrium are funereal monuments of the 16th and 17th centuries. The chapel of S. Andrea, by Flaminio Ponzio, has frescoes by Reni and Domenichino. The chapel of S. Silvia has a fresco by Reni and sculpture by Cordier. In the chapel of S. Barbara, which has frescoes by Viviani, there is a sculpture by Cordier. 204.

S. Ignazio (CH) *Piazza S. Ignazio.* Designed by Maderno, Orazio Grassi and possibly Algardi (the façade), it was built between 1626 and 1650. The sculptured decoration of the interior is by Algardi. Andrea Pozzo painted the frescoes on the ceiling, in the apse and the right transept, and the imitation cupola. This is a painting on canvas to make up for the absence of a real dome. Other sculptures in the chapels and on the altars are by Le Gros, Valle, Bracci, Rusconi, and Monnot. 204.

S. Ivo alla Sapienza (BH) *In the courtyard of the Palazzo della Sapienza, in Corso Rinascimento.* A fine work of Borromini, typical of his agitated style (especially the spiral form of cupola and lantern) and with an unexpected quality about the interior. On the altar there is a large picture by Pietro da Cortona and his assistants. *195,* 198.

S. Lorenzo in Damaso (BI) *Piazza della Cancelleria.* Incorporated into the palace of Cardinal Riario (Palazzo della Cancelleria). An Early Christian church, it was completely rebuilt at the end of the 15th century, and restored by Valadier. Frescoes by Corrado Giaquinto (*c.* 1735), paintings by Federico Zuccari and Sebastiano Conca. Sculptures by Stefano Maderno (S. Carlo Borromeo) and Tenerani (1854). 88, 224.

S. Lorenzo fuori le Mura *Piazzale del Verano.* Two early Christian churches have been combined in this building, one of the 4th and the other of the 5th century, and they had both been altered several times before they were joined together. The building was bombed in 1943, and after careful restoration, it was re-opened in 1949. The campanile is Romanesque. The portico, by Vassalletto, is of the 13th century. The interior is divided into three aisles, with ambos, a Cosmatesque candelabrum, and a canopy which is the work of the Roman masons, Pietro, Augusto and Sassone di Paolo (1148). The bishop's throne is of the 13th century. There is a mosaic on the inner side of the triumphal arch (originally meant to correspond with the front of the presbytery). There are catacombs, and a Romanesque cloister. 56, 69, 149.

S. Lorenzo in Lucina (CH) *Piazza S. Lorenzo in Lucina.* First built in the 5th century, it was rebuilt in the 12th and altered by Cosimo Fanzago *c.* 1650. The campanile and the porch with its lions are of the 12th century. Monument to Nicolas Poussin (1829). A painting of the Crucifixion by Guido Reni. A chapel and a bust by Bernini. Paintings in the chapels by Simon Vouet and Carlo Saraceni. 64.

S. Luigi dei Francesi (BH) *Piazza S. Luigi dei Francesi.* The building was begun in 1518, and taken over by Domenico Fontana in 1580. It is the French national church. The façade is possibly by Giacomo della Porta, with 18th-century sculpture. The stucco decoration of the interior is by Dérizet (1756-64). Ceiling fresco of the same period by Natoire. In the second chapel on the right, frescoes by Domenichino, and Guido Reni's *Santa Cecilia,* after Raphael. Over the high altar, a painting of the Assumption by Francesco Bassano. Caravaggio's three paintings of episodes from the life of St Matthew are in the Cappella Contarelli (or Cointrel), the fifth on the left. On the ceiling of this chapel there is a fresco by Cavalier d'Arpino. There is a monument to Claude Lorraine (1836) by Lemoyne. 108, 150, 162, 197.

S. Marco (CI) *Piazza S. Marco.* Founded in the 4th century, it was restored in the 8th, the 9th (the mosaics of the apse and the triumphal arch are of this period), the 15th (when it was annexed to the Palazzo Venezia, and so became the Venetian church), and again between 1740 and 1750. Its elegant Renaissance façade is of uncertain authorship. It has been attributed to Alberti. Campanile is Romanesque. The wooden ceiling is richly carved and gilded. Paintings by Melozzo da Forlì, Palma il Giovane, and Maratta. Sculptures by Isaia da Pisa, Mino da Fiesole, Cosimo Fancelli, Raggi and Canova. 86, 223.

S. Maria degli Angeli (DH) *Piazza dell'Esedra.* Designed by Michelangelo (1563-66) and utilizing the Tepidarium of the Baths of Diocletian, the church was re-modelled by Vanvitelli (1749). It has no true façade, its entrance being part of an exedra of the baths. Paintings by Daniele da Volterra, Maratta, Baglioni, Trevisani, Subleyras, Batoni, Costanzi and a fresco of St Peter by Domenichino. Sculptures by Houdon (S. Bruno) and Tenerani, and monuments. 32, 145.

S. Maria Antiqua (CI) *Roman Forum.* Founded possibly in the 5th century, this is another imperial building transformed into a church. Restored and decorated with frescoes by Popes John VII (705-07), Zachariah (741-52) and Paul I (757-67), it was abandoned in the second half of the 10th century for S. Maria Nova (otherwise known as S. Francesca Romana, *q.v.*). Restored in 1902. It consists of vestibule, atrium, narthex, and a nave divided into three, with presbytery, apse, and two side chapels. Mural paintings in three layers. 26.

S. Maria d'Aracœli (CI) *At the top of the steps, in Piazza S. Maria d'Aracœli, near the Campidoglio.* It stands on the site where the sibyl predicted the birth of Christ to Augustus. Early Christian, rebuilt by the Benedictines in the 13th century in Romanesque and Gothic styles. In the Middle Ages it became a rallying point of civil liberty. The marble staircase of 122 steps was put up in 1348 at the people's wish. The interior is divided into three, with columns from classical buildings, and it contains sculpture by Donatello, Andrea Bregno, the school of Michelangelo, and Sansovino. The Cappella Bufalini (S. Bernardino), the first on the right, has frescoes by Pinturicchio (*c.* 1485). 74, 78, 80, 82, 86, *127*, 137, 145.

S. Maria in Campitelli (CI) *Piazza Campitelli.* Commissioned by Alexander VII, and built by Rainaldi (1662-67), this is a masterpiece of Baroque. The magnificent interior has interesting perspective effects. There are paintings by Luca Giordano, Baciccia, Passeri, Conca, and sculptures by Melchiorre Cafà and Mazzuoli. The tabernacle on the high altar, by Cafà (1667), has a 13th-century French type enamel of the Virgin which was at one time in the Portico of Octavia. 201, *219*.

S. Maria in Cappella (CI) *Via dei Genovesi, in Trastevere.* Consecrated in 1090, it was completely restored in 1875. It has a simple brick façade and a Romanesque campanile. The columns are antique, in marble and granite, with Corinthian capitals. 64.

S. Maria della Concezione (DH) (or **S. Maria dei Cappuccini**) *Via Veneto.* Built in 1626 by Antonio Casoni for the Capuchin brother of Urban VIII. Paintings by Reni, Lanfranco, Domenichino, Gherardo delle Notti, Andrea Sacchi, Pietro da Cortona and Camassei. Sculptures by Rusconi. In the sacristy, a painting of St Francis at prayer attributed to Caravaggio, another version of which is in the church of S. Pietro at Carpineto Romano (76 km. from Rome). There are underground chapels with a macabre decoration of skulls and bones.

S. Maria in Cosmedin (CI) *Piazza Bocca della Verità.* Built in the 6th century, and enlarged in the 8th, when it acquired its present title on account of being used by the Greeks (*cosmedini* = ornament). Remodelled in the 9th and 12th centuries, and restored in 1899 to its 8th-century design, with a few of the 12th-century additions left. The Romanesque campanile is 12th century. The interior is divided by columns into a tripartite nave. Cosmatesque marble work in the iconostasis, the ambo, the throne, the candelabrum, and the canopy over the altar, signed by Deodato, 1294. Cosmatesque floor of *opus alexandrinum.* Crypt and museum attached. 36, 57, 64, *129, 130*.

S. Maria in Domnica (DL) *Piazza della Navicella.* An Early Christian church, enlarged by Paschal I (817-24), rebuilt at the beginning of the 16th century, and restored in 1820. Renaissance façade by A. Sansovino (1513-14). 9th-century mosaics in the apse, and a fresco frieze by Perin del Vaga on designs by G. Romano. 57 ff.

S. Maria di Loreto (CI) *Largo del Foro Traiano.* Built in 1507 by Antonio da Sangallo il Giovane, it was completed in 1585 by Jacopo del Duca, who is responsible for the dome and campanile. It is built on an octagonal plan. There is a 15th-century picture of the school of Antoniazzo Romano, and paintings by Cavalier d'Arpino. Baroque sculptures by Duquesnoy, Finelli and Stefano Maderno.

S. Maria Maggiore (DI) *Piazza S. Maria Maggiore.* It goes back to the time of Sixtus III (432-40), although a tradition which is no longer accepted attributes the foundation to Pope Liberius (360). Nicholas V rebuilt the apse in 1288-92. The principal façade was put up by Fuga in 1743-50. The façade at the back was built in the time of Clement X (1670-76) by Flaminio Ponzio, Carlo Rainaldi, and Domenico Fontana. Mosaics of Filippo Rusuti in the portico. Romanesque campanile of 1377. For the interior, the mosaics, etc., see pp. 54-5. 51, 54 ff., 74, 78, 80 ff., 145, 148 ff, 195, *203*, 217, 218.

S. Maria dell'Orazione e Morte (BI) *Via Giulia.* Built in 1575, it was altered by Fuga in 1732-37. The façade is decorated with stone skulls. The interior is elliptical. Frescoes by Lanfranco, paintings by Ciro Ferri and Pier Leone Ghezzi. In the crypt, there is a macabre composition of skeletons.

S. Maria dell'Orto (CL) *Via della Madonna dell'Orto in Trastevere.* Built in 1566 by Guidetto Guidetti. The façade is crowned with obelisks, after a design attributed to Vignola. Works by Baglioni, the Zuccari, and Corrado Giaquinto. The altar, of bronze and semi-precious stones, was designed by Giacomo della Porta. 150.

S. Maria della Pace (BH) *Vicolo della Pace.* Built in 1480, and restored in 1656 by Pietro da Cortona who put up the convex Baroque façade. The adjoining cloister is the first work which Bramante did in Rome (1500-04). Among the frescoes there are Raphael's *Sibyls,* and work by Timoteo Viti and Baldassarre Peruzzi; also painting by Peruzzi, Venusti, Maratta, Orazio Gentileschi. Sculptures by Stefano Maderno, Fancelli and Ferrata. The second chapel on the right was designed by Antonio da Sangallo il Giovane, and has elegant reliefs by Simone Mosca. The choir and the high altar are by Carlo Maderno. 111, 132, 201.

S. Maria del Popolo (CG) *Piazza del Popolo.* A medieval foundation, rebuilt by Sixtus IV and enlarged by Julius II. Renaissance façade with added side-pieces by Bernini, who also restored the interior (1655-60). Among the many works of art in the chapels the following are of note: in the first chapel on the right, frescoes by Pinturicchio and Tiberio d'Assisi, sculptures by Bregno and Mino da Fiesole. The second chapel was built by Carlo Fontana and has paintings by Maratta and Seiter. In the third chapel, frescoes by Tiberio d'Assisi and Antonio da Viterbo, sculpture by Bregno and Vecchietta. On the left-hand side, the Cappella Cerasi has two paintings by Caravaggio, the *Crucifixion of St Peter* and the *Conversion of St Paul,* and an *Assumption* by Annibale Carracci. The third chapel on the left (Cappella Chigi) was designed by Raphael, who also did the cartoons for the mosaics in the dome. It contains frescoes by Salviati, a painting by Sebastiano del Piombo, and sculpture by Bernini. In the fourth chapel, there is sculpture by Algardi. The tombs in the main chapel are by Andrea Sansovino. The altar in the right transept bears the signature of Andrea Bregno. 108, 112, 165, 194.

S. Maria del Priorato (CL) *Piazza dei Cavalieri di Malta, on the Aventine.* G. B. Piranesi's only work of architecture, built in 1765. He also designed the piazza in front of the garden where the church stands. The interior is remarkable for its elegance and its all-white decoration. The high altar was also designed by Piranesi who was buried here in 1780. 220.

S. Maria dei Sette Dolori (BI) *Via Garibaldi.* Built by Borromini *c.* 1662. The façade remained unfinished. Altar-piece by Maratta. 198.

S. Maria sopra Minerva (CI) *Piazza della Minerva.* Founded in the 8th century on the ruins of a temple of Minerva, and rebuilt in the Gothic style *c.* 1280. The interior largely restored in the 19th century, but alterations have been made at various times since the 15th. Michelangelo's *Risen Christ* at the side of the high altar. The Cappella Carafa in the right transept was frescoed in 1489 with episodes from the life of St Thomas by Filippino Lippi, who also painted the altar-piece. Numerous paintings and sculptures in the chapels put up in the Baroque period. Works by Antoniazzo Romano, Melozzo da Forlì, Venusti, Barocci, Maratta, Sacchi, Bregno, Bernini, and Cordier. Fra Beato Angelico is buried in a chapel on the left. 80, 82, *132*, 136, 144, 195.

S. Maria in Trastevere (BI) *Piazza S. Maria in Trastevere.* A very ancient foundation, traditionally of the 3rd century (Pope Callistus), it was completely rebuilt in the first half of the 12th century by Innocent II, and altered several times, especially in 1870 under Pius IX. The portico is by Carlo Fontana (1702). Mosaics of the 13th century, much restored, on the upper part of the inward sloping façade. Romanesque campanile. Typical basilica interior, with granite columns. Decorated wooden ceiling designed by Domenichino, who also painted the *Assumption* (1617). Mosaic panels in the apse by Pietro Cavallini, depicting the life of the Virgin (1291). Above these are mosaics of a slightly later period. Among the many works of art in the nave and chapels, there are medieval fragments in fresco and marble, 15th-century tombs including that of Cardinal Pietro Stefaneschi by Paolo Romano (1417). The fifth chapel on the left was built by A. Gherardi (1680) with a fanciful cupola. At the left-hand side of the apse, in the Cappella Altemps (designed by Martino Longhi il Vecchio), a picture of the *Madonna della Clemenza* (temporarily removed). Baptistery by F. Raguzzini. 68, 75.

S. Maria in Vallicella (or **Chiesa Nuova**) (BH) *Piazza della Chiesa Nuova.* Begun in 1575 and completed a few years later, it was designed by Martino Longhi il Vecchio. The façade is of 1605. Frescoes by Pietro da Cortona on the ceiling, also in the apse and dome. An altar-piece by Maratta in the Cappella Spada, designed by Carlo Rainaldi. On the high altar, a large triptych by Pieter Paul Rubens (1606-08). *Presentation of the Virgin* on the altar of the left-hand transept, and *Visitation* in the fourth chapel on the left, both by Barocci. The sacristy, designed by P. Marucelli in 1629, is interesting both for its architecture and for its decoration. Marble group by Algardi, ceiling fresco by Pietro da Cortona, and a painting by Guercino in the adjacent chapel. On the left-hand side of the church is the Oratory of the Filippini by Borromini.

S. Maria in via Lata (CI) *On the Corso, next to the Palazzo Doria Pamphilj.* Old foundation, rebuilt at its present level at the end of the 15th century, and enlarged in the Baroque period by Fansago and Fancelli. Façade and campanile by Pietro da Cortona (1658-62) considered among his best work. Thirteenth-century Madonna on the high altar in a richly decorated tabernacle. Tombs of the Bonapartes. Remains of earlier building (6th to 13th centuries) in the crypt. 86, 193, 200, *218*.

S. Maria della Vittoria (DH) *Via 20 settembre.* Built by Carlo Maderno for Cardinal Scipione Borghese (1608-20). Façade by G. B. Soria (1626). A sumptuous Baroque interior. Paintings by Domenichino in the second chapel on the right. In the Cappella Cornaro (left transept), Bernini's *Ecstasy of St Teresa* (1646). Works by Guercino and Reni in the third chapel on the left. In the sacristy there are paintings of Ferdinand II Habsburg's victory at Prague (1620) which gave the church its name. 194.

S. Martino ai Monti (DI) *Viale del Colle Oppio.* Built in the 5th century, and rebuilt in the 8th, using antique columns, it was completely altered in mid-17th century by Pietro da Cortona, who also did the façade (keeping the porch, which is of 1575). On the walls of the side aisles, frescoes of the Roman Campagna by Dughet, and views of the interior of the old St Peter's and St John Lateran by an unknown artist. Beneath Pietro da Cortona's fine crypt are the remains of a 13th-century oratory. 52.

S. Paolo fuori le Mura (St. Paul's outside the walls). The old basilica, founded by Constantine over the apostle's tomb was successively enriched and enlarged, but completely burned down on 16 July 1823. Restored in 1854 under Pius IX. Little of the original structure remains, and the decoration of the interior reflects the eclectic taste of 19th-century artists. The principal remains of the original building are the apse mosaic, and some restored mosaic fragments, the altar canopy by Arnolfo di Cambio, and the Cosmatesque work in the cloister and on the candelabrum. There is a small museum attached to the basilica, which contains the 11th-century bronze doors of the old building. 51, 69 ff, *116*.

S. Pantaleo (BI) *Piazza S. Pantaleo.* Founded in the 13th century, and rebuilt in the first half of the 17th by Giovanni Antonio de Rossi. Façade by Valadier (1806). Richly decorated Baroque interior. Ceiling frescoes by Filippo Gherardi (1690). On the second altar on the left is a painting by Mattia Preti. 224.

St Peter's, *see* **S. Pietro in Vaticano.**

S. Pietro in Montorio (BI) *On the Janiculum.* Founded in the early Middle Ages, rebuilt at the end of the 15th century by order of Ferdinand IV of Spain, possibly by Baccio Pontelli. Restored in the 19th century. Renaissance façade attributed to the school of Andrea Bregno. Works by Sebastiano del Piombo, Baldassarre Peruzzi, Vasari, Daniele da Volterra, Dirck van Baburen. Sculptures by Bartolomeo Ammannati. The second chapel on the left

built by Bernini. Beatrice Cenci is buried beneath the high altar, although there is no commemorative inscription. In the courtyard on the right of the church stands the Tempietto of Bramante, built in 1502. This is one of the most classically perfect and harmonious buildings of the Renaissance. Near the courtyard is the Accademia di Spagna di Belle Arti. 111, *150.*

S. Pietro in Vaticano (AH) For the original basilica, built under Constantine, see p. 50.
For its history see pp. 50-54.
For works now lost p. 73; works which have survived pp. 82-83.
The building of the new basilica was begun by Bramante on 18 April 1506 at the behest of Julius II. Many other architects followed him, including Raphael and Michelangelo. Giacomo della Porta built the dome on Michelangelo's design, Carlo Maderno built the façade and Bernini the colonnade.
Bernini is also responsible for the interior, the throne and the baldacchino. For principal works of art see pp. 108-16. These are of various periods. The *Pietà* of Michelangelo is in the first chapel on the right. Funereal monuments are found in the nave, the chapels, and against the pilasters. The underground part of the basilica is a museum in itself, also the sacristy, the treasure, and the Sagrestia dei Beneficiati. Michelangelo's magnificent dome, one of the most remarkable works of architecture ever conceived, is accessible by lift. 30, 50 ff., 51-54, 58, 59, 62, 73 ff., 82 ff., 108, 110 ff., 129, 135, 145, 150 ff., *168, 170, 175, 177,* 180 ff., 193 ff., 222 ff., 231.

S. Pietro in Vincoli (St Peter in Chains) (DI) *Piazza S. Pietro in Vincoli.* This church was built as a shrine for St Peter's chains (hence its title) on a site where buildings had stood at the time of the Republic. It has often been altered, especially in the 15th and 18th centuries. The portico is *c.* 1475, and the upper part late 16th century. The nave is of three aisles, with fluted columns. Julius II's tomb stands in the right transept. Michelangelo had originally designed it for St Peter's, but after many vicissitudes his plans were reduced to what we see today. Paintings by Domenichino, Guercino, Pier Francesco Mola. Sculptures by Andrea Bregno and Caradosso. Antonio and Piero del Pollaiuolo are buried here, to the left of the entrance. Early Christian sarcophagus in the crypt. 124, 135, 207.

S. Prassede (DI) *Via S. Prassede.*
Built in 817-24 by Paschal I, restored in the 15th, 17th and 19th centuries. It has an atrium and portico. The interior, much restored, contains various works of art. Ninth-century mosaics on the triumphal arch and in the apse. The Anchero sarcophagus by Arnolfo di Cambio, and the bust of a young man by Bernini. Paintings by Zuccari, Cavalier d'Arpino and Ciro Ferri. The chapel of S. Zeno, halfway down the nave, was put up by Paschal I as a mausoleum for his mother, Theodora, This is one of the finest Byzantine works in Rome, decorated with fine mosaics on a gold ground. 56, 58 ff, 74.

S. Pudenziana (DH) *Via Urbana.* Built in the 4th century on the site of a Roman bath, it was altered in the 8th, 11th, 13th and 16th centuries. An 11th-century frieze is visible on the 19th-century façade. There is a fine 4th-century apse mosaic. The Cappella Caetani is decorated with marbles and stucco work of the late 16th century. The Oratorio Mariano is of the 11th century, and has some notable frescoes. 56, 73.

S. Rocco (CH) *Near Piazza Augusto Imperatore.* Built in 1499 by the innkeepers and boatmen of the nearby port of Ripetta, it was rebuilt in the 17th century. Neo-classical façade by Valadier. A fresco of the Nativity is attributed to Peruzzi, and a painting by Baciccia. 224.

S. Sabina (CL) *Piazza Pietro d'Illiria on the Aventine.* Founded in the 5th century, and enriched with works of art in the 9th. Campanile and cloister of the 13th century. Restored between 1914 and 1938 to its original 5th-century design. Fifth-century doors of cypress wood in the middle entrance. Three-aisle nave with Corinthian columns of Parian marble. A band of the original mosaic decoration still remains on the wall at the entrance. Fifth-century marble frieze of *opus sectile* in the nave and apse. Frescoes by the Zuccari brothers in the vault of the apse and in the chapel of S. Giacinto. Altar-piece by Sassoferrato in the chapel of St Catherine. 54, *109.*

S. Salvatore in Lauro (BH) *Piazza S. Salvatore in Lauro.* Built in the Middle Ages near a grove of laurels, it was altered in 1594, 1669, and in 1727 (by Nicola Salvi). The façade is 19th century. The interior is as Mascherino designed it in 1594. Paintings by Pietro da Cortona, Giuseppe Ghezzi and Turchi. Renaissance cloister attached. Frescoes by

Salviati in the refectory, and a monument to Eugene IV, by Isaia da Pisa, from old St Peter's. 106.

S. Sebastiano *Via Appia antica.* Dedicated to the apostles Peter and Paul in the 4th century, it later became a shrine for the relics of St Sebastian. It was altered in the 13th century, and in 1609 underwent a Baroque transformation at the hands of Flaminio Ponzio and Giovanni Vasanzio, who were commissioned by Scipione Borghese. Sculptures by Cordier and Antonio Giorgetti (who did the St Sebastian lying beneath the altar). The Cappella Albani is 18th century. Entrance to the catacombs of St Sebastian to the right of the church. 49, 157.

S. Silvestro in Capite (DL) *Piazza S. Silvestro.* Built in the 8th century on the ruins of the temple of the sun. Rebuilt at the end of the 17th century by Domenico de Rossi. The church gets its name from the relic of the head of John the Baptist venerated here. Paintings by Orazio Gentileschi and Giacinto Brandi. Romanesque campanile (1210). Michelangelo designed an altar for the church, but nothing came of it. 145.

S. Stefano Rotondo (DL) *Via S. Stefano Rotondo, on the Celio.* Built in the 5th century on a circular plan, it has a five-arched portico of the 12th century, and once had a double ambulatory, but the outside one was demolished in 1453. Seventh-century mosaics in the chapel of SS. Primo and Feliciano. Wall fresco of Martyrs by Pomarancio, Tempesta and assistants. 56, 153.

S. Spirito in Sassia (Arciospedale di) (BH) *Lungotevere in Sassia.* Rebuilt by Sixtus IV in 1473-78, after the original 12th-century foundation was burned down. Entrance is by request only. There is an altar canopy attributed by Lavagnino to Palladio. The church of S. Spirito adjacent to this building was designed by Antonio da Sangallo il Giovane, and contains some Mannerist paintings. 92.

S. Susanna (DH) *Largo S. Susanna.* National church of the Americans. Early Christian foundation in basilica form, with 8th-century mosaics in the apse. Altered in 1475, 1595, and finally in 1603 by Maderno, who produced the very noble façade. Sculptures by Valsoldo and Vacca (?), a painting by Tommaso Laureti on the high altar, and frescoes by Baldassarre Croce. The sculptor Filippo Valle is buried here. 151.

SS. Apostoli (CI) *Piazza SS. Apostoli.*
Sixth-century foundation, restored in
the 15th and 16th centuries, and rebuilt by Francesco and Carlo Fontana (1702-14). Façade by Valadier
(1827). The 15th-century portico by
Baccio Pontelli was given Baroque
windows, balustrade and statues by
Rainaldi (1681). Ceiling fresco by
Baciccia, and altar paintings by Benedetto Luti (1723), Domenico Mura-
tori (1703), Sebastiano Ricci (1701).
Sculptures by Bregno, Mino da Fiesole, Giovanni Dalmata, Ludovisi and
Canova. There is an adjoining cloister.
69, 86, 212, 222, 224.

SS. Cosma e Damiano (CI) *Via dei
Fori Imperiali.* Consecrated by Pope
Felix IV in 527, the church was
in fact part of the library in the
Forum Pacis. It was rebuilt in the
Baroque period. The vestibule on
the side of the Roman Forum was
originally the Temple of Romulus.
Sixth-century mosaics of high quality on the triumphal arch and in the
apse. Paintings by Baglione and Spa-
darino. Frescoes by Francesco Alle-
grini (17th century). 58, *109.*

SS. Giovanni e Paolo (DL) *Piazza
SS. Giovanni e Paolo.* Early Christian foundation (4th century), often
rebuilt. Restored in 1949. Twelfth-
century portico and campanile. The
upper gallery is 13th century. Early
Christian and medieval frescoes in
the church and crypt, where there
are remains of various buildings, including a Roman house, a Christian
house and a medieval oratory. 64.

SS. Luca e Martina (CI) *Via del
Foro Romano.* Built by Pietro da
Cortona (1634-50) for Cardinal Francesco Barberini, protector of the Accademia di S. Luca, which was housed in a nearby building, demolished
in 1933. It was built over an underground church of the 6th century,
dedicated to S. Martina, which is
accessible by a staircase on the left
of the high altar. Baroque paintings
and sculptures in the upper and
lower churches. 200.

SS. Nereo e Achilleo (DL) *Via delle
Terme di Caracalla.* Fourth-century
foundation, rebuilt several times, in
the 9th, 15th and 16th centuries.
Typical basilica type. Ninth-century
mosaic on the triumphal arch. Frescoes and paintings by Pomarancio.

SS. Quattro Coronati (DL) *Via SS.
Quattro Coronati.* Fourth-century
foundation, enlarged in the 7th and
9th centuries. Burned by the Nor-
mans in 1084 and rebuilt in 1111
by Paschal I. It is dedicated to the
four Roman soldiers who were mar-
tyred for refusing to worship a statue
of Aesculapius. Preceded by two
courtyards, the basilica has traces
of the earlier church in the apse,
and an adjoining 13th-century cloister. Medieval and 17th-century frescoes. There are also interesting frescoes in the Oratorio di S. Silvestro
which is approached through the
adjoining convent. 57, 64.

Scalinata della Trinità dei Monti (CH)
("Spanish Steps") This leads from
the Piazza di Spagna to the Trinità
dei Monti. It was built with a legacy
from the French Ambassador Guef-
fier by Francesco de Sanctis (1723-
26). There are 138 steps which,
together with the travertine ramps,
create a picturesque ensemble and
recall the lay-out of the now demolished Porto di Ripetta (*q.v.*). 108,
213, *217,* 220.

Sepolcro degli Scipioni *Via di Porta
S. Sebastiano 9.* Discovered in 1780
and restored in 1926-29. An important family mausoleum of the period
of the Republic. It is approached by
means of a winding path (3rd century AD). Roman house with a columbarium and catacombs. Many sarcophagi and inscribed slabs. In the
garden at the entrance to the sepulchre is the columbarium of Pompo-
nius Hylas, discovered in 1830. This
is perfectly preserved, with stuccoes
and paintings of the 1st century. At
the exit on via di Porta Latina is the
octagonal Tempietto di S. Giovanni
in Oleo, built by a French prelate
at the beginning of the 16th century.
The upper part, and the arrangement
of the interior, are by Borromini.
Frescoes by Lazzaro Baldi.

"Spanish Steps" (CH) *see* **Scalinata
della Trinità dei Monti.**

Stadio Flaminio *Near Viale Tiziano.*
An ingenious construction by Pier
Luigi Nervi, built in 1959. It holds
45,000 spectators and includes a
covered swimming pool, gymnasia,
etc.

Tabularium (CI) *Entrance on via del
Campidoglio.* Built in 78 BC by the
Consul Quintus Lutatius Catulus as
a state archive, it was used as a
prison in the Middle Ages. It has
the oldest arched portico now in existence, almost intact. Palazzo Senatorio was built over it. 13.

Teatro Argentina (BI) *Largo Teatro
Argentina.* Built by Girolamo Theodoli in 1730, and rebuilt a century
later by Pietro Camporese. Façade by
Pietro Holl. Recently restored. *215.*

Teatro di Marcello (CI) *Via del Mare.* Begun under Julius Caesar, it was enlarged by Augustus and dedicated to the memory of his son-in-law and nephew, Marcus Claudius Marcellus, who died in 23 BC before he was twenty years old (Virgil, *Aeneid* VI, 860 *et seq.*). The Palazzo Caetani, formerly Orsini and Savelli, was later built over it. It was restored and separated in 1926-29. Alongside it are three columns of the Temple of Apollo (435 BC, rebuilt in 179 BC and AD 32) and the old Albergo della Catena, recently restored. 15, *53, 62,* 228.

Teatro dell'Opera (DH) *Piazza dell'Opera.* Built in 1880 by Achille Sfondrini for the impresario Costanzi, after whom it was originally named. Restored in 1926 and again in 1959 by Marcello Piacentini, who is responsible for the new façade. 231.

Teatro Valle (BI) *Via del Teatro Valle.* The neo classical façade is by Valadier (1819-22). 215, 224.

Tempietto di S. Andrea (BF) *Via Flaminia.* Built by Vignola in 1554 for Julius III. Square in shape, sober and harmonious in style, it has the first elliptical dome to be put up in the Renaissance. 150.

Temple of Antoninus and Faustina (CI) *Roman Forum.* Built by decree of the Senate in the 2nd century AD and dedicated to the Emperor Antoninus Pius and his wife. Hexastyle Corinthian prostyle, in peperino, with monolithic columns of cipollino and marble decoration. The *cella* is now the church of S. Lorenzo in Miranda, rebuilt in 1602. 26, *45.*

Temple of Castor and Pollux (or **the Dioscuri**) (CI) *Roman Forum.* Built in 484 BC and restored several times. Peripteral. Three fluted columns of Parian marble still remain, together with a part of the trabeation, both of the period of Augustus. *16,* 26.

Temple of Divus Romulus (CI) *Roman Forum.* Erected by Maxentius in 309 for his divinized son Romulus, it was possibly completed under Constantine. The bronze doors of the original building have survived. Some scholars maintain that the building is a vestibule of the Forum Pacis. The church of SS. Cosma e Damiano (*q.v.*) is built against it. 26.

Temple of Fortuna Virilis (CI) *Foro Boario, Piazza Bocca della Verità.* The title is a misnomer. It was built in greco-Italic style *c.* 100 BC. Tetrastyle Ionic pseudoperipteral of tufa and travertine, finished in stuc-

co. In the 9th century the building was used as a church. There are remains of medieval painting. 9, 10, 36, *55.*

Temple of Mars Ultor (CI) *Forum of Augustus. Via dei Fori Imperiali.* The remaining fragments are of the podium, the staircase, a few columns and the front part of the *cella.* 15, 28.

Temple of Venus Genetrix (CI) *Foro di Cesare, on the right-hand side of the via dei Fori Imperiali immediately after the Victor Emmanuel monument.* Consecrated in 46 BC and rebuilt by Trajan. The podium with three columns and a part of the trabeation still stands. 13, 27.

Temple of Venus and Rome (DI) *On the Velia, in front of the Colosseum.* An imposing building erected by Hadrian between 121 and 136 AD, completed by Antoninus Pius and then rebuilt by Maxentius. This was the largest temple in Rome. It was built on the vestibule of Nero's *Domus Aurea,* after the famous Colossus had been removed from it. Peripteral, with the two apses facing away from each other, that of Venus towards the Colosseum and that of Rome towards the Forum. It originally had 150 columns. It was restored in 1935. The missing columns were replaced with privet bushes, the steps with hedges of box, and the walls with hedges of laurel. 28.

Temple of Vesta (CI) *Foro Boario, Piazza Bocca della Verità.* The temple is misnamed. It belongs to the Augustan age. Corinthian peripteral, built on a round plan, with 19 of its original 20 fluted columns still standing. 15, *90.*

Temple and House of the Vestals (CI) *Roman Forum.* The temple is circular, and was built in 191 by Septimius Severus. Corinthian peripteral with 20 columns. The sacred flame was kept alight in the *cella.* The house is adjacent to the temple. There are remains of a rectangular atrium with portico. It was decorated with sculptures which are now in the Museo Nazionale Romano. There is a bust believed to be of Numa Pompilius, who founded the order of Vestal priestesses. 9, 26.

Tomb of Cecilia Metella *Via Appia Antica.* Cylindrical structure on a square base with travertine revetment. It belongs to the last years of the Republic. Dedicated to Cecilia, daughter of Quintus Metellus (the conqueror of Crete). She was the wife of Crassus, son of one of Caesar's generals in the Gallic war.

It was fortified in 1302 by the Caetani, who owned the nearby medieval castle. 16.

Tomb of Romulus, *see* **Lapis Niger.**

Torre dei Conti (CI) *Largo Corrado Ricci.* Only the lower part remains, the rest having fallen in the earthquake of 1348. It was built at the beginning of the 13th century by Riccardo dei Conti di Segni, a brother of Innocent III. Petrarch mentions it as one of the marvels of Rome. 64.

Torre del Grillo (CI) *Salita del Grillo.* Built in the 13th century. It gets its name from the Marchesi del Grillo who lived in the nearby palace, and gained possession of it in the 17th century. The crenellation was added by them.

Torre delle Milizie (CI) *Largo Magnanapoli.* The largest of the medieval towers to have survived in Rome. It was erected by Gregory IX in 1227-41 on the foundations of a building of the Servian age. It was cut down to its present height in the 14th century, and battlements added. It belonged to the Annibaldi and the Caetani families. It leans slightly to one side. Tradition maintains that it was here that Nero watched Rome burning. 64, *120.*

Torre Millina (BH) *Via di S. Agnese, near piazza Navona.* In the Middle Ages it belonged to the Mellini family. Their name is still visible in large letters on the upper part with its Guelph battlements. 64.

Trajan's Column (CI) *Forum of Trajan.* It has some of the most interesting sculpture to have survived from ancient Rome. 27, 28, 32, 33, *86, 88,* 148.

Triclinio del Patriarchio Lateranense (EL) *Piazza di Porta S. Giovanni.* In the great building erected by Ferdinando Fuga in 1743, one can see a partial reconstruction, with the very few fragments that remain, of the exedra of the dining room (Triclinium) of the patriarchio (the old papal palace of the Lateran). It was built by Leo III (795-816) on the site where the Lateran Palace now stands, and from which the mosaic was taken, and not very successfully installed here.

Trinità dei Monti (CH) *Piazza Trinità dei Monti.* Built between 1502 and 1587. The façade is by Carlo Maderno. The steps in front of it are by Domenico Fontana. Notable frescoes by Daniele da Volterra and monuments by Leonardo Sormani. 108, 148, 153, 167, 213, 220, 226.

Trinità dei Spagnoli (CH) *Via Condotti.* Built in 1741-46 and designed by the Portuguese Manoel Rodriguez dos Santos. Elliptical interior with frescoes by Gregorio Guglielmi and paintings by Giaquinto and Benefial. 218.

Umbilicus Urbis (CI) *Roman Forum.* This was the symbolic centre of Rome. It stands next to the rostra, towards the Arch of Septimius Severus. The circular base remains, and it was on this that the Umbilicus Urbis stood. 26.

Vatican (AH) 62, 82-83, 110 ff., 118 ff., 129 ff.
Biblioteca Apostolica 88.
Cappella Niccolina. Paintings by Angelico 82.
Cappella Paolina. Paintings by Michelangelo 194
Cappella Sistina (Sistine Chapel) 82, 88 ff., 94, 103 ff., 110, 120, 129 ff., 135, 145, 194, 214.
Cortile del Belvedere 111 ff., 222.
Cortile di S. Damaso 177
Gardens. Casina di Pio IV and Loggia by Pirro Ligorio *124.*
Grottoes. Sarcophagus of Junius Bassus 51, 74, 106.
Tomb of Paul II Tomb of Sixtus IV by Antonio del Pollaiuolo 107.
Logge of Raphael 30, 129, 152.
Museums 18, 30, 36 ff., 112, 222.
Sacri Palazzi 74, 82, 110, 231.
Pinacoteca 78, 88, 112, 118, 129, 204 ff., 230.
Bramante staircase 112, 119.
Stanze by Raphael 118 ff., 131, 152.

Via Appia Antica This is the most important of the consular roads, and is famous for the tombs of notable people buried alongside it, and for the romantic quality of its landscape. It used to connect Rome with Brindisi, its principal eastern port. Begun in 312 BC by Appius Claudius the Censor, and was re-opened by Pius VI (1775-99). The original paving is still visible in many places. 16, 40, 49, 50, *84.*

Via Ardeatina It goes off from the Via Appia Antica towards Ardea in front of the little church of Domine quo vadis, the place where Christ is supposed to have appeared to Peter. In the Ardeatine caves, 1 km. along the road from here, the Nazis killed 335 innocent people in 1944. The bronze gate at the entrance is by Mirko Basaldella (1910-70). 49.

Via delle Botteghe Oscure (CI) So called on account of the shops which were installed in the arches of the theatre of Cornelius Balbus (1st century BC) in the Middle Ages. The

Palazzo Caetani is of the late Renaissance. Archaeological remains on one side of the street, excavated in 1935. 117.

Via Condotti (CH) Joins the Corso and the Piazza di Spagna. One of the most elegant and frequented streets in Rome. It gets its name from the conduits of the Acqua Vergine which came this way. The Caffè Greco (established in 1760) near the Piazza di Spagna, was a favourite meeting place for artists and men of letters, such as Goethe, Stendhal, Gogol, Baudelaire, Schopenhauer, Anatole France, Berlioz, Mendelssohn, Wagner, Liszt, Leopardi, d'Annunzio and Buffalo Bill. 218, 225.

Via dei Coronari (BH) *In the Parione district.* A street full of character, noted for the number of its antique shops. 148.

Corso (CH) The continuation of the consular Via Flaminia as far as the Campidoglio. Once called via Lata, it was laid out by Domenico Fontana in the time of Sixtus V. 148, 191, 193, 201.

Via Flaminia (BF-CG) From the Porta del Popolo it takes a north-easterly direction. Opened by the censor Caius Flaminius, it reaches the Adriatic at Rimini in front of the Arch of Augustus, at which point the via Emilia goes off to the north-west. 35, 150, 229.

Via dei Fori Imperiali (CI-DI) Opened in 1932 as a direct route between Piazza Venezia and the Colosseum, dividing the Forum area into two. This destroyed the unity and completeness of the excavations. 13, 27, 64.

Via Giulia (BI) Opened by Julius II in the early 16th century, it was for a long time one of the most important thoroughfares in the city, and some magnificent palaces were built here. 117 ff., 154.

Via della Lungara (BI) Opened by Julius II, this is one of the longest straight roads laid out in the 16th century. Its length gave rise to its new name. It was originally the Via Settimiana, and this name is still applied to the entrance from Trastevere. In this street are the Farnesina of Agostino Chigi, the Palazzo Corsini, the Palazzo Salviati, and Rome's prison, the Regina Cœli. 117 ff.

Via Nazionale (DH-CI) The largest Roman thoroughfare to be opened after 1870, from the station to Piazza Venezia. It is straight for almost its whole length, and follows the old Vicus Longus between the Quirinal and the Viminal. Halfway down is the Palazzo delle Esposizioni (*q.v.*). 26, 227 ff.

Via Nomentana (EG) It leaves Porta Pia in the direction of Nomentum, the present-day Mentana. It follows more or less the old Consular Via Nomentana. Some 6 km. outside Rome there is a fine view of the battlemented Ponte Nomentano. 57.

Via Ostiense It leaves the Porta Ostiensis (Porta S. Paolo, *q.v.*) and follows the old Consular route to Ostia. Of great artistic and archaeological interest are the Sepolcreto Ostiense, catacombs of Commodilla, and basilica of St Paul outside the walls. 51.

Via Sacra (CI) It crosses the Roman Forum from east to west, from the Arch of Septimius Severus to the Arch of Titus. It gets its name from the sanctuaries which stood on both sides of it. Polygonal paving is visible at a number of points. 26, 34.

Via Salaria (EF-DE) So called on account of the salt trade which the Romans carried on with the Sabines. The present-day road connects Rome not only with the Sabine region, but also with Reatino, the Abruzzi and the Marche. 49.

Via Veneto (CG-DH) This runs from Piazza Barberini to the Pincio and Villa Borghese. Most of the large hotels are situated here, and the street is very popular. It was opened after 1870 and immediately became a fashionable meeting place. Especially noteworthy are the Fontana delle Api (*q.v.*) of Bernini, near Piazza Barberini, the church of S. Maria della Concezione (dei Cappuccini) *q.v.* The United States Embassy occupies the Palazzo Margherita (built by Gaetano Koch, 1886-90) and its adjacent palazzine. At the top of the street stands the Porta Pinciana, a double arch with cylindrical towers, built in the 6th century under Belisarius. 183, 228.

Villa Albani (DG) (now **Villa Torlonia**) *Via Salaria.* Built by Carlo Marchionni between 1743 and 1763 for Cardinal Alessandro Albani who, under Winckelmann's guidance, assembled a valuable collection of antique sculpture, much of which was taken to Paris by Napoleon. It consists of a small palace facing an exedra. In a room on the first floor is Raphael Mengs' fresco of Parnassus (1756). There is a collection of paintings in the adjoining rooms. Fine classical sculptures in the exedra and on ground floor of the palazzina. The villa is not open to the public, but permission to view is sometimes granted. 36, 218, 226.

Villa Giulia (CG) *Viale delle Belle Arti.* Built for Julius III by Vignola and Bartolomeo Ammannati, between 1551 and 1553. Vignola is responsible for the Palazzo and the hemicycle of the first courtyard. Ammannati designed the loggia and the ninfeo, in elegant late Renaissance style. The villa is now the Museo Nazionale Etrusco, or Museo di Villa Giulia. 36, 150, 217.

Villa Madama (AF) *Via Villa Madama, on the slope of Monte Mario.* Begun by Raphael for Cardinal Giulio dei Medici (later Pope Clement VII) in 1516, and continued by Antonio da Sangallo il Giovane. It belonged to Madama Margherita of Parma, natural daughter of Charles V. It is now used by the Presidenza del Consiglio dei Ministri. Permisson to view is granted by the Ministero degli Affari Esteri (Cerimoniale). There is a loggia with grotesques and stucco decorations by Giovanni da Udine. Also paintings by Giulio Romano. 112.

Villa Medici (CG) *Viale Trinità dei Monti.* Built by Annibale Lippi in 1544 for Cardinal Ricci, from whom it passed to the Medici. In 1803 Napoleon had the French Academy transferred here from the Palazzo Salviati (*q.v.*). The garden front is very much decorated with sculpture and friezes (some of these are from the Ara Pacis). Galileo was imprisoned here by the Holy Office from 1630 to 1633. Recently restored. 19, 149, 158, 166, 226.

Viminale One of the seven hills of Rome. 11, 32, 147.

Vittoriano (CI) This is the name usually given to the monument to Vittorio Emanuele II in Piazza Venezia. It is also called the Altare della Patria, since it contains the grave of an unknown soldier of the First World War. Built between 1885 and 1911 by Giuseppe Sacconi, the work continued for ten years after that. It is built of Lombard limestone, instead of the usual travertine of Roman monuments, which creates a striking contrast with its surroundings. Its eclectic architecture likewise has little in common with the majestic ruins round about it, or with the complex of the Aracœli and the Campidoglio which it adjoins. It is decorated with a large number of academic sculptures. There is an entrance in the right hand side to the Museo storico del Risorgimento. 27, *227*.

Other localities mentioned:

Ariccia. Church of S. Maria della Assunzione, built by G.L. Bernini in 1664, who also enlarged the important Palazzo Chigi (once the Palazzo Savelli) in the picturesque ensemble of Piazza della Repubblica. 194.

Boville Ernica. The parish church contains an angel from a Giottesque fragment of the mosaic of the Navicella in old St Peter's. 80.

Caprarola. Palazzo Farnese. Built by the nephew of Paul III on the foundations of a fortress which the pope had constructed by Antonio da Sangallo il Giovane. The Palazzo was built by Vignola, who made it his masterpiece. It is pentagonal, with a round courtyard, all magnificently proportioned. Parts of the interior may be visited, and these are very fine, containing some Mannerist frescoes. 150.

Castelgandolfo. Summer residence of the Popes. The papal palace was built under Urban VIII between 1624 and 1629 by Carlo Maderno and his assistants. The church of S. Tommaso da Villanova is by Bernini (1661). 194.

Cerveteri. One of the principal Etruscan cities, named Caere. It is famous for its necropolis. The tombs are decorated with paintings, polychrome stuccoes and friezes. The most important ones are: Tomba dell'Alcova, Tomba dei rilievi, Tomba degli Scudi e delle sedie, and Tomba Regolini-Galassi, the furnishings of which are in the Vatican Museums. 40.

Ostia antica. See description on pp. 38 ff.

Tarquinia. A picturesque medieval town. (Palazzo Vitelleschi, Museo Nazionale, Duomo, churches of S. Maria di Castello, S. Pancrazio, and S. Francesco.) Necropolis with tombs famous for their mural paintings. The most important ones are: Tomba della Caccia e della Pesca, Tomba del Letto funebre, Tomba del Triclinio, Tomba di Polifemo, Tomba dei Tori.

Tivoli. Hadrian's Villa. Temple of the Sibyl. Villa d'Este. Duomo. Church of S. Maria Maggiore (13th century), S. Silvestro (Romanesque), S. Giovanni Evangelista (15th century), Villa Gregoriana and Cascate dell'Aniene. 30, *62*, *64*, *68*, *71*, 111, 184, 193, *222*.

Painters, Sculptors and Architects

Accardi, Carla (Trapani 1927). Abstract painter specializing in Op art. Living in Rome since 1950. Paintings in the Galleria Nazionale d'Arte Moderna, and aluminium panels in the FAO building, Via della Passeggiata archeologica. 232.

Afro (Afro Basaldella; Udine 1912). One of the most important and most representative Italian abstract painters. Lives in Rome. Paintings in Galleria Nazionale d'Arte moderna. 232.

Agesander (Agesandros) son of Paeonius (Rhodes, 2nd century BC). Sculptor. Together with his sons Athenodorus and Polydorus (*q.v.*) he produced the *Laocoön* in the Vatican Museum. 30.

Agresti, Livio (Forlì, *c.* 1508-Rome *c.* 1580). Mannerist painter. Decorated the Sala Regia in the Vatican and the Oratorio del Gonfalone. 154.

Alberti, Leon Battista (Genoa 1404-Rome 1472). Architect, humanist and author. He came of a Florentine family, spent several years in Rome studying and measuring the monuments of antiquity. Restored S. Stefano Rotondo (*q.v.*) and possibly helped in designing the Palazzo Venezia and its adjoining garden.

Algardi, Alessandro (Bologna 1595-Rome 1654). Baroque sculptor and architect. Came to Rome in 1625, where his first works were the *Baptist and the Magdalen* in S. Silvestro al Quirinale (1628-29). Outstanding paintings in S. Maria del Popolo, S. Marcello al Corso, and the Galleria Doria. Bronze monument to Innocent X in the Palazzo dei Conservatori, altar-piece with *Attila and Leo the Great* in St. Peter's. Stucco sketch in Palazzo Vallicelliano. Designed the Casino Pamphilj in the Villa on the Janiculum. 190, 195 ff., 222.

Ammannati, Bartolomeo (Settignano 1511-Florence 1592). Sculptor and architect. One of the most typical exponents of late Romano-Tuscan Mannerism. Came to the court of Julius III in Rome in 1550. Collaborated with Vignola and Vasari in the Villa Giulia, where he was responsible especially for the loggia. Other Roman works: the Collegio Romano (?), Palazzo Ruspoli in the Corso, Palazzina of Pius IV (?) in the Via Flaminia (now occupied by the Italian Embassy to the Holy See), the roof-terrace of Palazzo Vecchiarelli (now Emo-Capodilista) near via dei Coronari. Collaborated in the Palazzo Firenze in Piazza Firenze (centre of the Società Dante Alighieri). Sculptures in S. Pietro in Montorio and in the Sala dei Pontefici in the Borgia Apartment. 193.

Angelico, Fra (Guidolino di Pietro, name in religion Fra Giovanni da Fiesole, also known as Beato Angelico; Vicchio di Mugello *c.* 1400-Rome 1455). Florentine painter and Dominican friar. Came to Rome *c.* 1445. Frescoes for Pope Nicholas V in the Cappella Niccolina in the Vatican. His works in Rome: a triptych with the *Ascension, Pentecost* and the *Last Judgment,* in the Galleria Nazionale d'Arte antica in Palazzo Barberini. *Madonna with the child and saints* and two predella panels of the life of St Nicholas of Bari, in the Pinacoteca Vaticana. He is buried in the church of S. Maria sopra Minerva. 80, 82 ff., 120.

Antonello (Antonello di Antonio, known as Antonello da Messina; Messina *c.* 1430-1479). Painter. The fine portrait of a man, *c.* 1473, in the Galleria Borghese is his only work in Rome. *186.*

Apollodorus (Apollodorus of Damascus). Greek architect and sculptor, 2nd century AD. Worked in Rome in the first half of the century, especially on the great complex of the Forum of Trajan, and the Ulpian Basilica. According to a recent hypothesis, he may be the sculptor of the reliefs on Trajan's Column, and of some slabs which were originally in the Forum of Trajan and later incorporated into the Arch of Constantine. Banished from Rome Hadrian, and condemned to death. 27.

Arnolfo di Cambio (Colle Val d'Elsa *c.* 1245-Florence 1302). Sculptor and architect. After working with his master, Nicola Pisano, at Bologna and Siena, came to Rome and spent many years there. His Roman works, which cannot be exactly dated: the Annibaldi tomb in St John Lateran, the statue of Charles of Anjou in the Palazzo dei Conservatori (1277), canopies of St Paul outside the walls (1289) and of S. Cecilia in Trastevere (1293), bronze statue of St Peter in St Peter's (?), crib in S. Maria Maggiore, and tomb of Boniface IV in the Vatican Grottoes. 58, 69 ff., *131.*

Athenodorus of Rhodes (Rhodes 2nd-1st century BC). Son of Agesander (*q.v.*). Sculptor. Worked with his father and Polydorus on the *Laocoön* group in Vatican Museum. 30.

Baburen (Theodor, also called Dirck, van; Utrecht *c.* 1590-?). Dutch painter of the Caravaggio circle. In Rome 1619-20 with David de Haen, with whom he worked in S. Pietro in Montorio. Here he painted a *Deposition*, which is a free version of Caravaggio's treatment of the same subject. His *Betrayal of Christ* is in the Galleria Borghese, and a *Christ among the Doctors* in the Palazzo Venezia.

Balla, Giacomo (Turin 1874-Rome 1958). Futurist painter (after an early period devoted to impressionism and pointillisme). Works in the Galleria Nazionale d'Arte moderna. 231 ff.

Balthus (Balthazar Klossowski de Rola; b. 1908). Director of the French Academy in the Villa Medici since 1961.

Barocci (Federico Fiori; Urbino 1535-1612). Mannerist painter. Frescoes in the Casina di Pio IV and the Sala del Museo Gregoriano Etrusco in the Vatican. His paintings in the Pinacoteca Vaticana include a *Rest on the flight into Egypt* (1573). His *Communion of the Apostles* is in S. Maria sopra Minerva, and his *Presentation of the Virgin* in the Chiesa Nuova. (1594). Other works in the Galleria Borghese, the Galleria Doria, and the Accademia di S. Luca.

Basaldella, see **Afro** and **Mirko**.

Basile, Ernesto (Palermo 1857-1932). Architect in the Art Nouveau style, he designed the new wing of the Camera dei Deputati, and the façade in Piazza del Parlamento. 228.

Batoni, Pompeo Girolamo (Lucca 1708-Rome 1787). Apprenticed as a goldsmith in his father's workshop, before he became a painter. His works are in the Pinacoteca Capitolina (*Madonna and Child*), the Gesù, S. Gregorio Magno al Celio, SS. Celso e Giuliano (the altar-piece of *Christ with saints* is a masterpiece of his early period), the Museo di Roma, the Colonna and Borghese galleries, the Accademia di S. Luca, Palazzo Barberini, Villa Albani. 218.

Bellini, Giovanni (also called Giambellino; Venice *c.* 1430-1516). Father of Venetian Renaissance painting with its mastery of light and colour. Rome possesses two of his Madonnas, one in the Galleria Borghese, the other in Galleria Doria Pamphilj. He also painted the upper part of the great polyptych (Pinacoteca Vaticana, room IX) which was commissioned for the church of S. Francesco in Pesaro. *142*.

Benefial, Marco (Rome 1684-1764). One of the first painters in the neoclassical reaction to Baroque academicism. His works are to be seen in the churches of SS. Giovanni e Paolo (1716), Aracœli (1729), Trinità degli Spagnoli (1750) and St John Lateran, also in the Galleria Nazionale d'Arte antica di Palazzo Barberini, and the Galleria Spada. 218.

Bernini, Gian Lorenzo (Naples 1598-Rome 1680). Architect, sculptor and painter. He came from Naples as a child, with his father, Pietro Bernini (*q.v.*). As a creator of the Baroque style, he contributed greatly to the architecture of Rome. For his architectural work see pp. 171-184. He destroyed most of his paintings, but there is a striking self-portrait in the Galleria Borghese. 113, 149, 170, 177, 180 ff., 186 ff., 193 ff., *196*, 222.

Bernini, Pietro (Sesto Fiorentino 1562-Rome 1629). Father of Gian Lorenzo Bernini. He began as a painter, under the influence of Cavalier d'Arpino, and took up sculpture in Rome with the late Mannerists then working in S. Maria Maggiore. His Roman works are the Baptist in S. Andrea della Valle, the Fontana della Barcaccia (?) in Piazza di Spagna, a relief of the Assumption in S. Maria Maggiore, and other sculptures in the Cappella Paolina of the same basilica. 183, 195, 207.

Biagio (d'Antonio). Florentine painter of the second half of the 15th century. He worked on the first series of frescoes in the Sistine Chapel. 94.

Boccioni, Umberto (Reggio Calabria 1882-Verona 1916). Futurist painter and sculptor. Author of the Futurist painters' manifesto of 11 February 1910, also signed by Carrà, Russolo, Balla and Severini. In the Galleria Nazionale d'Arte moderna are a few of his most important works. 231.

Bonvicino, Ambrogio (Milan *c.* 1552-1622). Sculptor and worker in stucco. His works are in S. Maria sopra Minerva (statues of Urban VII and St John the Baptist), S. Andrea della Valle, S. Maria Maggiore and St John Lateran. He also did the bas relief of the *Giving of the Keys to Peter* under the Loggia delle Benedizioni, on the façade of St Peter's (*c.* 1614) and the 32 seated statues pontiffs, in stucco, placed laterally on the vault of the nave of St Peter's. 207.

Borgianni, Orazio (Rome *c.* 1578-1616). Painter, and follower of Caravaggio. His works are to be seen in the Galleria Spada (a *Pietà*), the Galleria Colonna and the Galleria di Palazzo Barberini. There is an *Assumption* by him in the modern church (1887) of the Sacro Cuore in via Marsala, and *St. Charles Borromeo* in the church of S. Carlo alle Quattro Fontane. 205.

Borromini (Francesco Castelli; Bissone, Canton Ticino 1599-Rome 1667). In 1628 he changed his name, possibly to distinguish himself from the many others who bore the name of Castelli. See pp. 196-98 for his works. With Bernini, he is the creator of Roman Baroque, contributing his own special rhythm to the dramatic play and tension between space and light. His Roman works, in chronological sequence: S. Carlo alle Quattro Fontane, 1634-41, work in the Palazzo Spada and the Palazzo Falconieri, 1637-50, Oratorio dei Filippini, rebuilding of St John Lateran, completion of the Palazzo Carpegna, S. Ivo alla Sapienza, 1642-60 (his most brilliant work), S. Agnese in Piazza Navona, 1653-61, S. Maria dei Sette Dolori, *c.* 1662, the front of the Collegio di Propaganda Fide and its church, and the campanile of S. Andrea delle Fratte, 1665. 26, 51, 170, 177, 186 ff., *193*, 196 ff., 220.

Botticelli (Sandro Filipepi; Florence 1445-1510). Painter. Pupil of Filippo Lippi, Verrocchio, and Antonio del Pollaiuolo. He was in Rome in 1481-82 working on the frescoes in the Sistine Chapel, where he produced his *Moses as a Young Man,* the *Punishment of the Israelites,* the *Temptation of Christ,* and some of the figures of popes in niches. 91.

Bracci, Pietro (Rome 1700-1773). One of the most outstanding 18th-century Roman architects and sculptors. His sculptures are in St Peter's (tombs of Clement XIV and Maria Clementina Sobieski), San Marcello al Corso, and the Corsini Chapel in St John Lateran. He also worked on the Fontana di Trevi. 184, 217.

Bramante (Donato di Pascuccio d'Antonio; Monte Asdruvaldo, near Urbino, 1444-Rome 1514). Painter and architect. He was architect to Julius II, and put in charge of the building of the new St Peter's. 52, 86-88, 110 ff., 117, 118, 129, 145, *151*, 177.

Bramantino (Bartolomeo Suardi; Milan *c.* 1465-1530). Pupil of Bra-

mante but not a slavish imitator. He worked in the Vatican *Stanze,* between 1507 and 1509. 118.

Bregno, Andrea (Osteno, Como, 1418-Rome 1503). Architect and sculptor, one of a large family of artists. 106.

Brunelleschi, Filippo (Florence 1377-1446). Architect, sculptor and goldsmith. He was often in Rome after 1402, studying classical architecture and its techniques. None of his work is in Rome. 80, 82.

Burri, Alberto (Città di Castello 1915). Painter. Has been in Rome since his first exhibition in 1947. His work is exhibited in the Galleria Nazionale d'Arte moderna. 232.

Cafà, Melchiorre (Malta *c.* 1630-1667). Sculptor of the Bernini circle, and collaborator of Ferrata. His works in Rome: high altar in S. Maria in Campitelli, and reliefs in S. Agnese in Agone and S. Caterina a Magnanapoli.

Calderini, Guglielmo (Perugia 1837-Rome 1916). Architect. He designed the Palazzo di Giustizia (1887-1911) in eclectic style. 228.

Campi, Pietro Paolo (Massa Carrara; there is information about him from 1702 to 1735). Sculptor. His work can be seen in S. Agnese in Agone and in the left transept of St Peter's.

Canova, Antonio (Possegno 1757-Venice 1822). Sculptor. One of the great creative talents of the neoclassical period. He came to Rome for the first time in 1774, and settled there in 1781. The street in which he had his studio now bears his name (it lies between the Corso and Via di Ripetta). 222 ff., *234*.

Capogrossi, Giuseppe (b. Rome, 1900). He began as a tonal painter, and after joining the 'Origine' group at its foundation in 1949, along with Burri and Colla, he took up abstract painting. He is one of the most outstanding and individual artists of the new school. He lives in Rome, and there is a room devoted to his work in the Galleria Nazionale d'Arte moderna. 232.

Caravaggio (Michelangelo Merisi; Caravaggio 1573-Porto Ercole 1610). Painter. One of the greatest names in western painting. He began painting in Lombardy, and arrived in Rome *c.* 1593, where he worked for a long time and revealed himself as a very great artist. For his many works in Rome, and his tempestuous life, see pp. 162-67. Also 124, 151, 154-5, 156 ff., 194, 196 ff., 207, *209*, *210*, *211*.

Carrà, Carlo (Quargnento 1181-Milan 1966). Originally a pointilliste painter, he became a Futurist and was one of the signatories of the Manifesto of Futurist painters (1910). His works can be seen in the Galleria Nazionale d'Arte moderna. 231.

Carracci, Agostino (Bologna 1557-Parma 1602). Painter and engraver. He joined his brother Annibale in Rome in 1596 for the decoration of the Galleria di Palazzo Farnese, which he may have designed. His works are in the Galleria Colonna, the church of S. Onofrio al Gianicolo, and the church of S. Michele at Velletri (40 km. from Rome). 145, 167, 205.

Carracci, Annibàle (Bologna 1560-Rome 1609). Painter. He arrived in Rome in 1595 and worked in the Palazzo Farnese, first in the camerino with the story of Hercules, and then, with his brother and other assistants, on the walls and ceiling of the gallery. This was his major work, and the first of the great Baroque decorative ensembles. Many of his works are in Rome. One of the most important paintings of his later period, the *Flight into Egypt,* is in the Galleria Doria Pamphilj, where there is also a *Pietà* and a *Christ entombed.* His *Assumption* is in the Cappella Cerasi in S. Maria del Popolo. Other paintings in the Pinacoteca Capitolina, S. Maria di Monserrato, S. Caterina dei Funari, the Abbey church of Grottaferrata (21 km. from Rome), and the Borghese, Spada, Colonna and Pallavicini galleries. 145, 151, 165, 167, 205.

Castagno, Andrea del (Andrea di Bartolo; Castagno nel Mugello 1421-Florence 1457). Florentine painter. He came to Rome to work in the Vatican, but none of his painting there remains. 118.

Cavalier d'Arpino (Giuseppe Cesari; Arpino 1568-Rome 1640). Mannerist painter. Pupil of Roncalli. A prolific decorator. Frescoes in the hall of the Palazzo dei Conservatori, in the Lateran Baptistry, the Cappella Paolina in S. Maria Maggiore, the ceiling of the Cappella Contarelli in S. Luigi dei Francesi, the ceiling of the loggetta of the Palazzetto of Sixtus V, in Via di Parione 7 (on which he collaborated with Federico Zuccari). He designed the cartoons for the mosaics in the dome of St Peter's. Other works in S. Maria di Loreto, the Chiesa Nuova, Trinità dei Pellegrini, S. Silvestro al Quirinale, S. Vitale, S. Prassede, S. Cesareo, S. Crisogono, S. Onofrio, S. Maria in Traspontina, the Borghese,

Capitolina and Vatican galleries, and Accademia di S. Luca. 152, 158 ff

Cavallini, Pietro (Rome *c.* 1240/50-1330 ?). Painter. The most important Roman name in art between the late 13th century, and the beginning of the 14th. His real name was Cerroni, but he was nicknamed Cavallino, and this was the name he adopted. His first works were the frescoes and mosaics of St Paul outside the walls (1270-79), which were destroyed in the fire of 1823. In 1291 he produced the seven mosaic panels in the apse of S. Maria in Trastevere. In 1293 he painted the fresco in S. Cecilia in Trastevere. His lunette over the Acquasparta tomb in the Aracœli is of later date. He was in Naples 1316-20. 59, 75 ff., *122*, 163.

Ceroli, Mario (Castelfrentano 1938). Sculptor. His large sculpture in stainless steel, *Squilibrio* (1970), is in the Officina Carte-Valori in via Tuscolana. 232.

Cerquozzi, Michelangelo (Rome 1602-1660). Painter, pupil of Cavalier d'Arpino. Specialist in historical scenes, battles and 'bambocciate' (genre pieces with elaborate details of Roman life after the manner of Van Laer, known as il Bamboccio (*q.v.*). His *Revolt of Masaniello* is in the Galleria Spada. Other works in the Pinacoteca Capitolina, the Doria, Colonna and Corsini galleries, and the Villa d'Este at Tivoli. 207.

Codazzi, Viviano (Bergamo *c.* 1600-Rome 1672). Painter. Specialist in architectural landscapes. His works are in the Museo di Roma and the Galleria Nazionale di Palazzo Corsini. 207.

Colla, Ettore (Parma 1899-Rome 1968). Sculptor. His work in the Galleria Nazionale d'Arte moderna includes the *Great Spiral* (1962) on the outside of the building, originally designed for Spoleto. 232.

Conca, Sebastiano (Gaeta *c.* 1680-Naples 1764). Painter. Pupil and assistant of Solimena. With his brother Giovanni he painted frescoes in many Roman churches: S. Cecilia in Trastevere, Maddalena, San Clemente, SS. Luca e Martina, also the Sala delle Muse in the Vatican. Paintings in S. Lorenzo in Damaso, S. Maria della Luce, St John Lateran, and in the Spada, Corsini and Vatican galleries. 59, 217 ff.

Consagra, Pietro (Mazara del Vallo 1920). Sculptor. His works are in the Galleria Nazionale d'Arte moderna and in the courtyard of the Ministry of Foreign Affairs in the Farnesina. 232.

Cordier, Nicolas (known in Rome as il Franciosino; Lorraine *c.* 1567-Rome 1612). Sculptor. Worked extensively in Rome. Marble statues in the Cappella Paolina in S. Maria Maggiore, the colossal Henry IV in bronze in St John Lateran; statues and busts of the Aldobrandini family in S. Maria sopra Minerva. 195.

Costanzi, Placido (Naples 1688-1759). Painter. Frescoes on the ceiling of S. Gregorio al Celio (1727) and the apse of S. Maria in Campo Marzio. Paintings in S. Maria degli Angeli and in St Peter's. Worked with Van Bloemen, putting figures in his landscapes. Works in the Galleria Colonna. 217.

Cozza, Francesco (Stilo, Calabria, 1605-Rome 1682). Pupil of Domenichino, influenced by the Neapolitan school of Caravaggio, also by Preti, and by the luminous quality of Lanfranco. Frescoes in S. Andrea delle Fratte, on the ceiling of the Biblioteca del Collegio Innocenziano in Piazza Navona, and in a room of the Palazzo Pamphilj at Valmontone (42 km. from Rome). Paintings in the Galleria Colonna, the Ospedale di S. Spirito, and S. Maria della Cima at Genzano (30 km. from Rome). 207.

Daniele da Volterra (Daniele Ricciarelli; Volterra 1509-Rome 1566). Mannerist painter. Worked with Perin del Vaga in S. Marcello. Admirer of Michelangelo, of whom he made a bronze bust. After Michelangelo's death, Pius V made him paint clothes on the nudes in the *Last Judgment* in the Sistine Chapel. Fresco of the *Deposition* in Trinità dei Monti. Other frescoes in the Palazzo Massimo, and stuccos in the Sala Regia in the Vatican. 153.

De Chirico, Giorgio (Volos, Greece, 1888). Son of a Sicilian engineer, he studied in Athens. Some of his work, although nothing from his Metaphysical period, is in the Pinacoteca Vaticana and the Galleria Nazionale di Arte moderna.

Del Grande, Antonio (Rome 1625-1671). Architect. Designed the front of the Palazzo Doria Pamphilj in Mannerist style, the Galleria di Palazzo Colonna (1654) and the new prison in via Giulia. This was put up under Innocent X and is his most significant work. 193.

Della Gatta, Bartolomeo (Piero Dei; Florence 1448-1502/03). Painter and architect. One of the group of Florentine and Umbrian painters working on the decoration of the Sistine Chapel. Probably an assistant of Luca Signorelli. 92, 94.

Della Porta, Giacomo (? *c.* 1540-Rome 1602). Architect. He came from Lombardy. Assistant to Vignola, he became the chief architect of Rome *c.* 1580. He is responsible for the façade, the dome, and some of the chapels of the Gesù, the façade of S. Luigi dei Francesi, and the completion of S. Giovanni dei Fiorentini. Entirely his are the churches of the Madonna dei Monti, S. Atanasio dei Greci, and S. Giuseppe dei Falegnami. Together with Fontana he worked on the erection of the dome of St Peter's on the already existing drum. He completed other projects of Michelangelo: the Campidoglio, and the Sforza Chapel in S. Maria Maggiore. 113, 138, 144 ff., 148, 150, 167, 184, 205, 207.

Della Porta, Giovanni Battista (Porlezza, Como, *c.* 1542-Rome ? 1597). Sculptor. Collaborated on the Fontana dell'Acqua Felice, in Piazza S. Bernardo. In S. Pudenziana there is his marble group of the *Giving of the Keys to Peter*. Other sculptures in the Cappella Sistina of S. Maria Maggiore. He also produced eight nymphs for the Fontana dell'Ovato in the Villa d'Este at Tivoli. 147.

Della Porta, Guglielmo (Porlezza, Como, *c.* 1500-Rome 1577). Follower of Michelangelo, and restorer of many classical sculptures, including the Farnese Bull. His monument to Paul III in St Peter's (completed by his son Teodoro) is his masterpiece. His statues of Justice and Peace recall Michelangelo's Medici tombs in Florence. It is said that the head of Justice (originally nude) is a portrait of the pope's sister, Giulia Farnese. Other works in Palazzo Farnese (Abundance and Peace, also designed for the monument to Paul III), S. Maria del Popolo, the Galleria Borghese (a bas-relief in wax), the Sforza Chapel in S. Maria Maggiore (built by Giacomo della Porta). 195.

Della Porta, Tommaso (Porlezza ?-1618). Sculptor. Worked with Leonardo Sormani on the bronze statue of St Peter which was put on Trajan's Column in 1587. The statue of St Paul on the Antonine Column is also attributed to him. It was put up by Fontana in 1589. 32, 148.

De Pisis, Filippo (Luigi Filippo Tibertelli de Pisis; Ferrara 1896-Milan 1956). Painter and poet.

De Rossi, Mattia (Rome 1637-1695). Architect. G. L. Bernini's favourite pupil. He completed a number of Bernini's projects: a wing of the colonnade of St Peter's, the balustrade of Ponte S. Angelo, and the churches at the end of the Corso, in Piazza del Popolo. 183, 201 .

De Sanctis, Francesco (Rome 1693-1740). Architect. His name is associated principally with the picturesque Spanish Steps (Piazza di Spagna), built between 1723 and 1726, after projects by various other architects had been dropped. 213.

Diamante, Fra' (Terranuova Bracciolini, Arezzo, c. 1430-after 1498). Painter. One of the painters responsible for the upper part of the fresco in the Sistine Chapel, which showed a series of popes. 94.

Domenichino (Domenico Zampieri; Bologna 1581-Naples 1641). Painter. Followed Annibale Carracci to Rome in 1602 for the decoration of the Galleria di Palazzo Farnese. Here he painted the *Death of Adonis, Apollo and Hyacinth, Narcissus* and the *Girl with a Unicorn*. He produced many frescoes and altar-pieces for Roman villas, palaces and churches. His lunettes in S. Onofrio have a certain constricted feeling, but his great fresco cycles in S. Andrea della Valle, S. Carlo ai Catinari and S. Gregorio al Celio reveal his true quality and grand manner. His *Communion of St Jerome* is in the Pinacoteca Vaticana and there are other of his major paintings in the Doria Pamphilj and Borghese galleries. 145, 167, 202, 204, 206.

Donatello (Donato di Niccolò di Betto Bardi; Florence 1386-1466). Sculptor. His first visit to Rome was in 1409, possibly in the company of Brunelleschi. He came back in 1432-33, and created the canopy for the Blessed Sacrament in St Peter's, and the tomb of Giovanni Crivelli in S. Maria in Aracœli. 82.

Dorazio, Piero (Rome 1927). Abstract painter. 232.

Dughet, Gaspard (also known as Le Guaspre Poussin. He was a brother-in-law and also a pupil of Nicolas Poussin. Rome 1613-Florence 1675). Painter of romantic landscapes, usually with picturesque ruins. Paintings in the Doria Pamphilj, Colonna and Spada galleries, and also in the churches of S. Vitale and S. Martino ai Monti. 204.

Dujardin, Karel (Amsterdam c. 1622-Venice 1678). Painter of portraits and landscapes, mainly Italian. 208.

Dupérac, Etienne (Bordeaux c. 1525-Paris c. 1604). Painter, engraver and architect. He came to Rome when very young, and drew antique monuments and works of 16th-century architecture, especially that of Michelangelo. He published his *Vestigia delle Antichità di Roma* in 1575, also plans and views of the city and its environs

Duquesnoy, François (Brussels 1594-Leghorn 1643). Flemish sculptor. Studied in Rome in 1618 together with Poussin. His works in Rome: St Andrew, on the tribune of St Peter's, S. Susanna (1630) in S. Maria di Loreto, the putti of the Vryburch monument in S. Maria della Anima, stuccos and marbles with putti (his favourite motif) in the Spada and Doria Pamphilj galleries, and a Bacchanal in the Galleria Borghese. He also worked with Bernini on the Baldacchino of St Peter's.

Fancelli, Cosimo (Rome 1620-1688). Sculptor. Pupil and collaborator of Bernini and Pietro da Cortona. He decorated a number of Roman churches. His work is in S. Marco, SS. Luca e Martina, S. Maria in via Lata, S. Maria della Pace, etc. 193.

Fanzago, Cosimo (Clusone, near Bergamo, 1591-Naples 1678). Architect and sculptor. He worked in several Roman churches, including S. Agostino and S. Maria in via Lata. 193.

Ferrata, Ercole (Pellio Inferiore, Como 1610-Rome 1686). Sculptor of the Bernini circle. His works in Rome, which are remarkable for the perfection of their technique: S. Agnese and two marble altars in S. Agnese in Agone, tombs in S. Giovanni dei Fiorentini, S. Anastasia in the church of S. Anastasia, sketches in the Museo di Palazzo Venezia, portraits in the Sale dei Conservatori, and an angel on the façade of S. Andrea della Valle.

Filarete (Antonio Averulino; Florence 1400-Rome c. 1469). Sculptor, architect and goldsmith. Commissioned by Eugene IV, he designed the bronze doors of the central entrance of St Peter's (1433-35). Also attributed to him is a bronze bust of the Byzantine Emperor John Paleologos in the Sala dei Pontefici in the Vatican. 82, 116, 230.

Finelli, Giuliano (Carrara c. 1601-Rome 1657). Sculptor of the Bernini circle, he collaborated on the Baldacchino of St Peter's. Other Roman works: S. Cecilia in S. Maria di Loreto, fine tombs in S. Caterina a Magnanapoli (1648), and a bust of Cardinal Santori in St John Lateran.

Fontana, Carlo (Brusate, Canton Ticino, 1634-Rome 1714). Architect, and disciple of Bernini, he collaborated in much of the Baroque architecture of Rome: altar in style of Bernini in S. Maria in Traspontina, façade of S. Marcello al Corso, Cappella Cybo in S. Maria del Popolo, portico of S. Maria in Trastevere, and fountain in the piazza, a chapel in S. Andrea della Valle. His masterpiece is the Ospizio di S. Michele a Ripa. 68, 207, 212.

Fontana, Domenico (Melide, Lugano, 1543-Naples 1607). Chief architect to Sixtus V. He designed the Cappella del Presepe in S. Maria Maggiore, began the building of the Palazzo del Quirinale, built the Lateran Palace, and moved the Egyptian obelisk from Nero's Circus to the Piazza S. Pietro in 1585. Worked on St Peter's dome with G. della Porta. 55, 74, 113, 146 ff., 167, 193.

Fouquet, Jean (Tours *c.* 1420-1477/81). French painter and miniaturist. He was in Rome at the time of Eugene IV and painted his portrait (now lost). 52, 82, 232.

Fragonard, Jean Honoré (Grasse 1732-Paris 1806). French painter and engraver.

Franchina, Nino (Palmanova di Udine, 1912). Sculptor. His works are in the Galleria Nazionale d'Arte moderna. 232.

Fuga, Ferdinando (Florence 1699-Naples 1781). He came to Rome at 18 and became chief architect to the pope, working in Rome for about 20 years. 55, 58, 149, 212, 217.

Galilei, Alessandro (Florence 1691-Rome 1736). Architect. In 1732 he won the competition for the façade of St John Lateran. It was completed three years later and is his major work. He also did the Corsini Chapel (the first chapel in the left hand aisle of the basilica) and the façade of S. Giovanni dei Fiorentini. 217.

Gaulli, Giovan Battista (also known as Baciccia; Genoa 1639-Rome 1709). Painter. On arriving in Rome, he joined the circle of Bernini. Among his principal frescoes are: the ceiling of the Gesù (a sketch of which is in the Galleria Spada), SS. Apostoli, S. Marta in Piazza del Collegio Romano, the sacristy of S. Maria di Montesanto, S. Agnese in Agone (allegories at the base of the dome). Among his portraits, the one of Clement IX in the Galleria dell'Accademia di S. Luca is outstanding. Many altar-pieces, sketches, and paintings, including the Maddalena, S. Maria in Campitelli, S. Andrea al Quirinale, S. Rocco, S. Francesco a Ripa, S. Nicola da Tolentino, Palazzo Chigi, the Spada, Capi-

toline and Vatican galleries, the Galleria Nazionale d'Arte antica. 204.

Gentile da Fabriano (Fabriano *c.* 1370-Rome 1427). Painter. One of the great exponents of international Gothic. In Rome in 1425 where he worked for Martin V. Frescoes of St John the Baptist in St John Lateran. All his Roman work has been lost except for the *Virgin with angels* now in the Museo Capitolare di Velletri (40 km. outside Rome), and parts of the Quaratesi polyptych in the Pinacoteca Vaticana, where there is also an *Annunciation* attributed to him. 80, 82, *137, 138.*

Gentileschi, Artemisia (Rome 1597-Naples after 1651). Painter. Daughter and pupil of Orazio Gentileschi (*q.v.*). A self-portrait (?) in the Galleria Nazionale d'Arte antica, and a S. Cecilia in the Galleria Spada. 205.

Gentileschi, Orazio (Orazio Lomi; Pisa *c.* 1562-London 1647). Painter. Frescoes in S. Maria Maggiore, St John Lateran, the loggia of Palazzo Pallavicini-Rospigliosi (in collaboration with Agostino Tassi), the Salone Sistino of the Biblioteca Vaticana. His works are also in the churches of S. Silvestro in Capite and S. Maria della Pace, in the Galleria Spada, the Galleria Nazionale d'Arte antica (*St Francis* and *St Cecilia*) and the Pinacoteca Vaticana. 205.

Géricault, Théodore (Rouen 1791-Paris 1824). Painter.

Ghezzi, Pier Leone (Rome 1674-1755). Painter and engraver. He painted the martyrdom of St Ignatius in S. Clemente, and S. Giuliana Falconieri in S. Maria dell'Orazione e Morte in Via Giulia. A room of the Villa Falconieri (22 km. outside Rome) is decorated with his caricatures and a self-portrait. 215 ff.

Ghiberti, Lorenzo (Florence 1378-1455). Sculptor, goldsmith, painter, architect and writer on art. 75 ff., 82.

Ghirlandaio, Domenico (Domenico Bigordi; Florence 1449-1494). Painter. Summoned to Rome in 1481 to decorate the Sistine Chapel. With the help of his brother, Davide, he produced two frescoes, of which the only remaining one is that of the *Vocation of the Apostles.* 94.

Giaquinto, Corrado (Molfetta 1703-Naples 1765). Painter. He came to Rome from Naples in 1723 and became a pupil of Solimena. His works are in: S. Nicola dei Lorenesi (1731), S. Lorenzo in Damaso (Cappella Ruffo), S. Giovanni Calibita, S. Croce in Gerusalemme (1751). He painted a fine *Trinity* in the Trinità degli Spagnoli, a *Baptism of Christ* (1750) in S. Maria dell'Orto, and an *Assumption* in the Collegiale di Rocca di Papa. 218.

Giocondo (Fra Giovanni da Verona; Verona *c.* 1433-Rome 1515). Architect. He worked with Raphael on plans for the new building of St Peter's. 112.

Giotto di Bondone (Colle di Vespignano nel Mugello, *c.* 1267-Florence 1337). He came to Rome for the first time probably after doing the upper part of the frescoes in the upper church at Assisi. The Cross in S. Tommaso dei Cenci, recently discovered by I. Toesca, was presumably painted during this first visit, together with the tondi in S. Maria Maggiore. The rest of his Roman works were done during a second, and possibly a third visit (*c.* 1313). These are the fresco of the *Jubilee* in St John Lateran (of which a small fragment survives), the *Navicella* in St Peter's (completely restored). His Stefaneschi polyptych is in the Pinacoteca Vaticana. It includes work by his assistants. 74 ff., 116.

Giovanni da Udine (Udine 1487-Rome 1564). Painter. One of Raphael's most talented pupils. He specialized in 'grotesques' in the Logge Vaticane (1517-19), the Sala di Psiche in the Farnesina, the Villa Madama, and Castel S. Angelo. He worked with Perin del Vaga on the decoration of the Sala dei Pontefici, under Leo X. 110, 132.

Giovanni Dalmata (G. Ducnovic; Traù *c.* 1440-after 1509). Sculptor and architect. He worked with Mino da Fiesole on the screen and the choir of the Sistine Chapel, on the altar in the sacristy of S. Marco (1474), the tomb of Paul II and other works in the Vatican Grottoes. His Roverella tomb in S. Clemente (1477) shows the influence of Mino. Other sculptures in S. Maria sopra Minerva and SS. Apostoli. 106.

Giuliano da Maiano (Maiano di Fiesole *c.* 1432-Naples 1490). Vasari maintains that he designed the Palazzo Venezia.

Giulio Romano (Giulio Pippi; Rome 1499-Mantua 1546). Painter and architect. The most brilliant of Raphael's pupils, and eventually his heir. He collaborated in the *Stanze* and *Logge* of the Vatican, also the Farnesina and Villa Madama. He built the Palazzo Maccorani (1535) in Piazza S. Eustachio, and produced many designs for architects and decorators. Paintings are in the Galleria Nazionale d'Arte Antica, the Borghese and Villa Albani galleries, and the Pinacoteca Vaticana. Two of his altar-pieces are in S. Maria dell'Anima and the sacristy of St Peter's. 118, 125, 132, 152.

Gozzoli (Benozzo di Lese; Florence 1420-Pistoia 1497). Painter. He came to Rome with Fra' Angelico *c.* 1445 and worked with him on the frescoes of the Cappella Niccolina in the Vatican, thus introducing to Rome the painting of the Florentine Renaissance. He seems to have made a second visit, and to this period belong his surviving works: fragments of a fresco in S. Maria di Aracœli, an altar-piece with the *Virgin and St Thomas* in the Pinacoteca Vaticana, and the *Madonna with angels* in Cathedral of Sermoneta. 82, 108.

Gramatica, Antiveduto (Rome 1571-1626). Painter. His works in Rome are a *Nativity* in the Galleria Doria Pamphilj, a *Magdalen* in the Galleria Borghese, a *Guardian angel* in S. Agostino. *St Hyacinth* in S. Maria della Scala, and *St Romuald* in the Camaldolese monastery above Frascati (26 km. from Rome). 158.

Guercino (Giovanni Francesco Barbieri; Cento 1591-Bologna 1666). Painter. Summoned to Rome by Gregory XV in 1621 to decorate the Loggia delle Benedizioni in St Peter's. This work was interrupted at the pope's death. He also painted the large picture of the *Burial of S. Petronilla* (now in the Pinacoteca Capitolina) also destined for St Peter's. This is one of the most famous paintings of the 17th century, for the influence that it had on other artists. In the Casino of Villa Ludovisi he painted an allegorical fresco of Dawn and Night, which is his masterpiece. Many of his paintings are to be seen in the Doria, Spada, Colonna, Borghese and Corsini galleries, and in the churches of S. Agostino, S. Maria della Vittoria, and the Chiesa Nuova. His *Magdalen in a landscape* is in the Pinacoteca Vaticana. 167, 202, 204.

Guidetti, Guidetto (Lombard; ?-1564). Architect. Disciple of Michelangelo, he carried out the master's plans for the Palazzo dei Conservatori. He designed the Cappella Cesi in S. Prassede (*c.* 1550), the church of S. Maria dell'Orto in Trastevere, and the façade of S. Caterina dei Funari, which was his last work. 144.

Guttuso, Renato (Bagheria 1912). Painter. His works are in the Galleria Nazionale d'Arte moderna. 232.

Hackert, Philipp (Prenzlau, Brandenburg, 1737-Caregi, Florence, 1807). German painter. Some of his pictures hang in Villa d'Este at Tivoli. 226.

Isaia da Pisa (his activities are recorded from 1447 to 1464). Sculptor. His most complete work in Rome is the tomb of Eugene IV, which was designed for St Peter's and was eventually transferred to S. Salvatore in Lauro. Other fragments of his are to be found in S. Marco, S. Agostino, S. Maria sopra Minerva, and the Vatican Grottoes. There is also a lavabo by him in the sacristy of the Sistine Chapel. 106.

Jacopino del Conte (Florence 1510-Rome 1598). Painter. Trained in the school of Andrea del Sarto. He worked with Salviati on the decoration of the Oratorio di S. Giovanni Decollato (1537-41). Portraits in the Borghese and Spada galleries, and other works in S. Luigi dei Francesi and Villa Albani. 153.

Jacopo di Andrea (Florence, active c. 1487). Sculptor. He carved the Albertoni tomb in S. Maria del Popolo. 106.

Jacopo da Camerino (Fra'; Camerino, Macerata, active in 1290-92). Mosaicist and architect. Worked with Torriti on the apse mosaic of the Lateran basilica, dated 1291.

Juvarra, Filippo (Messina 1678-Madrid 1736). Architect. His only building is the Cappella Antamoro in S. Girolamo della Carità (c. 1708-10). Some ascribe to him the atrium of the Convent of S. Agostino in via della Scrofa, also the loggia of Palazzetto Zuccari at Trinità dei Monti. 215.

Kauffmann, Angelica (Chur, Grisons, 1741-Rome 1807). Swiss painter. Her work is in the Galleria dell'Accademia di S. Luca. 226.

Lanfranco, Giovanni (Terenzo, Parma, 1582-Rome 1647). Painter. Pupil of Agostino Carracci. Sent to Rome by Ranuccio Farnese in 1602, where he worked with Annibale Carracci on the last phase of the decoration of the Galleria del Palazzo Farnese. In the same building there is a small room entirely decorated by him. There are three frescoes of hermits by him in S. Maria dell'Orazione e Morte in via Giulia. Of a later date are his frescoes in S. Andrea della Valle, S. Agostino, St Peter's and S. Carlo ai Catinari. Other works of his are in the Pinacoteca Capitolina, and the Doria Pamphilj, Colonna, Borghese and Barberini galleries. 145, 167, 206.

Le Nain, Louis (Laon 1593-Paris 1648). Painter, in Rome between 1629 and 1630. 208.

Leonardo (Vinci 1452-Cloux 1519). He came to Rome when he was sixty as a protégé of Cardinal Giuliano de' Medici, and stayed until 1517. His only painting in Rome, the *Saint Jerome* in the Pinacoteca Vaticana, is early. 108 ff., 111 ff., 118, *144*.

Libera, Adalberto (Villalagarina, Trento, 1903-Rome 1963). Architect. He planned the Palazzo dei Congressi at the EUR. 228 ff.

Ligorio, Pirro (Naples c. 1510-Ferrara 1583). Painter and architect. He did some frescoes in the Oratorio di S. Giovanni Decollato, and after that devoted himself entirely to architectural works: the Villa d'Este at Tivoli, and the Casino or Villa of Pius IV in the Vatican gardens. 153, 193.

Lippi, Annibale (mid-16th century). Architect. Of Florentine origin and Mannerist in style, he worked on the Villa Medici in Rome. He also designed the apse of S. Marcello al Corso (1569), and the Palazzo Caetani alle Botteghe Oscure is attributed to him. 149.

Lippi, Filippino (Prato 1457-Florence 1504). Painter. Son of Filippo Lippi (*q.v.*). Pupil of Botticelli. In Rome from 1489 to 1493, where he painted the frescoes in the Cappella Carafa in S. Maria sopra Minerva.

Lippi, Filippo (Florence c. 1406-Spoleto 1469). Painter. In the Galleria Nazionale d'Arte antica in Palazzo Barberini are his *Madonna of Tarquinia* (1437) and an *Annunciation* (c. 1443). A triptych with the *Coronation of the Virgin with angels and monks* is in the Pinacoteca Vaticana.

Longhi, Martino (Il Vecchio; Viggiù ?-Rome 1591). Architect. In Rome from 1537, where he worked with Giacomo della Porta on the Palazzo Borghese and the buildings on the Capitol. He also built the tower of the Palazzo Senatorio. 138.

Lorrain (Claude Gellée; Champagne, Vosges, 1600-Rome 1682). French painter. He came to Rome before 1620 and worked with Cavalier d'Arpino and Agostino Tassi on the decoration of the Villa Lante at Bagnaia, Viterbo. In the Galleria Doria Pamphilj are his *Rest on the Flight into Egypt*, also *A view of Delphi with a procession*, and *Mercury and the bulls of Apollo*. Other works in the Galleria Colonna. 203 ff.

Lotto, Lorenzo (Venice *c.* 1480-Loreto 1556). Painter. In Rome in 1509, working with Bramantino, Peruzzi and Sodoma on the *Stanze* of Julius II. Their frescoes were later destroyed to make room for those of Raphael. His works are in the Pinacoteca Capitolina, and the Pallavicini, Doria Pamphilj, and Colonna galleries. There is a *Sacra Conversazione* signed and dated 1508 in the Galleria Borghese. 118, 159.

Maderno, Carlo (Capolago, Canton Ticino 1556-Rome 1629). Architect. His first important work was the façade of S. Susanna (1603). He designed the interiors of S. Andrea della Valle and S. Maria della Vittoria, and the domes of S. Giovanni dei Fiorentini and S. Andrea della Valle, and built St Peter's façade in 1607-12. 113, 149, 151, 177, 180 ff., 193 ff., 205.

Maderno, Stefano (Bissone, Canton Ticino 1576-Rome 1636). Sculptor. In Rome from 1597. His first work in Rome was the *S. Cecilia* in S. Cecilia in Trastevere. Other sculptures are in S. Maria Maggiore (Cappella Paolina), S. Maria sopra Minerva (Cappella Aldobrandini), S. Maria di Loreto, S. Maria della Pace, S. Lorenzo in Damaso. 49, 58, 195.

Mafai, Mario (Rome 1902-1965). Painter. His works are in the Galleria Nazionale d'Arte moderna. 231.

Manfredi, Bartolomeo (Ostiano, Mantua *c.* 1580-Rome 1624). Painter. His *Bacchus* and *Good Fortune* are in the Galleria Nazionale d'Arte antica in Palazzo Corsini. 205.

Mantegna, Andrea (Isola di Carturo, Padua 1431-Mantua 1506). Painter and engraver. One of the greatest Renaissance artists, with a passion for classical antiquity. Summoned to Rome in 1488 by Innocent VIII for the decoration of his private chapel in the Belvedere, which was destroyed in 1780.

Manzù, Giacomo (Bergamo 1908). Sculptor. In 1949, after much controversy, he won the competition for the new side doors of St Peter's. These were put in place in 1964. He lives at Ardea (36 km. from Rome) where in 1969 a museum for his works was opened. 82, 116, *228*, 230, 232.

Maratta, Carlo (Camerano di Ancona 1625-Rome 1713). Painter. One of his first works was the *Nativity* in S. Giuseppe dei Falegnami (1650). Later came his *Death of St Francis* in the Gesù, a *Madonna with saints* in S. Maria del Popolo (1685), the *Baptism of Christ* in S. Maria

degli Angeli, the portrait of Clement IX in the Pinacoteca Vaticana, *St Ambrose and St Charles in glory* in the church of SS. Ambrogio e Carlo on the Corso, etc. He painted frescoes in the Palazzo Altieri, the Villa Falconieri at Frascati (22 km outside Rome), and there are various other works of his in the museums of Rome. 204.

Marchionni, Carlo (Ancona 1702-Rome 1786). Architect and sculptor. His most notable work is the Villa Albani, built for Cardinal Alessandro between 1743 and 1763, and celebrated by Winckelmann. He designed the Sacristy of St Peter's and the picturesque passage between it and the basilica. (This is visible from the Arco delle Campane, on the left-hand side of the façade; 1776-84). His sculptures include the monument to Benedict XIII in S. Maria sopra Minerva, and others in S. Apollinare, S. Crisogono, and S. Maria Maggiore. 218.

Martini, Arturo (Treviso 1889-Milan 1947). Sculptor. There is a room devoted to his work in the Galleria Nazionale d'Arte moderna. 230.

Masaccio (Tommaso di Ser Giovanni di Simone Guidi, S. Giovanni Valdarno 1401-Rome 1428?). Painter. An artist of the greatest genius, he was in Rome in 1425 with Masolino. Frescoes in S. Clemente and a triptych with double front for the Cappella Colonna in S. Maria Maggiore. Parts of this are now in various museums. 80 ff.

Masolino da Panicale (Tommaso di Cristofano Fini; Panicale in Valdarno 1383-1440 (1447). Painter. Working in Rome in 1425 on a cycle of frescoes in the Cappella di S. Caterina in S. Clemente, depicting scenes from the lives of S. Caterina and S. Ambrogio; also a *Crucifixion* in which Masaccio collaborated with noticeable independence of style. His collaboration with Masaccio is also noticeable in the double-fronted triptych for the Cappella Colonna in S. Maria Maggiore, parts of which are now in various galleries. There is a *Crucifixion* in the Pinacoteca Vaticana, also a *Dormition of the Virgin* attributed to him. 80 ff.

Matteo da Città di Castello (Matteo Bastolani; Città di Castello between 1566 and 1616). Architect. He designed the Cappella Barberini in S. Andrea della Valle, also the Ponte Rotto on the Tiber.

Maturino da Firenze (Florence 1490-Rome 1527/28. Painter. Assisted Raphael in the Vatican, and was one of his most faithful followers. With Polidoro da Caravaggio he decorated the fronts of many Roman palaces with frescoes, and especially with graffiti. The Palazzo Ricci in Piazza Ricci was one of these. Some of his detached graffiti can be seen in the Museo di Rome. Landscapes, also done in collaboration with Polidoro, are in S. Silvestro al Quirinale. 148.

Mazzoni, Giulio (Piacenza c. 1525-c. 1618). Painter, sculptor and stucco worker. Pupil and assistant of Giorgio Vasari in Florence and Naples. His talents in stucco were recognized in Rome, where, between 1556 and 1560, he decorated the façade and courtyard of the Palazzo Spada, begun by Giulio Merisi. Also attributed to him is the so-called Palazzetto dei Pupazzi in Via dei Banchi Vecchi, where Sixtus V resided. In the Cappella Cerasi in S. Maria del Popolo is a *St Catherine* sculpted and signed by him, together with some very fine stuccos.

Melozzo da Forlì (Marco Ambrogi or Melozzo degli Ambrosi; Forlì 1438-1494). Painter. He may have followed Piero della Francesca to Rome in 1459 at the invitation of Sixtus IV. In the Pinacoteca Vaticana there is a fresco by him of the humanist Bartolomeo Platina. His frescoes for the apse of SS. Apostoli are now divided between the Pinacoteca Vaticana and the Palazzo del Quirinale. In 1489 he designed the mosaic decoration of the Cappella di S. Elena in S. Croce in Gerusalemme. Works in S. Maria sopra Minerva. 88.

Mengs, Anton Raphael (Ústí nad Labem, 1728-Rome 1799). Bohemian painter and writer on art. His *Parnassus* (1761) fresco in the Casino della Villa Albani became the fulcrum of neo-classical theories expounded by himself and Winckelmann in opposition to the Baroque. There is another fresco of his in the church of S. Eustachio in Piazza Vittorio. Also allegories by him in the Sala dei Papiri in the Museo Sacro in the Vatican. 218, 226.

Michelangelo (Michelangelo Buonarroti; Caprese 1475-Rome 1564). Architect, painter, sculptor and poet. He first came to Rome in 1496, and his *Pietà* dates from this period. He returned several times, finally settling there from 1534 to his death. He painted the ceiling of the Sistine Chapel, the *Last Judgment*, and the Cappella Paolina. His sculpture in Rome includes the *Pietà*, the tomb of Julius II in S. Pietro in Vincoli, the *Risen Christ* in S.

Maria sopra Minerva. His architectural works in Rome are the chapel in Castel S. Angelo, S. Maria degli Angeli, the dome of St Peter's, the Campidoglio, and the Porta Pia. 16, 32, 33, 88 ff., 94, 103 ff., 108 ff., 112 ff., 118, 124, 132-45, 150, *158, 160, 161, 165, 166, 168,* 181, 200, 207, 227.

Michelin, Jean (Langres, Champagne, c. 1616-Paris c. 1670). French painter of Roman views. 208.

Michelozzo (Michelozzo Michelozzi di Bartolomeo; Florence 1396-1472). Sculptor and architect, he worked with Donatello on the altar canopy in old St Peter's. 82.

Miel, Jan (Beveren-Waas 1599-Turin 1663). Flemish painter. He worked on the decoration of Palazzo Barberini, and in 1651 painted a *Crossing of the Red Sea* for Alexander VII in the Palazzo del Quirinale. Other works in S. Martino ai Monti and the Galleria Nazionale d'Arte antica. 208.

Mino da Fiesole (Fiesole 1429-Florence 1484). Sculptor. His chief works (usually done with many assistants) are the screen and choir in the Sistine Chapel, the Forteguerri tomb in S. Cecilia, the Tornabuoni tomb in S. Maria sopra Minerva, and the tomb of Paul II, part of which is now in the Louvre, and other parts in the Vatican Grottoes. 86, 106.

Mirko (Mirko Basaldella; Udine 1910-Cambridge, Mass., 1970). Sculptor. He designed the commemorative bronze doors of the Fosse Ardeatine (1949-51). Other works in the Galleria Nazionale d'Arte moderna.

Mochi, Francesco (Montevarchi 1580-Rome 1654). Sculptor. Trained in Tuscany and later in Rome, he worked in the Cappella Paolina in S. Maria Maggiore. His best works are the statues for the Cappella Barberini in S. Andrea della Valle. Works in Palazzo Braschi and S. Silvestro al Quirinale, and the *Veronica* in the tribune of St Peter's. 195, 207.

Modigliani, Amedeo (Leghorn 1884-Paris 1920). Painter. Two of his paintings are in the Galleria Nazionale d'Arte moderna, the *Lady with the collar*, and a *Nude.* 231.

Mola, Pier Francesco (Coldrerio, Canton Ticino, 1612-Rome 1666). Painter. Pupil of Cavalier d'Arpino and one of the major exponents of the neo-Venetian style. Many of his works are in Rome, in the churches of S. Pietro in Vincoli, S. Anastasia, S. Carlo al Corso, SS. Domenico e Sisto, and in the Doria, Borghese,

Colonna, Corsini, and Spada galleries, the Accademia di S. Luca, the Pinacoteca Capitolina and Vaticana. 204.

Morandi, Giorgio (Bologna 1890-1964). Painter. Works are in the Pinacoteca Vaticana and the Galleria Nazionale di Arte moderna. 230.

Morandi, Riccardo (Rome 1902). Architect and engineer, specializing in the techniques of pre-stressed concrete. 229 ff.

Morelli, Cosimo (Imola 1732-1812). Architect. Designer of the Palazzo Braschi with impressive stairway. 221.

Moretti, Luigi (Rome 1907). Architect. His buildings in the Foro Italico in 1936 and in Trastevere. One of the most gifted of contemporary Italian architects. He designed the Palazzina del Girasole (*q.v.*), and the office blocks at the entrance to the EUR quarter (1967). 228 ff.

Nebbia, Cesare (Orvieto 1512-1590). Painter. He worked in Rome under Sixtus V with the Mannerists. His works are in S. Maria Maggiore, St John Lateran, the Palazzo del Quirinale, and the Oratorio del Gonfalone. 154.

Nervi, Pier Luigi (Sondrio 1891). Architect and engineer. His most important works in Rome are the Palazzo and the Palazzetto dello Sport, the Stadio Flaminio (1960), and the Olympic viaduct (in which he collaborated with others). More recently he has built the Officina Carte-Valori and the new Audience Hall in the Vatican. 229, *230*.

Nolli, Giovan Battista (Como 1692-1756). Architect and engraver. In 1748 he published a plan of Rome. Previous plans had been drawn up by Leonardo Bufalini in 1551, Antonio Tempesta in 1606, and Giovan Battista Falda in 1676. A complete collection of historic plans of Rome is in the Biblioteca Vaticana (Galleria Clementina, 2nd section). 219.

Overbeck, Johannes Friedrich (Lübeck, *c.* 1789-Rome 1869). Painter. He came to Rome in 1810 with the painters Pforr and Vogel. 226.

Pannini, Giovanni Paolo (Piacenza *c.* 1691-Rome 1765). Painter and architect. In Rome in 1715, as a pupil of Benedetto Luti, he was famous for his historical paintings and stupendous views of the city, two of which are in the coffee house of the Quirinal. He frescoed the library adjoining the monastery of S. Croce in Gerusalemme, and the Villa Grazioli at Frascati. Other paintings of his are in the Museo di Roma, the Galleria dell'Accademia di S. Luca, the Galleria di Villa Albani and the Galleria Corsini. He designed the altar of S. Teresa in S. Maria della Scala. 210 ff., 215, 217.

Paolo Romano (Paolo Salvati or Salviati; early 15th century). Sculptor. Work in S. Maria in Trastevere, and S. Francesco at Capranica (Viterbo). 106.

Paolo Taccone (Paolo di Mariano da Sezze. Also called Paolo Romano. There is information regarding him from 1451 to 1477). Sculptor and decorator, working in Rome. There is an *Angel*, signed by him, on the façade of S. Giacomo degli Spagnoli (now N.S. del Sacro Cuore) in Piazza Navona, and a *St Paul* on the Ponte S. Angelo. 106.

Penni, Giovanfrancesco (known as il Fattore; Florence 1488-Naples 1530). Pupil and assistant of Raphael in the Farnesina, the Vatican *Stanze* and *Logge*. 125, 132.

Perin del Vaga (Pietro Bonacolsi or Buonaccorsi; Florence *c.* 1501-Rome 1547). Painter. Pupil and assistant of Raphael in the Vatican *Logge*. He frescoed the Palazzo Baldassini (1520-22) and painted a *Pietà* in S. Stefano del Cacco. Frescoes in Trinità dei Monti, S. Marcello al Corso (1536), Castel S. Angelo and the Vatican. 110, 152.

Perugino (Pietro Vannucci; Città della Pieve *c.* 1448-Fontignano di Perugia 1523). Painter. He was in Rome between 1480 and 1482 and played a major part in the early decoration of the Sistine Chapel and the Vatican *Stanze*. The *Giving of the keys to Peter* in the Sistine Chapel is one of his finest works. There is an altar-piece with the *Virgin and Saints* in the Pinacoteca Vaticana. Other works in the Galleria Borghese, Palazzo Barberini, Villa Albani and S. Cecilia in Trastevere, 90, 93 ff., 105, 118.

Peruzzi, Baldassarre (Siena 1481-Rome 1536). Painter and architect. His frescoes in the apse of S. Onofrio show his debt to Pinturicchio and Sodoma. His buildings are the Farnesina, for Agostino Chigi, the Palazzo Savelli (later Orsini) on the Theatre of Marcellus, and the Palazzo Massimo alle Colonne. 62, 118, 132 ff., 148, 150.

Peterzano, Simone (from Bergamo, but active in Milan 1573-96). 153.

Piacentini, Marcello (Rome 1881-1960). Architect. Son of Pio Piacentini, and principal architect in Rome during the Fascist régime. He was responsible for pulling down the old houses in front of Piazza S. Pietro known as the 'Spina dei Borghi', and laying out the rather unfortunate Via della Conciliazione (1941-50). 230.

Piacentini, Pio (Rome 1846-1928). Architect. Academic and eclectic in style, his principal works are the Palazzo delle Esposizioni in Via Nazionale (1880-82), the Palazzo del Ministero di Grazia e Giustizia in Via Arenula (1920). 228.

Pier Matteo da Amelia (Amelia *c.* 1450-1503/08). Painter of the Umbrian school. He worked on the early decoration of the Sistine ceiling and with Pinturicchio in the Borgia Apartment. 106, 110.

Piero della Francesca (Borgo San Sepolcro 1410/20-1492). Painter. Vasari maintains that Piero came to Rome for the first time under Nicholas V (before 1455) and it may be during this visit that he painted the fresco in S. Maria Maggiore, of which fragments survive. He came again in 1459-60, at the time of Pius II, to paint in the Vatican, but these works are lost. 81, 118, 123.

Piero di Cosimo (Piero di Lorenzo di Chimenti; Florence 1462-1521). Painter. Pupil and assistant of Cosimo Rosselli on the wall frescoes of the Sistine Chapel. 94.

Pietro da Cortona (Pietro Berrettini da Cortona; Cortona 1596-Rome 1699). Painter and architect. He is responsible for the church of SS. Luca e Martina near the Forum, the façade of S. Maria della Pace and that of S. Maria in Via Lata, the dome of S. Ambrogio e Carlo al Corso, and the alteration of S. Martino ai Monti. In painting, his works are: a fresco of the Barberini family on the ceiling of the largest room of the Palazzo, the story of Turnus and Aeneas in the Galleria del Palazzo Pamphilj, and mosaics for three chapels in St Peter's. Numerous paintings in S. Salvatore in Lauro, the Palazzo dei Conservatori, the Pinacoteca Capitolina, S. Lorenzo in Miranda, S. Ivo, the Galleria Colonna, Galleria Doria, Accademia di S. Luca, Galleria Borghese and Galleria Barberini. 51, 180, 186, 193, 198 ff.

Pinelli, Bartolomeo (Rome 1781-1835). Painter and engraver. 226.

Pinturicchio (Bernardino di Betto; Perugia 1454-Siena 1513). Painter of the Umbrian school. Worked with Perugino on the Sistine Chapel frescoes between 1481 and 1483 (*Circumcision of the sons of Moses,* and

Baptism of Christ). He later adopted the Florentine manner, as we can see in his frescoes in the Cappella di S. Bernardino in S. Maria di Aracœli, the Borgia Apartment (1491-94), and the chapels in S. Maria del Popolo. Other works in Galleria Borghese and the Pinacoteca Vaticana. 94, 110.

Piranesi, Giovan Battista (Mogliano di Mestre 1720-Rome 1779). He began his artistic training in Venice, and came to Rome to study engraving under Vasi. The Prisons (*Carceri*) of 1750 were his first collection of Roman engravings, followed by the Views of Rome, the Antiquities of Rome (1756) and the *Trattato della Magnificenza e Architettura dei Romani* (1761). His complete works are in the Calcografia Nazionale. His only building in Rome is the church of S. Maria del Priorato on the Aventine, put up in 1765 for the Knights of Malta. 210 ff., 218 ff.

Pisanello (Antonio Pisano; Pisa, before 1395-1455). Painter and medal designer. Trained in the Verona school, he worked with Gentile da Fabriano whom he assisted in Rome in 1426 with the frescoes of St John Lateran, now lost. 80, 82.

Polydorus. Rhodian sculptor, 2nd-1st century BC. He worked with Agesander (*q.v.*) and Athenodorus on the *Laocoön*. 30.

Polydoro da Caravaggio (Polidoro Caldara; Caravaggio *c.* 1500-Messina 1546). Painter. Disciple of Raphael and assistant to Giovanni da Udine in the decoration of the Vatican *Logge*. His outstanding work was the graffito decoration on the façades of 16th-century palaces, *e.g.* Palazzo Ricci, and a house, No. 9, Via della Maschera d'oro. 148.

Pollaiuolo (Antonio del Pollaiuolo; Florence 1431 or 1432-Rome 1498). Painter, sculptor and goldsmith. Son of a poulterer, Jacopo di Antonio Benci, hence the name. He came to Rome with his brother Piero in 1484, where he produced the tomb of Sixtus IV, now in the Vatican Grottoes, which was his finest work. He also did the tomb of Innocent VIII in St Peter's, but this one was dismantled in 1621 and badly put together again. Commonly attributed to him are the bronze twins added to the Capitoline she-wolf. Some claim that these were done by his brother Piero. 107 ff, 152.

Pollaiuolo (Piero del Pollaiuolo; Florence *c.* 1443-Rome 1496). Painter, sculptor and goldsmith. Younger brother of Antonio. 107 ff.

Pomarancio (Niccolò Circignani; Pomarance, Pisa, 1517-after 1596). Mannerist painter. His is one of the hands involved in an unusual martyrdom fresco in S. Stefano Rotondo, striking for its crude realism. Other frescoes in S. Giovanni e Paolo, S. Cecilia in Trastevere, S. Pietro in Montorio, the Sala dei bronzi in the Museo Gregoriano Etrusco, and in the Vatican. 152 ff.

Pomodoro, Arnaldo (Morciano di Romagna 1926). Sculptor. A large work, which was exhibited in the Expo at Montreal, stands on the Piazzale in front of the Ministero degli Affari Esteri. His *Colonna del viaggiatore* stands in front of the Galleria Nazionale d'Arte moderna, which contains other sculpture by him. 232.

Pontelli, Baccio (Florence, where he is mentioned c. 1450-Urbino 1492). Architect. Working in Rome in 1483 for Sixtus IV. According to a recent hypothesis, he may have built the Sistine Chapel. 88.

Ponzio, Flaminio (Milan c. 1560-Rome 1613). Architect. He collaborated with other architects on S. Maria Maggiore, the Villa Borghese, the church of S. Sebastiano, and the façades of the Palazzo Sciarra, the Palazzo Colonna and the Palazzo Borghese. 55, 156 ff.

Poussin, Nicolas (Villers, Les Andelys, 1594-Rome 1665). He came to Rome in 1624 and settled there. None of his painting of this period is in Rome, apart from the *Martyrdom of St Erasmus* (1630) in the Pinacoteca Vaticana (originally designed for an altar in St Peter's), and a few landscapes. 12, 157, 202 ff.

Pozzo, Andrea (Trento 1642-Vienna 1709). Jesuit painter and architect. He came to Rome in 1681 and worked from 1685 to 1694 in S. Ignazio, producing the cycle of frescoes that covers the apse, the tribune, the false dome and the ceiling. At some time between 1695 and 1699 he designed the altar. 204.

Preti, Mattia (known as il Cavalier Calabrese; Taverna 1613-La Valletta, Malta, 1699). Painter and architect. Works are in S. Pantaleo, S. Giovanni Calibita, and the painting of the *Tribute money* in Galleria Doria. Frescoes (c. 1642) in S. Carlo ai Catinari (in collaboration with his brother Gregorio), and others in the apse of S. Andrea della Valle. Paintings in the Spada and Corsini galleries. There are some frescoes in poor condition on a ceiling in the

Palazzo Pamphilj at Valmontone (42 km from Rome). 205 ff.

Raffaellino da Reggio (Raffaellino Motta; Codemondo, Reggio Emilia, c. 1550-78). Mannerist painter. Worked on the decoration of the Oratorio del Gonfalone, and with Federico Zuccari in S. Caterina dei Funari. Other frescoes in S. Silvestro al Quirinale. One of his paintings is in the Galleria Borghese. 154.

Raggi, Antonio (Vico Morcote, Canton Ticino, 1624-1686). Sculptor. Pupil and assistant of Bernini. His works are in S. Maria dei Miracoli, S. Maria del Popolo, the Gesù, and S. Agnese in Agone. He carved the figure representing the Danube on the Fontana dei Fiumi in Piazza Navona, and the upper part of S. Marcello al Corso. Works in S. Andrea della Valle, S. Giovanni dei Fiorentini, S. Andrea al Quirinale. 207.

Raguzzini, Filippo (Benevento 1680-Rome 1771). Architect. He built the Ospedale di S. Gallicano and the Cappella di S. Domenico in S. Maria sopra Minerva. He is best known for his elegant design for the Piazza di S. Ignazio (1727-28). He also built the Chiesetta di S. Filippo Neri in Via Giulia, the church and convent of S. Sisto Vecchio (1724-30), the baptistery of S. Maria in Trastevere. He restored S. Maria della Quercia and designed the altar in the transept of S. Maria d'Aracoeli in 1727, and the façade of the church of SS. Quirico and Giulitta near the Forum (1733) where he kept the 16th-century marble doorway. 213 ff.

Rainaldi, Carlo (Rome 1611-1691). Architect, one of the most outstanding of the Baroque period. He is responsible for planning the three roads converging on S. Maria del Popolo, the church of S. Maria in Campitelli (1662-67), the façade of S. Andrea della Valle, and many other Roman buildings contain his work. 55, 145, 186, 198, 201, 205.

Raphael (Raffaello Sanzio; Urbino 1483-Rome 1520). Painter and architect. He came to Rome in 1508 at the instance of his countryman, Bramante, and painted the *Stanze* and the *Logge* of the Vatican. 30, 94, 103, 112, 118 ff., 134, 148, 151, 155, *162, 167, 187,* 203.

Raphaël, Antonietta (Kovno, Lithuania, 1900). Painter and sculptress. In Rome since 1924. She is the wife of the painter Mario Mafai. 231.

Reni, Guido (Calvenzano, Bologna, 1575-Bologna 1642). He came very young to Rome as a protégé of

Cavalier d'Arpino, staying till 1610. Returning a second and third time, he produced notable work: the *Crucifixion of St Peter* in the Pinacoteca Vaticana, frescoes in S. Gregorio al Celio, the *Aurora* of Casino Rospigliosi, a youthful self-portrait and other paintings in the Pinacoteca Capitolina, a *Crucifixion* in S. Lorenzo in Lucina. Other works in the Doria, Spada, Colonna and Borghese galleries, the Accademia di S. Luca, the Galleria Corsini. Frescoes in Trinità dei Pellegrini, S. Carlo ai Catinari, Palazzo del Quirinale (Cappella dell'Annunciata), the Cappella Paolina in S. Maria Maggiore. One famous work is the St Michael in S. Maria della Concezione in Via Veneto (this, and the *Crucifixion of St Peter* are copied in mosaic in St Peter's). 55, 159, 167, 202, 205.

Robert, Hubert (known as 'Hubert des ruines'; Paris 1733-1808). Painter. His works are in the Galleria Nazionale d'Arte antica in Palazzo Barberini (Cervinara bequest). 211.

Rodriguez dos Santos, Manoel. Portuguese architect, in Rome from 1733 to 1771. Between 1741 and 1746 he built the Trinità degli Spagnoli in Via Condotti, with an elegant concave façade. 218.

Rosselli, Cosimo (Florence 1439-1507). Painter. Summoned to Rome in 1481 by Sixtus IV with other Florentine artists for the frescoes of the Sistine Chapel. Three scenes are attributed to him: the *Adoration of the Golden Calf,* the *Sermon on the Mount,* and the *Last Supper.* Vasari claims he did these with the help of Piero di Cosimo. 94.

Rossellino, Bernardo (Settignano 1409-Florence 1464). Architect and sculptor, brother of Antonio Rossellino. 52.

Rubens, Peter Paul (Siegen, Westphalia, 1577-Antwerp 1640). He came to Italy in the spring of 1600 and stayed eight years. Besides the three large pictures in the Chiesa Nuova, there are many other of his paintings in Rome. Outstanding among these is the *Wolf suckling Romulus and Remus* (1617-18), in the Pinacoteca Capitolina. In the Galleria Pallavicini is a group of his early works, in the Galleria Doria Pamphilj the portrait of a Franciscan, and in the Galleria Spada a portrait of a cardinal. Other works in the Galleria Colonna and the Accademia di S. Luca. Two early works, a *Deposition of Christ* and a *St Sebastian,* are in the Galleria Borghese and the Galleria Corsini. 159, 166.

Russolo, Luigi (Latisana, Venice, 1885-1947). Futurist painter. His works are in the Galleria Nazionale d'Arte moderna. 231.

Rusuti, Filippo (Rome, 13th century-*c.* 1317/21?). Painter, and follower of Cavallini, he executed and signed the mosaic on the old façade of S. Maria Maggiore. 55.

Rutelli, Mario (Palermo 1859-1951). Sculptor. His most successful work is the Fontana delle Naiadi in Piazza della Repubblica (late dell'Esedra). 228.

Sacchi, Andrea (Nettuno 1599-Rome 1661). Painter. The *Vision of St Romuald,* in the Pinacoteca Vaticana, is one of his best works. Other pictures by him are in S. Maria sopra Minerva, S. Carlo ai Catinari, S. Maria della Concezione, S. Isidoro, S. Bernardo alle Terme, the Borghese, Doria, Pallavicini and Palazzo Barberini galleries. His paintings of John the Baptist are in the Lateran Baptistry. 204.

Sacconi, Giuseppe (Montalto, Ascoli Piceno, 1854-Collegigliato di Pistoia, 1905). Architect. He designed the monument to Vittorio Emanuele in Piazza Venezia (also known as the Vittoriano), begun in 1885 and inaugurated in 1911. 228.

Sadun, Piero (Siena 1919). Painter. His works are in the Galleria Nazionale d'Arte moderna. 232.

Salvi, Nicola or **Niccolò** (Rome 1697-1751). Architect. He worked with Vanvitelli on the Palazzo Odescalchi. His major work is the Fontana di Trevi, which occupied him from 1732 until his death. It was completed in 1762. 184, 217.

Salviati (Francesco de' Rossi, known as Cecchino Salviati; Florence 1510-Rome 1563). Painter. Some of his works are in the Doria and Colonna galleries, but most of them are in churches and palaces: S. Marcello, the Chigi Chapel in S. Maria del Popolo, the old refectory of the church of S. Salvatore in Lauro, the Oratorio di S. Giovanni Decollato, the Sala Regia in the Vatican, a room in the Palazzo Sacchetti (Via Giulia, 66), and the Cappella del Pallio of the Palazzo della Cancelleria. 152 ff.

Sangallo (Antonio da Sangallo il Giovane; Florence 1483-1546). Architect. His first works were the church of S. Maria di Loreto and the Palazzo Farnese, and he worked on the latter throughout his life. A number of buildings in Via Giulia and Via Monserrato are attributed to him, including the Palazzetto

Leroy (also known as the Farnesina ai Baullari). He worked, together with other architects, on the churches of S. Giacomo degli Spagnoli, S. Giovanni dei Fiorentini, S. Maria di Monserrato, and S. Marcello. With Raphael he worked in the Villa Madama. 112, 132, 145, 149 ff.

Sangallo (Giuliano da S. di Francesco Giamberti; Florence 1473-1516). Architect. The design of the coffered nave ceiling in S. Maria Maggiore is attributed to him. He built the portico of the monastery of Grottaferrata. 112.

Saraceni, Carlo (Venice 1580-1620). Painter. One of the best of Caravaggio's followers. In Rome before 1605. Many altar-pieces in Roman churches. *Rest on the flight into Egypt* in the Camaldolese monastery above Frascati, *Death of the Virgin* in S. Maria della Scala, *St Charles* in S. Lorenzo in Lucina. Other paintings in S. Maria in Aquiro, S. Maria dell'Anima (1617-18) and the Pinacoteca Capitolina. 205.

Sardi, Giuseppe (S. Angelo in Vado, Pesaro, *c.* 1680-1753). Architect. His principal work is the Rococo façade of the Maddalena. Previous to this he had built the façade of S. Paolo alla regola (the lower part of which was designed by Giacomo Cioli). His last work was the rebuilding of the church of S. Paschal Baylon in Trastevere. 218.

Scialoja, Toti (Rome 1914). Painter. His works are in the Galleria Nazionale d'Arte moderna. 232.

Schadow, Wilhelm (Berlin 1798-1862). Painter. His works are in S. Andrea delle Fratte. 226.

Scipione (Scipione Bonichi; Rome 1904-1933). Painter. His works, including the portrait of the Cardinal Deacon, are in the Galleria Nazionale d'Arte moderna. 231.

Schnorr (Julius von Carolsfeld; Leipzig 1794-Dresden 1872). Painter, one of the group known as the 'Nazarenes', in Rome in 1817. His works are in the Casino Massimo. 226.

Scordia, Antonio (Santa Fé, Argentina, 1918). Abstract painter, living in Rome. His works are in the Galleria Nazionale d'Arte moderna. 232.

Sebastiano del Piombo (Sebastiano Luciani; Venice *c.* 1485-Rome 1547). Brought to Rome by Agostino Chigi for the decoration of the Villa Farnesina. He painted the Polyphemus and the scenes from Ovid's *Metamorphoses* in the lunettes. Other works by him in Rome: the portrait

of Andrea Doria in the Galleria Doria Pamphilj, the *Birth of the Virgin* in the Chigi Chapel in S. Maria del Popolo, the *Flagellation of St Peter* in S. Pietro in Montorio. His magnificent *Pietà* (1514-17) is in the Museo Civico di Viterbo. 132, 134.

Seitz, Ludovico (Rome 1844-Albano 1908). Painter of German origin. Belonged to the Nazarene group. 226.

Serodine, Giovanni (Ascona, Switzerland, *c.* 1594-Rome *c.* 1630). Painter. 205.

Severini, Gino (Cortona 1883-Paris 1966). Painter. He went over to Futurism after a pointilliste period, and signed the Manifesto of 1910. In 1953-54 he decorated the Palazzo dei Congressi of the EUR. His works are in the Galleria Nazionale d'Arte moderna. 231 ff.

Signorelli, Luca (Cortona *c.* 1441-1523). Painter. In Rome 1481-82 with a group of painters working on the Sistine Chapel frescoes. He painted the scene of *Moses giving his staff to Joshua.* He also painted in the *Stanze,* before Raphael. One of his paintings is in the Galleria Pallavicini, and there is an altarpiece by him in the Museo di Castel S. Angelo. 92, 118.

Sironi, Mario (Sessari 1885-Milan 1961). Painter. There is glass by him in the Palazzo del Ministero dell'Industria e Commercio in Via Veneto (1932). His works are in the Galleria Nazionale d'Arte moderna, and in the Pinacoteca Vaticana. 230.

Sodoma (Giovanni Antonio Bazzi; Vercelli 1477-Siena 1549). Painter. He worked in the Vatican *c.* 1508 although nothing of what he did there survived. Also in the Farnesina *c.* 1511-12 where he produced his masterpiece, the *Marriage of Alexander and Roxana.* There is a *Pietà* by him in the Galleria Borghese. Three other paintings of his are in the Galleria Nazionale d'Arte antica in Palazzo Barberini. 118, 134.

Sormani, Leonardo (Savona ? before 1530-after 1589). Sculptor. One of the artists responsible for the Fontana dell'Acqua Felice. He worked with Tommaso della Porta on the statue of St Peter that was placed on Trajan's Column. He carved two tombs in Trinità dei Monti, and sculptures for Domenico Fontana's monument to Nicholas IV in S. Maria Maggiore. 147.

Specchi, Alessandro (Rome 1668-1729). Architect and engraver. Pupil of Carlo Fontana. He designed the

Porto di Ripetta on the Tiber, now demolished, also the Palazzo de Carolis on the Corso, now the Banco di Roma. A collection of his engravings is in the Museo di Roma. 212, 217.

Stati, Cristoforo (Bracciano 1556-Rome 1619). Sculptor. There is a *Magdalen* by him in the Barberini Chapel in S. Andrea della Valle, bas-reliefs in the Cappella Paolina of S. Maria Maggiore, and a group of *Venus and Adonis* in the Palazzo Comunale at Bracciano. 195, 207.

Subleyras, Pierre (Saint-Gilles-du-Gard 1699-Rome 1749). Painter. His works are in S. Francesca Romana (1744), the Galleria dell'Accademia di S. Luca, and S. Maria degli Angeli. Some of his work is copied in mosaic in St Peter's. 218.

Sweerts, Michael (Brussels 1624-Goa 1664). Painter. In Rome from 1646, possibly until 1654. He painted vivid scenes of Roman life. His works are in the Pinacoteca Capitolina and the Galleria dell'Accademia di S. Luca. 208.

Tadolini, Adamo (Bologna 1788-1868). Sculptor. He finished Canova's statue of Pius VI in St Peter's. Other works by him in the Protomoteca Capitolina and the Galleria Comunale d'Arte moderna. 222.

Testa, Pietro (Lucca 1611-Rome 1650). Painter. Influenced by Poussin and the Venetians. His works are in the Pinacoteca Capitolina, the Galleria dell'Accademia di S. Luca, and S. Martino ai Monti. His *Slaughter of the Innocents* in the Galleria Spada is specially noteworthy. 204.

Tintoretto (Jacopo Robusti; Venice 1518-1594). Painter. His paintings in Rome are: *Portrait of a man* in Galleria Doria Pamphilj (where the portrait of a prelate is also attributed to him), a double portrait, the *Portrait of a man,* and a *Spinet-player* in Galleria Colonna, *Christ with the woman take in adultery* in the Galleria Nazionale d'Arte antica in Palazzo Barberini.

Titian (Tiziano Vecellio; Pieve di Cadore *c.* 1490-Venice 1576). Painter. His early paintings in Rome are: *Herodias* in the Galleria Doria, the *Baptism of Christ, c.* 1512 in the Pinacoteca Capitolina, the *Portrait of a musician* in the Spada gallery (in rather poor state). His masterpiece, the *Sacred and Profane Love* (*c.* 1515) is in the Galleria Borghese. In the Galleria Doria is his painting representing *Spain coming to the help*

of Religion. There are three late works, *St Dominic, Venus blindfolding Cupid* (*c.* 1565) and the *Flagellation of Christ* in the Galleria Borghese. The portrait of Onofrio Panvinio is in the Galleria Colonna, and that of Ippolito Riminaldi in the Galleria dell'Accademia di S. Luca (where there is also a *St Jerome* by him). The Pinacoteca Vaticana possesses his portrait of Doge Marcello, and the altar-piece with the *Madonna and Saints* originally in the Frari at Venice. His *Venus and Adonis* (with much work by his pupils) is in the Galleria Nazionale di Arte antica in Palazzo Barberini. 184, 203.

Torriti, Jacopo (Rome, late 13th century). Mosaicist. His name, associated with that of Fra' Jacopo da Camerino (*q.v.*) appears for the first time in the apse mosaic of St John Lateran (1291) which has been much restored. The apse mosaic in S. Maria Maggiore (1295) gives a better idea of his art. 55, 78.

Turcato, Giulio (Mantua 1912). Abstract painter. One of the most active artists in the Roman avant-garde, his works are in the Galleria Nazionale d'Arte moderna. 232.

Vacca, Flaminio (Rome *c.* 1538-d. between 1592 and 1605). Sculptor. His work is to be seen in a number of Roman churches: a *St Francis* in the Sistine Chapel in S. Maria Maggiore, a *St John Evangelist* and a *Baptist* in the Chiesa Nuova, and two angels, in the Lateran basilica and in the Gesù. He collaborated on the Fontana del Moro in Piazza Navona, and the Acqua Felice in Piazza S. Bernardo. 147.

Valadier, Giuseppe (Rome 1762-1839). Architect, and the first designer involved in the modern planning of the city. He is responsible for the Ponte Milvio area, the gardens of the Pincio, the Piazza del Popolo, and the restoration of such monuments as the Arch of Titus and the Colosseum. He built the Teatro Valle, the Palazzetto della Stamperia, the façade of S. Pantaleo and S. Rocco, the Casa dei Lezzani on the Corso, a palazzo in Via del Babuino, and the Casina Valadier on the Pincio terrace. 113, 222 ff.

Valentin (Louis de Boulogne; Coulommiers, Brie, 1591-Rome 1634). Painter. His works are in the Galleria Spada, the Galleria Corsini, and the Pinacoteca Vaticana (*Martyrdom of St Processus and St Martinianus,* of which there is a mosaic copy in St Peter's). 205, 232.

Valle (Filippo, also known as Della Valle; Florence 1693-Rome 1770). Sculptor. Among his most important works are: *Temperance* in the Corsini Chapel in St John Lateran (where there is also a bas-relief of the *Beheading of John the Baptist*), and his relief of the *Annunciation* in S. Ignazio. He carved two of the statues on the Fontana di Trevi (*Fertility* and *Health*). There are more works in St Peter's, S. Maria Maggiore, and S. Giovanni dei Fiorentini. 217.

Valvassori, Gabriele (Rome 1683-1761). Architect. His best work is the Rococo façade of the Palazzo Doria Pamphilj on the Corso. 193, 217.

Van Aelst, Pieter (Enghien, ?-1536). Flemish weaver. It was in his workshop at Brussels that ten tapestries were woven for the Sistine Chapel, on cartoons by Raphael. Their subject-matter is the Acts of the Apostles, and they are now in the Pinacoteca Vaticana. This workshop produced the tapestries in the Galleria degli Arazzi in the Vatican, on cartoons by Bernard van Orley (*q.v.*) and Raphael's pupils. 129.

Van Bloemen, Jean-François (Antwerp 1662-Rome 1748). Painter. Works by him in the Galleria Nazionale di Palazzo Corsini, the Galleria Doria Pamphilj, the Coffee house of the Quirinale gardens. 217.

Van Dyck, Anthony (Antwerp 1699-London 1641). Painter. He came to Rome in February 1622 and returned during the following year to paint some of his most famous portraits. There are two portraits in the Pinacoteca Capitolina of Pieter de Jode the elder, and Pieter de Jode the younger. In the Galleria dell'Accademia di S. Luca, a *Madonna with angels;* a portrait in the Galleria Pallavicini; a *Rest on the Flight into Egypt* in the Galleria Nazionale di Palazzo Corsini; a *St Francis Xavier* in the Pinacoteca Vaticana. 157.

Van Heemskerk, Martin (Heemskerk, Holland, 1498-1574). Painter and engraver. Famous for his detailed drawings of Rome in the 16th century. In the Galleria Nazionale di Palazzo Barberini there is a *Deposition* attributed to him.

Van Laer, Pieter (known in Rome as 'Il Bamboccio'; Haarlem, *c.* 1592-1642). Painter. His works were known as 'Bambocciate', and his followers as 'Bamboccianti.' His works are in the Galleria Nazionale di Palazzo Corsini, the Galleria Spada, and the Villa d'Este at Tivoli. 207.

Van Orley, Bernard (Brussels 1488 ?-1541). Painter and designer of cartoons for tapestries and windows. In Brussels he supervised the weaving of the Raphael designs in the workshop of Pieter van Aelst (*q.v.*). His works are in the Galleria Colonna (the *Seven joys and seven sorrows of the Virgin*) and the Galleria Borghese (a portrait of Charles V, replica of a lost original). 129.

Van Santen, Jan (known in Italy as Giovanni Vasanzio; Utrecht, mid-16th century-Rome 1621). Architect. His principal works are the Casino Borghese, (which houses the Museo and Galleria Borghese), and the Palazzo Borghese (now Rospigliosi Pallavicini) where he may have designed the *teatro d'acqua.* He designed these buildings in collaboration with Maderno. He completed the new basilica of S. Sebastiano on the catacombs of S. Sebastiano, begun by Ponzio. He designed two fountains (the Fontana dell'Aquilone and the Fontana del Sacramento) in the Vatican gardens. 159 ff.

Van Staverden, Jacob (Amersfoort, Holland, second half of the 17th century). Painter of Roman views. One of his works is in the Galleria Nazionale di Palazzo Corsini. 208.

Vanvitelli (Gaspar van Wittel, also called Gaspare dagli Occhiali; Amersfoort, Holland 1655-Rome 1736). He came to Rome in 1674 and settled there. One of the best painters of Roman views in his time. There are many works by him in the Musei Capitolini, the Galleria Doria Pamphilj, Accademia di S. Luca, and Galleria Nazionale d'Arte antica in Palazzo Corsini. 59, 132, 208 ff, 232.

Vanvitelli, Luigi (Naples 1700-Caserta 1773). Architect. Son of Gaspare Vanvitelli and pupil of Juvarra. Most of his work in Rome was done in collaboration with others. He was involved in the façade of Palazzo Odescalchi, completion of S. Maria degli Angeli, modernizing of the convent next to the church of S. Agostino, and the Cappella delle Reliquie in S. Cecilia in Trastevere. 217 ff.

Vasari, Giorgio (Arezzo 1511-Florence 1574). Painter, architect and author. Pupil and biographer of Michelangelo. He came to Rome in the entourage of Cardinal Ippolito dei Medici in 1531, and joined the circle of Mannerist artists. He was again in Rome in 1538, 1545 and 1550, after the election of Julius III, for whom he designed the tomb of Cardinal del Monte in S. Pietro in

Montorio. He wrote the *Lives of the Painters, Sculptors and Architects*. His works in Rome are: allegorical frescoes on the life of Paul III in the Palazzo della Cancelleria, and others in the Sala Regia in the Vatican; a *Beheading of John the Baptist* on the high altar of the Oratorio di S. Giovanni Decollato; other works in the Galleria Borghese and Pinacoteca Vaticana. 80, 88, 91, 103, 106, 108, 120, 136, 152,, 153.

Vasi, Giuseppe (Corleone, Palermo, 1710-Rome 1782). Engraver. 220.

Vassalletto (the name of a family of Roman sculptors active in the 12th and 13th centuries, also known as the Cosmati, since a number of them were named Cosma). The two most important artists in the family were Pietro Vassalletto (Rome, 1154-1186), and Niccolò di Angelo Vassalletto (Rome 1215-1263). Their work is to be seen in S. Paolo and S. Lorenzo fuori le Mura, St John Lateran, and the SS. Apostoli. 69 ff.

Vecchietta (Lorenzo di Pietro; Castiglione d'Orcia, Siena, 1412 ?-1480). Painter, sculptor, architect and military engineer. His works in Rome are: the tomb of bishop Gerolamo Foscari (1463-64) in S. Maria del Popolo (where there is also a small lavabo attributed to him, with two busts of female saints); a painting of a miracle-working saint in the Pinacoteca Vaticana. 108.

Veit, Philipp (Berlin 1793-Mainz 1877). Painter. One of the 'Nazarene' group who worked on the decoration of the Casino Massimo. Other works by him: a *Triumph of Religion* in the Vatican, and an altarpiece in Trinità dei Monti. 226.

Velasquez (Diego Rodriguez de Silva y Velasquez; Seville 1599-Madrid 1660). Painter. He came to Rome twice, between 1629 and 1631, and again between 1649 and 1651, where he painted some of his finest work. Only one of his paintings remains, and that is the superb portrait of Innocent X in the Galleria Doria Pamphilj. 190, 201.

Veronese (Paolo Caliari; Verona 1528-Venice 1588). His works in Rome are a *Narcissus at the spring* in the Galleria Colonna, a *St Helen* and an *Allegory* in the Pinacoteca Vaticana, and other paintings in the Pinacoteca Capitolina.

Verrocchio (Andrea del Verrocchio; Florence 1435-Venice 1488). Goldsmith, sculptor, painter and engineer. He worked as goldsmith and sculptor in Rome, but little remains of what he produced. There is a relief in the Ospedale di S. Spirito, and two statuettes in the Sala dei Trionfi di Mario in the Palazzo dei Conservatori on the Campidoglio, which at least resemble his work in style. 108.

Vignola (Jacopo Barozzi; Vignola 1507-Rome 1573). Architect and author. The most important builder in the late Renaissance. He came to Rome *c.* 1534 and joined the circle of Antonio da Sangallo. His best works are the Gesù and the Palazzo di Caprarola. He was also involved in work on the Villa Giulia, the portico of the Campidoglio, the Palazzo Farnese, Palazzo Borghese, Palazzo della Cancelleria and St Peter's. He built the Tempietto of S. Andrea on the Via Flaminia. 113, 145, 149 ff.

Vitellozzi, Annibale (Anghiari 1902). Architect. Collaborated with P.L. Nervi on the Palazzetto dello Sport, and with others on the front of the Stazione Termini and the Museo delle Arti e Tradizioni popolari at EUR.

Vouet, Simon (Paris 1590-1649). Painter. His works in Rome: paintings of the life of St. Francis in S. Lorenzo in Lucina; an *Allegory of Vanity* in the Pinacoteca Capitolina; *Herodias* in the Galleria Nazionale d'Arte antica di Palazzo Corsini, and the *Birth of the Virgin* in S. Francesco a Ripa. 202.

Zuccari, Federico (S. Angelo in Vado, Pesaro 1542/1543-1609). Painter and author. A brilliant and eclectic Mannerist. Founder of the Accademia di S. Luca, which was first established in the palazzetto which he designed and decorated in Via Gregoriana, near the Trinità dei Monti. Frescoes in the Sala Regia and the Cappella Paolina in the Vatican. Many of his paintings are in churches, palaces and galleries in Rome: the Gesù, S. Marcello, the Palazzetto di Sisto V in Via di Parione, S. Lorenzo in Damaso, the Oratorio del Gonfalone, S. Caterina dei Funari, the Galleria Borghese, the Galleria Capitolina, the Galleria Nationale d'Arte antica di Palazzo Barberini, the Accademia di S. Luca, etc. 148, 152, 154.

Zuccari, Taddeo (S. Angelo in Vado, 1528-1566). Painter. Elder brother of Federico Zuccari. Many of his paintings are in the churches and galleries of Rome. Frescoes in S. Maria della Consolazione (1556), the apse of S. Sabina (1560), S. Maria S. Marcello, the Sala dei Palafrenieri in the Vatican. Paintings in Galleria Doria Pamphilj, and Galleria Borghese. 148, 152.

R

S.ANGELO   PIGNA   CAMPIDELLI   TRASTEVERE   REGO

L' INSEGNE DELLI XIIII